Looking Back for Jehoiachin

Africanus Monograph Series

The *Africanus Monograph Series* is published by the Africanus Guild, based at Gordon-Conwell Theological Seminary's Boston campus, the Center for Urban Ministerial Education (CUME). Like the *Africanus Journal*, it strives to promote academic work by men and women that is globally evangelical in the historically orthodox, multiethnic, multicultural sense, with a commitment to biblical fidelity, in conversation with the realities of the world in which we live.

The journal is named in honor of Julius Africanus, a Christian scholar born around AD 200. He probably was born in Jerusalem; studied in Alexandria, Egypt; and later became bishop of Emmaus. He was considered by the ancients a man of consummate learning and sharpest judgment, a careful historian who sought to defend the truth of the Bible.

The journal may be read online at http://www.gordonconwell.edu/boston/africanusjournal.

The *Africanus Monograph Series* publishes academic dissertations and books by scholars who agree with its goals and have earned research degrees.

Looking Back for Jehoiachin

Yahweh's Cast-Out Signet

JAMES R. CRITCHLOW

Foreword by
STEPHEN L. DEMPSTER

WIPF & STOCK · Eugene, Oregon

LOOKING BACK FOR JEHOIACHIN
Yahweh's Cast-Out Signet

Africanus Monograph Series 1

Copyright © 2012 James R. Critchlow. All rights reserved. Except for brief quotations in critical publications or reviews, no part of this book may be reproduced in any manner without prior written permission from the publisher. Write: Permissions. Wipf and Stock Publishers, 199 W. 8th Ave., Suite 3, Eugene, OR 97401.

Wipf & Stock
An Imprint of Wipf and Stock Publishers
199 W. 8th Ave., Suite 3
Eugene, OR 97401

www.wipfandstock.com

ISBN 13: 978-1-62032-111-9

All English Scripture citations are from the Revised Standard Version of the Bible, copyright 1952 (2nd edition, 1971) by the Division of Christian Education of the National Council of the Churches of Christ in the United States of America. Used by permission. All rights reserved.

Contents

Foreword by Stephen L. Dempster | vii
Introduction | ix

1 Jehoiachin in the Narratives Concerning the Davidic Kings | 1
2 Jeremiah's Prophecies: Jeconiah in Babylon | 33
3 Jehoiachin in Other Prophetic and Narrative Literature | 75
4 Reflections of Jehoiachin in the Poetry of Israel | 100
5 Reflections of Jeconiah in Intertestamental and New Testament Literature | 121
6 Conclusions | 149

Bibliography | 155
General Index | 173
Ancient Documents Index | 177

Foreword

THIS IS THE FIRST full length monograph on a mysterious but important figure in biblical history—Jehoiachin, the last real king of Judah, who reigned only three months. Yet it is remarkable how important his life was deemed in later biblical and extra-biblical literature. Within the Old Testament, he becomes the locus of hope for the Davidic promise of an eternal covenant, and he is found in a strategic place in the genealogy of Jesus in the Gospel of Matthew, marking the beginning of exile from which the birth of Jesus the Messiah would bring final relief. It is no wonder that he is the subject of significant reflection in Jewish tradition.

Jim Critchlow's assessment of the pertinent facts relating to Jehoiachin and their wider significance is a welcome study filling an important gap in biblical study. His careful examination of the textual data, his exegesis of the texts in their historical setting and in their wider biblical context, as well as their canonical context, and his examination of the extra biblical literature makes this study a solid contribution to the field. One of the important results of his study for Old Testament and Hebrew Bible research is his important contribution to the debate on the hermeneutical significance of the last four verses of 2 Kings. Are these verses the last historical note the historian of Kings had at his disposal and therefore a simple footnote to a pessimistic assessment of Israel's history where the last word is divine judgment? Or are they words that seek to rekindle the Messianic hope that there would always be a descendant on David's throne? Significant biblical scholars weigh in on the side of Martin Noth for the former position and Gerhard von Rad for the latter. Jim Critchlow's work goes a long way to finally resolving this debate in favour of von Rad. All of which serves to explain why Jehoiachin becomes an important figure in later biblical and extra-biblical tradition.

Foreword

Critchlow's assessment of this biblical figure has not only relevance to the field of biblical inquiry and scholarship. It profoundly addresses the contemporary world where hope is at a premium in a time where it seems as if all the gods have failed. The situation was similar in ancient Judah. Isaiah spoke of a shoot springing up from the stump of Jesse as a sign of incredible hope (Is 11:1). The massive tree which nourished the Davidic covenant had been cut down. All that remained was a stump. There were no Davidic descendants anywhere to be found on the throne of Judah—in fact Judah was nothing but a wasteland—the temple demolished, cities burned to the ground, only a meagre population left in the land after a Babylonian holocaust. But there was a king in exile in a Babylonian prison—Jehoiachin of Judah, described as nothing more than a broken piece of pottery, thrown away on a garbage heap (Jer 22:28). When he is granted release from prison, surely this is the shoot springing up from the stump, an astonishing sign of hope. The broken pottery has been retrieved and fashioned into a beautiful piece of art. Yahweh has put on his signet ring again which he had tossed aside (Jer 22:24, cf. Hag 2:21). Was this not the beginning of Israel's resurrection from the grave of exile, a portent of a greater Resurrection in the future, the Resurrection of the Son of God? Such significance should speak into our seemingly hopeless world as it did into ancient Judah's, the Good News that while our idols have all failed, Yahweh is as alive as ever, specializing in resurrection and hope. Enjoy the book!

Stephen L. Dempster

Introduction

THIS STUDY EXAMINES THE life and legacy of Jehoiachin[1] son of Jehoiakim son of Josiah, the last living Davidic king[2] during the Babylonian captivity. It investigates the names Jehoiachin/Jeconiah/Coniah (יהויכין/יכוניה/כניהו) and their occurrences in the Hebrew Bible, intertestamental literature, and the New Testament. It develops composite portraits of this tragic historical figure from the biblical accounts, inscriptions, and the writings of Flavius Josephus and the rabbis.

THE VALUE OF THE STUDY

We are unaware of any scholarly study of Jehoiachin that has been undertaken. Summary articles about him appear in *NIDOTTE*,[3] *ABD*,[4] *ISBE*,[5] *IDB*,[6] and other encyclopedic reference works. There are numerous articles in scholarly journals, especially concerning inscriptions and the temple vessels taken with him to Babylon (see bibliography). However, it appears that no attempt to draw together the extensive biblical, postbiblical, and inscriptional accounts exists. This is surprising, given

---

1. For the reader's convenience, we adopt the convention of referring to this king as Jehoiachin in all general comments. Although not strictly accurate, this makes the argument easier to follow. When we move to the pericope level of detail, we reflect the king's name (and spelling) as recorded in that text.

2. Zedekiah was taken to Babylon, where he presumably died before the release of Jehoiachin in 560 BCE. Rabbinic and Josephan writings expand Jehoiachin's legacy beyond that of the biblical corpus.

3. Foulkes, "Theology of Jehoiachin," 4:744–45.

4. Berridge, "Jehoiachin," 3:661–63.

5. Genung, "Jehoiachin," 2:975–76.

6. May, "Jehoiachin," 2:811–13.

Introduction

the attention paid to him in ancient texts. Jehoiachin is the subject or object of (1) narrative passages in 2 Kings, 1 and 2 Chronicles, and Esther; (2) prophecies in Jeremiah and Haggai; (3) poetry in Ezekiel, Lamentations, Isaiah and Psalms; and (4) intertestamental writings in 1 Esdras, Additions to Esther, Baruch, the writings of Flavius Josephus, and the rabbinical tradition. Jehoiachin also features prominently in a genealogical record traced in Matthew wherein he is the linking name between Abraham and David and Jesus Christ. It is surely significant that a king who only reigned three months would provoke so much comment throughout different bodies of literature.

The biblical citations do more than merely comment on Jehoiachin. Jeremiah, Ezekiel, Psalms, and Chronicles, at the very least, help interpret the exile for the reader confused about the loss of king, temple, and independence. Modern scholars disagree about the significance of Jehoiachin's release from prison as described in the final pericopes in 2 Kings and Jeremiah, and on the implications for the deuteronomistic history (DtrH), including the "Messianic Hope."[7]

Jeremiah's prophecy (Jer 22:24–30) that Coniah would be a cast-out signet (חוֹתָם) and "childless" (עֲרִירִי) portended the end of the Davidic royal line. "The prophetic assertion was apparently intended not only to disqualify Jeconiah himself from kingship, but to exclude his entire posterity."[8] Curses on the last kings of Judah were prophesied against Hezekiah (2 Kgs 20:16–19), Manasseh (21:11–15), Jehoahaz (Jer 22:10–12), Jehoiakim (22:13–19; 36:29–31), Jehoiachin (22:24–30), and Zedekiah (21:3–7; 24:8–10; 24:2–3). These curses indicate a radical renegotiation of the Davidic covenant announced in 2 Samuel 7. Note also that Hananiah son of Azzur predicted that Jeconiah's exile would last only two years (Jer 28:4), but Jeremiah countermanded this sentiment with the letter to the exiles, "Settle down . . . build homes . . . do not believe your diviners . . ." (29:5–9).

---

7. Von Rad, *Deuteronomium Studien*, 63–64; *Old Testament Theology*, 334: "But the Deuteronomist saw yet another word as active in history, namely, the promise of salvation in the Nathan prophecy (2 Samuel 7). . . . 2 Kgs 25:27–30 . . . points to a possibility with which Yahweh can resume." Noth, *The Deuteronomistic History*, 98: "Clearly he (the DtrH) saw the divine judgment which was acted out in his account of the external collapse of Israel as a nation as something final and definitive and he expressed no hope for the future, not even in the very modest and simple form of an expectation that the deported and dispersed people would be gathered together."

8. Malamat, "Jeremiah and the Last Two Kings of Judah," 81–87.

Introduction

Although the end of the exile was years beyond Jehoiachin's lifetime, he was singled out for favorable attention by Nebuchadrezzar's[9] successor, Amel-marduk (Evil-merodach in 2 Kgs 25 and Jer 52). Indeed, it seemed that Yahweh was tending the "good figs" in Babylon in accordance with Jeremiah 24:1, of whom Jeconiah was the captive-in-chief. Yet, Jehoiachin never returned to Judah. He died in Babylon (52:34), although he had been elevated to preference by the Babylonian king. "This last event of Judean royalty"[10] marks the end of the Davidic royal line—the (dead) end of four centuries of kings on the throne of David. It seemed that Yahweh had promised David an eternal kingdom—an heir to reign on the throne—yet David's descendant Jehoiachin died, leaving no heir seated on that throne. Nevertheless, the house of David continued beyond the exile, traced in 1 Chronicles 3 from Jeconiah at least seven further generations. Furthermore, Matthew 1 selectively reproduces the genealogy of the patriarchs and kings of Israel in a mnemonic of fourteen generations each from Abraham to David, David to Jeconiah (and the exile), and Jeconiah to Jesus Christ.

Two recent historiographies of Davidic kings, McKenzie's *King David* and Sweeney's *King Josiah*,[11] have contributed to the understanding of key figures in the messianic line. We propose that this study of Jehoiachin similarly contributes to scholarly understanding. Although Jehoiachin briefly occupied the throne of David, the fact that he was the last remaining Davidic king, the sire of Zerubbabel, and the basis for intense biblical and postbiblical writings commends the study.

METHOD OF INVESTIGATION

In this textual/historical investigation of Jehoiachin, the organizing motif will be the thirty-two occurrences of the name "Jehoiachin" (and alternates Jeconiah and Coniah) in the Bible.[12] This study examines the

---

9. Although most often rendered *Nebuchadnezzar* in comtemporary Bible translations, the spelling *Nebuchadrezzar* is used in the Babylonian Chronicle and in Jeremiah.

10. Genung, "Jehoiachin," II:976. In the interests of brevity, we will footnote citations that are longer than a very brief phrase.

11. McKenzie, *King David: A Biography*; Sweeney, *King Josiah of Judah: The Lost Messiah of Israel*.

12. This investigation will go beyond the boundaries of the Hebrew Bible to the apocryphal writings of the Roman Catholic and Orthodox communities as well as the

Introduction

passages in canonical order (narrative, prophecy, and poetry) successively through the Hebrew Bible, the apocryphal books, intertestamental literature, and the New Testament. Within each pericope, the study sets forth (1) a reconstruction of the proposed Hebrew text with comments and translation; (2) background observations of pertinent linguistic, grammatical, or structural details; and (3) verse-by-verse exegesis and analysis of the texts read in light of the current literature. The texts examined in chapter 4 do not explicitly mention the name of the king, but rather make allusions to him. Among texts making such allusions are Ezekiel 17 and 19, which contrast his reign to that of Zedekiah. It is also possible that Lamentations 3 and 4, Isaiah 52:13—53:12, and Psalms 61 and 89 concern Jehoiachin's exile. The individual pericopes build to create composite portraits of Jehoiachin—a tragic, cast-off king of Judah whose dramatic story merits close investigation.

This study is essentially an optimistic portrayal of Jehoiachin. Despite his ignominious exile as the figurative signet of Yahweh to Babylon, Jehoiachin served as a source for intense commentary by later communities. At the end of his life, after thirty-seven years in Babylonian captivity, he was released from prison and seated preferentially at the table of the king of Babylon. There, he embodied the hopes of the Jews for a restoration of the golden age of King David. Although Jehoiachin was finally rejected as the last Davidic king, and his descendants would not rule on the throne of David, his grandson Zerubbabel rebuilt the temple and restored a semblance of the glory of the past and pointed forward to an expected Davidic Messiah.

IMPLICATIONS OF THIS STUDY

The drawing together of all historical and scholarly literature on this key figure is significant in its own right. Furthermore, the development of a reconstructed text for each pericope will allow scholars to consider them in a new light. The drawing together of postbiblical writings adds new dimensions to the portraits of the biblical accounts.

New Testament, thereby incorporating all four "Bibles."

Introduction

WHAT DO THE NAMES MEAN, AND WHERE DO THEY OCCUR?

The foundation of the study is the life and legacy of Jehoiachin son of Jehoiakim. The three names of this king have nearly identical meanings. Jehoiachin and Jeconiah may be rendered, "May Yahweh establish/uphold," whereas Coniah means "the establishing of Yahweh." These names are a transposition of the divine abbreviation for Yahweh (יְה) to the root, i.e., Jehoiachin (יְה begins the name) or Jeconiah/Coniah (יְה at end). Jeconiah reflects a *qal* imperfect inflection of כּוּן and Jehoiachin is a *hip'il* imperfect (כִּין). Additionally, as Davis observes,

> Among the kings in the line of David, the consciousness of their formal adoption by Yahweh to be His vice-regents on the throne of Israel (2 Sam 7; Ps 2) found expression in the royal names.... early in the 9th century ... it was conventional for the king of Judah to have for his name a sentence with Yahweh as its subject. The only exceptions ... were Manasseh and his son Amon, both of whom were notoriously apostate from Yahweh.[13]

The (given?) name Jeconiah (יְכָנְיָה and יְכָנְיָהוּ) occurs in 1 Chronicles 3:16, 17; Esther 2:6; Jeremiah 24:1; 27:20; 28:4; 29:2; Baruch 1:3, 9; Additions to Esther 11:4; 1 Esdras 1:9, 34.[14] The shortened form (hypocoristicon) Coniah (כָּנְיָהוּ) occurs in Jeremiah 22:24, 28; and 37:1. The (throne?) name Jehoiachin (יְהוֹיָכִין) occurs as follows: 2 Kings 24:6, 8, 12, 15, 17; 25:27 (twice), 29; 2 Chronicles 36:8, 9; Jeremiah 52:31 (twice), 33; Ezekiel 1:2; and 1 Esdras 1:43. In the New Testament, the name is spelled Jechoniah (Ieconia) in Matthew 1:11, 12 (RSV). In two important inscriptions, Jehoiachin's name is spelled "*Ya'u-kinu* (alt. *Yakû-kinu*)[15] king of the land of *Yahudu* (alt. *Yaudu, Yakudu*)" (Babylonian Chronicle) and *Yaukin* (Eliakim seal impressions).

---

13. Davis, "Names in the Hebrew Bible," 2:1011.

14. There is a variant in the LXX at 1 Sam 6:19 referring to the sons of Jechonias (οἱ υἱοὶ Ιεχονιου), whereas the Masoretic Text lists only the men of Beth Shemesh (בְּנֵי בֵית־שֶׁמֶשׁ). We have not counted this in the thirty-two occurrences of Jehoiachin in the Bible.

15. This study will follow the (standard) transliteration indicated in *NIDOTTE*, 1:li.

xiii

Introduction

Figure 1: The Davidic dynasty in Judah, post-721[16]

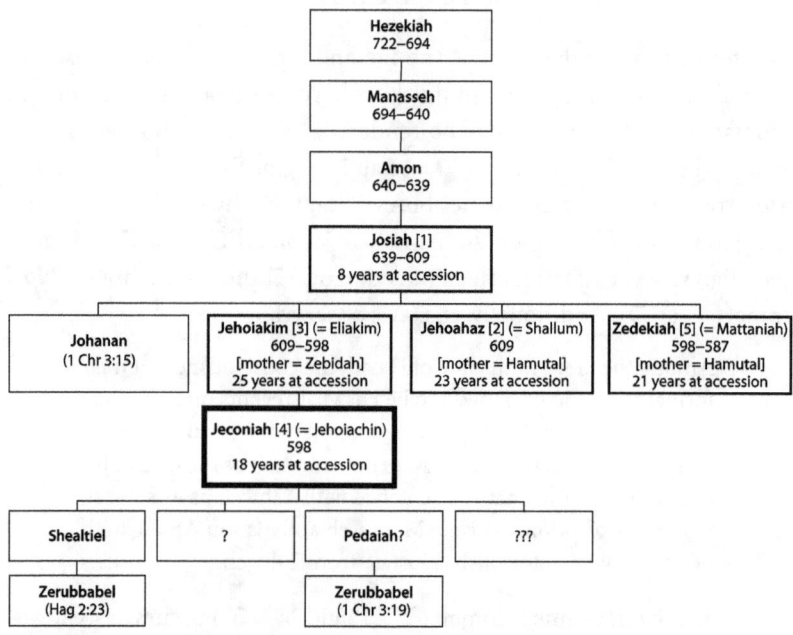

(Reign Order) Age Order
(1) Josiah, born 647
(3) Jehoiakim, born 634 (when Josiah was 13 years old)
(2) Jehoahaz, born 632
(5) Zedekiah, born 619
(4) Jehoiachin, born 616 (when Jehoiakim was 18 years old)

IN WHAT SETTING DID JEHOIACHIN LIVE?

The major events that shaped Jehoiachin's life (616–560? BCE) from the death of Josiah to the exile of the Judean kingdom may be summarized in the following manner. Pharaoh Neco killed Josiah (his grandfather) at Megiddo in 609 when Jehoiachin was about seven years old. Jehoahaz (Jehoiachin's uncle) was appointed king by the people of the land, but was deposed after a three-month rule by Neco and taken captive to Egypt. Jehoiakim (Jehoiachin's father) was appointed king by Neco and ruled

---

16. This chart originally designed by D. J. Reimer, unpublished class notes, New College, University of Edinburgh, Oct. 2001, but with modifications by the author.

Introduction

for eleven years in a series of shifting alliances and treaties. King Nebuchadrezzar of Babylon defeated Egypt in 605 at Carchemish; tribute and hostages were possibly taken from Judah at that time (2 Chr 36:6–7; Dan 1:1–2). Jehoiakim initially served Nebuchadrezzar for three years, but in 601/600 withheld tribute from Babylon. At some point during the Babylonian march to Judah, in order to punish Jehoiakim, Jehoiakim either died or was assassinated and Jehoiachin became king in December 598 (January 597) at age eighteen. When Nebuchadrezzar arrived to oversee the siege, Jehoiachin surrendered to him along with his family (mother and wives, possibly children; 2 Kgs 24:15) and officials. Jehoiachin and 10,000 captives (including Ezekiel) were deported to Babylon. His uncle Zedekiah was appointed king in his stead by Nebuchadrezzar. Nine years after Jehoiachin's exile, Zedekiah rebelled against Babylon, resulting in Nebuchadrezzar's reprisal. He summarily executed Zedekiah's children and nobles, razed Jerusalem, and deported the population with the now-blinded Zedekiah to Babylon. Jehoiachin would have been twenty-nine years old, though notification would have taken months to reach Babylon (Ezek 33:21). Gedaliah son of Ahikam was appointed governor of Judah, but was assassinated two months later, depriving the depleted population of any semblance of Israelite governance. Jehoiachin, now the putative king of Judah in exile, remained in prison until the age of fifty-five years, when he was freed and elevated above the other captive kings in Babylon. He died in Babylon some time during or slightly after 560 BCE. A *terminus ad quem* is difficult to fix, but Jehoiachin was released during the reign of Nebuchadrezzar's son Amel-marduk (562–560). Jehoiachin may have survived into the reign of Neriglissar. The Weidner Tablets verify that he had five sons in his household while he was in captivity (house arrest?). First Chronicles 3:16–17 records the names of seven sons. Jehoiachin's grandson Zerubbabel led the returning exiles to Judah after the decree of Cyrus (539) and rebuilt the temple in Jerusalem (Ezra 2:2; 3:2; 4:3; 5:2; Zech 4:9).

INSCRIPTIONS THAT INFORM OUR UNDERSTANDING OF JEHOIACHIN

Numerous inscriptions assist in piecing together the story of Jehoiachin. Pride of place goes to the Babylonian Chronicle, which establishes that in the eighth year of Nebuchadrezzar, in Kislev (November/December

Introduction

598), the Babylonian king marched to the land of *Hatti* (Palestine). He besieged the city of Judah (Jerusalem) on the second of Adar (15/16 March 597), took the city, captured the king (Jehoiachin), appointed one of his own choice (Zedekiah), imposed heavy tribute, and took captives back to Babylon.[17]

In addition to the Babylonian Chronicle, the Weidner Tablets unearthed in the vicinity of the Ishtar Gate in ancient Babylon (one of four texts dated 592/591) stipulate that the king (Nebuchadrezzar) provided Jehoiachin (*Ya'u-kinu*) supplies of oil and barley. "The Tablets also contain references to other Judeans, to inhabitants of Ashkelon, Tyre, Byblos, and Arvad, and to Egyptians, Elamites, Lydians, and others."[18] The Unger Prism additionally lists what may be the nations of captive kings in Babylon with Jehoiachin (kings of Tyre, Gaza, Sidon, Arvad, and Ashdod).

Numerous impressed storage jug handles known as the Eliakim seal impressions were discovered at Tell Beit Mirsim, Beth-shemesh, and Ramat Rahel. Although these are by no means conclusive, the inscription *l'lyqm n'r ywkn* ("to Eliakim servant of Yaukin") seems to point to Jehoiachin who at the time was in prison in Babylon. "Most scholars accept the identification of the Yaukin of this seal impression with Jehoiachin."[19]

Two seal impressions contemporaneous with the fall of Jerusalem in 586—inscribed, "to Jaazaniah, servant of the king" (see 2 Kgs 25:23) and "to Gedaliah, who is over the house" (2 Kgs 25:22–25)—may provide background information.[20]

Lachish Ostracon III describes Coniahu son of Elnathan (כניהו בן אלנתן), the commander of the army, "going down to Egypt," possibly to request assistance in breaking the Babylonian siege of Jerusalem in 587. Coniahu son of Elnathan is a contemporary of Zedekiah and obviously different from Jehoiachin son of Jehoiakim.

Excavations of the Ishtar Gate and the South Citadel of Babylon (potentially Jehoiachin's house-arrest location), signet rings from ancient Nineveh, and other finds are explained when they help establish the story of Jehoiachin within the chapters that follow.

---

17. Wiseman, *Chronicles of the Chaldean Kings*, 36.
18. May, "Jehoiachin," 3:811.
19. Berridge, "Jehoiachin," 3:662.
20. May, "Three Hebrew Seals and the Status of Exiled Jehoiachin," 146–48.

Introduction

OUTLINE OF OUR STUDY

Chapter 1: Jehoiachin in the Narratives Concerning the Davidic Kings

2 Kings 24:6–17: Jehoiachin's accession, surrender, and exile to Babylon

2 Chronicles 36:8–10: Jehoiachin's age, reign, and exile with the temple vessels

2 Kings 25:27–30: In the thirty-seventh year of his exile, Jehoiachin's release from prison

Jeremiah 52:31–34: Parallel account of Jehoiachin's release from prison and death

The pericopes chosen reflect the narratives of the demise of the last four kings of Judah and Jehoiachin's eventual release from the Babylonian prison. The international situation of the Levant is set in the appropriate historical timeline. We address these topics: (1) the Babylonian deportation of 597 in the light of the Babylonian Chronicle; (2) Jehoiachin's age at accession (eighteen in 2 Kgs 24:8 or eight in 2 Chr 36:9); (3) the relationship between Jehoiachin and Zedekiah (nephew in 2 Kgs 24:17 or brother in 2 Chr 36:10); (4) the Chronicler's emphasis on exile and tribute for each of the last four Davidic kings (2 Chr 36:1–21); (5) the accounts regarding the temple treasures (2 Kgs 24:13; 2 Chr 36:10); (6) Nebuchadrezzar's successor, Evil-merodach (Amel-marduk, 562–560); and (7) the minor date differences (twenty-fifth day in 2 Kgs 25:27, twenty-seventh day in Jer 52:31, twenty-fourth day in LXX$^{\text{Jer 52:31}}$).

Chapter 1, as in the two succeeding chapters, will begin with the proposed reconstructed Hebrew text for each pericope. This text is explained by critical notes and translated, followed by a discussion of the background, verse-by-verse discussion, and how the text informs our understanding of Jehoiachin.

Chapter 2: Jeremiah's Prophecies: Jeconiah in Babylon

Jeremiah 36:30–31: To Jehoiakim, "None to sit upon the Throne of David"

Introduction

> Jeremiah 13:18–19: To the king and queen mother, "All Judah is taken into exile"
>
> Jeremiah 22:24–30: Coniah, Yahweh's cast-out signet (חותם), dishonored and ערירי
>
> Jeremiah 24:1–3: Yahweh looks after "good" (Jeconiah) and "bad figs" (Zedekiah)
>
> Jeremiah 27:19–22: The remaining temple vessels to go to Babylon (like Jeconiah)
>
> Jeremiah 28:1–4: Hananiah predicts, "Jeconiah and vessels to return in two years"
>
> Jeremiah 29:1–3: Jeremiah's letter to (Jeconiah in) Babylon, "Build and multiply..."
>
> Jeremiah 37:1–2: Zedekiah to reign in Judah in place of the exiled Coniah

These pericopes refer to Jeconiah and Coniah, unlike the preponderant use of Jehoiachin in the narratives. The first two pericopes prophesy an end to the primogeniture succession of Davidic kings on the throne. Jeremiah 22:24–30 is the pivotal prophecy in this chapter. It records Yahweh's oath that Coniah and his mother were to be violently hurled into captivity in Babylon. Coniah is described as wretched, cast-out, and without offspring to sit on the throne of David. Jeremiah 24:1–3 is Yahweh's promise to look after the exiles as "good figs" and chastise those remaining in Jerusalem with Zedekiah as "bad figs." Jeremiah 27:19–22 includes the prediction that the temple vessels would end up in Babylon—just as Jeconiah did. Jeremiah 28:1–4 records the controversy between Hananiah and Jeremiah regarding the length of the exile. Jeremiah 29:1–3 is the letter stating that the exile would last longer than that specified by the prophets like Hananiah.

Chapter 3: Jeconiah in Other Prophetic and Narrative Literature

> Ezekiel 1:1–3: Ezekiel in Babylon in the fifth (through twenty-seventh) year of the exile of Jehoiachin
> 1 Chronicles 3:15–19: Sons born to Jeconiah... the captive (אסר)
> Haggai 2:20–23: Zerubbabel (Jeconiah's grandson) to be like a signet (כחותם)
> Esther 2:5–7: Mordecai in Susa, exiled with Jeconiah

Introduction

Ezekiel dates his prophecy from the fifth year of the exile of Jehoiachin. It is significant that the book uses dates from the exile of Jehoiachin instead of the fall of Jerusalem in 586 under Zedekiah (33:21).

The sons of Jeconiah are named in 1 Chronicles 3. The meaning of אסר in the MT of this pericope is carefully examined.

The prophecy of Haggai likens Zerubbabel to a returning signet. This is a reversal of Jeremiah 22:24–30, the prophecy that Coniah (his grandfather) was to be cast out as a signet.

Esther 2:5–6 implies that Mordecai's great-grandfather Kish was exiled with Jeconiah (cf. Add Esth 11:2–4).

Chapter 4: Reflections of Jehoiachin in the Poetry of Israel

Ezekiel 17: Allegory of top bough of cedar taken to a land of traders
    Ezekiel 19: Lament of a lioness left without a scepter to rule
    Lamentations 3 and 4: "I am the man who has known affliction"
    Isaiah 52 and 53: "Behold, my (Suffering) Servant!"
    Psalm 61: "Hear my cry, O God"
    Psalm 89: Lament over David's debased throne

Allusions in Ezekiel 17 and 19 are explained as they refer to Jehoiachin. Porteous and Rudolph opined that the sufferings of Jehoiachin might have suggested some of the imagery of Lamentations 3 and 4. Barnes proposed Psalm 61 as a prayer of Jehoiachin in exile. Goulder suggested that the "Suffering Servant" of Isaiah 52–53 and the subject of Psalm 89 are one and the same—Jehoiachin. These proposals are carefully examined.

Chapter 5: Reflections of Jeconiah in intertestamental and NT literature

    1 Esdras 1:9ff: Variant tradition of Jeconiah and Jehoiachin

    Josephus' Encomiums regarding Jeconiah/Jehoiachin

    Additions to Esther 11:2–4: Mordecai in Susa brought from Jerusalem with Jeconiah

    Rabbinical: Reading Rabbinic Judaism (Jeconiah's exile) back into the Bible

    Baruch 1:3–9: Baruch's letter read to Jeconiah in Babylon

Introduction

> Matthew 1:1–17: Fourteen generations after Jeconiah's exile—Jesus Christ

The Apocrypha records alternate traditions regarding Jeconiah. Specifically, 1 Esdras records Jeconiah, Jehoiakim, and Jehoiachin in the same pericope, an apparent confusion of the biblical account. The Greek additions to Esther record that Mordecai was exiled with Jeconiah. The text of Baruch was reportedly read by Baruch in the hearing of Jeconiah.

Josephus rewrites the canonical accounts to serve his purposes. He may have depended on the rabbinical tradition—an interesting "reading back into Scripture" of rabbinic Judaism. That both Josephus and the rabbis amend Jehoiachin's legacy is a fascinating topic by itself.

The genealogy in Matthew includes the allusive phrase "Jeconiah *and his brothers*" (emphasis added). The exile was the most momentous event in the history of Israel. The name linked to this exile is Jeconiah—not Zedekiah, as one might suspect.

Chapter 6: Conclusions

> Yahweh promised a Davidic king reigning as coregent and signet
>
> Curses excluded Hezekiah, Jehoahaz, Jehoiakim, Jehoiachin, and Zedekiah
>
> The Davidic throne fell, but hope for redemption remained in 2 Kings 25 and Jeremiah 52
>
> Zerubbabel, like a signet, rebuilt the Temple of Yahweh
>
> "Rewritten Bible" of Josephus and the rabbinics modified Jehoiachin's legacy
>
> NT: Royal lineage of David; "House and line of David"

The conclusions synthesize what has been stated about Jehoiachin in each of these chapters. Additional suggestions for further research are suggested. An extensive bibliography is included.

CHAPTER 1

Jehoiachin in the Narratives Concerning the Davidic Kings

INTRODUCTION

THIS CHAPTER EXAMINES THE narrative accounts of the life of Jeconiah (616–560? BCE), named Jehoiachin (יהויכין) in these four pericopes. The initial pericope, 2 Kings 24:6–17, is the most comprehensive account of the parentage, life, accession, siege, surrender, and exile of Jehoiachin and covers the years 616–597. Jehoiachin's parents were Jehoiakim son of Josiah and Nehushta daughter of Elnathan. Jehoiakim's death after withholding tribute (24:1) from Nebuchadrezzar led to the installation of the eighteen-year-old king during a chaotic period. Jehoiachin did evil according to that which his father had done (24:9).

The Babylonian Chronicle underscores the accuracy of the biblical record. In the eighth year of his reign, Nebuchadrezzar and the Chaldean army marched to Judah. The Babylonian host besieged Jerusalem, and Jehoiachin capitulated in March 597 with his family and officials. The royal family, priests, nobles, and 10,000 residents were exiled to Babylon. The prospects were decidedly bleak in Judah. "All" the treasures, vessels, princes, men of valor, craftsmen, and smiths were exiled.

The second pericope (2 Chr 36:8–10) paints a shaded version of the portrait of Jehoiachin. It adds to the evil characterization of Jehoiakim, records Jehoiachin's age as eight at accession, specifies his reign as three months and ten days, and notes that Nebuchadrezzar did not personally attend the siege of Jerusalem. It further states that Zedekiah was Jehoiachin's brother.

The narratives we selected for chapter 1 completely skip 596–563, the years of Zedekiah's reign in Judah and Jerusalem, Gedaliah's governorship, and the rest of Nebuchadrezzar's rule. This gap is filled by the prophecies of Jeremiah (chapter 2) and other prophetic and narrative literature (chapter 3).

We resume with the account of 2 Kings 25, Jehoiachin's release from prison after thirty-seven years in captivity. Evil-merodach (reigned 562–560), Nebuchadrezzar's son, in an apparent accession-year emancipation, set Jehoiachin free from prison, in preference to the other captive kings. (For the exiles in Babylon, this news must have been encouraging. Could the king's primacy signal a return to days of Joseph's favor in Pharaoh's court?)

The Jeremiah 52:31–34 pericope adds a few nuances in date and the death announcement to the 2 Kings 25:27–30 account. With the death of the last living king of Judah and Jerusalem, the focus must have shifted to his offspring, Shealtiel and Pedaiah (considered in chapter 3), and to the writings of the poets reflecting on Jehoiachin's exile (chapter 4).

2 KINGS 24:6–17: JEHOIACHIN'S ACCESSION, SURRENDER, AND EXILE TO BABYLON

Reconstructed text of 2 Kings 24:6–17

⁶ וישכב יהויקים ᵃ עם אבתיו וימלך יהויכין בנו תחתיו
⁷ ולא הסיף עוד מלך מצרים לצאת מארצו כי לקח מלך בבל מנחל מצרים עד נהר פרת כל אשר היתה למלך מצרים
⁸ בן שמנה עשרה שנה יהויכין במלכו ושלשה חדשים מלך בירושלם ושם אמו נחשתא בת אלנתן מירושלם ⁹ ויעש הרע בעיני יהוה ככל אשר עשה אביו ¹⁰ בעת ההיא ᵃ עלו עבדי נבכדנאצר מלך בבל ירושלם ותבא העיר במצור
¹¹ ויבא נבוכדנאצר מלך בבל על העיר ועבדיו צרים עליה
¹² ויצא יהויכין מלך יהודה על מלך בבל הוא ואמו ועבדיו שריו וסריסיו ויקח אתו מלך בבל בשנת שמנה למלכו
¹³ ויוצא משם את כל אוצרות בית יהוה ואוצרות בית המלך

Jehoiachin in the Narratives Concerning the Davidic Kings

ויקצץ את כל כלי הזהב אשר עשה שלמה מלך ישראל
בהיכל יהוה כאשר דבר יהוה 14 והגלה את כל ירושלם
ואת כל השרים ואת כל ᵃגבורי החיל ᵇ עשרת אלפים
גולה וכל החרש והמסגר לא נשאר זולת דלת עם
הארץ 15 ויגל את יהויכין בבלה ואת אם המלך
ואת נשי המלך ואת סריסיו ואת ᵃ אילי הארץ
הוליך גולה מירושלם בבלה 16 ואת כל אנשי
החיל שבעת אלפים והחרש והמסגר אלף הכל
גבורים עשי מלחמה ויביאם מלך בבל גולה בבלה
17 וימלך מלך בבל את מתניה דדו תחתיו ויסב את
שמו צדקיהו

Text notes

6a: LXXᴸ adds καὶ ἐτάφη ἐν κήπῳ Οζα, "and he was buried in the Garden of Uza." Neither LXXᴬ nor LXXᴮ has this addition. (LXX[2 Chr 36:8] inserts καὶ ἐτάφη ἐν κήπῳ Γανοζα.) Retain MT.

10a: MT has עבדי נבכדנאצר מלך בבל. The *Qere* has the plural verb עלו, reflecting the plural subject עבדי, "servants," in construct with Nebuchadrezzar. The *Kethib* has the singular verb עלה and would reflect deletion of the plural noun עבדי. LXX has the singular verb ἀνέβη, "came up," and refers to the king of Babylon. Jones,[1] Robinson,[2] Montgomery,[3] Hobbs,[4] and Seitz[5] all retain the plural noun and the plural *Qere*. Gray concludes that 24:11 "must refer to a parallel tradition of the initial activity of Nebuchadrezzar's officers, he himself arriving for the final stage of the siege."[6] Without additional offsetting evidence, we retain MT *Qere*.

14a: MT has ואת כל גבורי החיל, "and all the men of valor." LXX has καὶ τοὺς δυνατοὺς ἰσχύι, literally, "and those capable of strength." Retain MT.

14b: MT *Qere* עֲשֶׂרֶת "ten" in construct; *Kethib* עֲשָׂרָה. The *Qere* here is preferable.

1. G. Jones, *1 and 2 Kings*, 636.
2. Robinson, *The Second Book of Kings*, 235.
3. Montgomery and Gehman, *The Books of Kings*, 554.
4. Hobbs, *Second Kings*, 345.
5. Seitz, *Theology in Conflict*, 97.
6. Gray, *I and II Kings*, 691.

15a: MT *Qere* אֱיָלֵי and *Kethib* אוּלֵי. LXX has ἰσχυρούς "the mighty." Hobbs mentions Ehrlich's emendation to גְּדוֹלֵי, then dismisses it as unnecessary.[7]

Translation of 2 Kings 24:6–17

6So Jehoiakim slept with his fathers, and Jehoiachin his son became king in his place. 7Now the king of Egypt did not come out of his land again, for the king of Babylon had taken all that belonged to the king of Egypt from the brook of Egypt to the river Euphrates.

8Jehoiachin was eighteen years old when he became king, and he reigned three months in Jerusalem; and his mother's name was Nehushta the daughter of Elnathan of Jerusalem. 9And he did evil in the sight of the Lord, according to all that his father had done.

10At that time, the servants of Nebuchadrezzar king of Babylon came up to Jerusalem, and the city was besieged. 11And Nebuchadrezzar the king of Babylon came to the city, while his servants were besieging it; 12and Jehoiachin the king of Judah went out to the king of Babylon—he and his mother and his servants and his captains and his officials. So the king of Babylon took him captive in the eighth year of his reign. 13And he carried out from there all the treasures of the house of the Lord, and the treasures of the king's house, and cut in pieces all the vessels of gold which Solomon king of Israel had made for the temple of the Lord, just as the Lord had said. 14Then he led away into exile all Jerusalem and all the captains and all the mighty men of valor, ten thousand captives, and all the craftsmen and the smiths. None remained except the poorest people of the land. 15So he led Jehoiachin away into exile to Babylon; also the king's mother and the king's wives and his officials and the chief men of the land, he led away into exile from Jerusalem to Babylon. 16And the king of Babylon brought captive to Babylon all the men of valor, seven thousand, and the craftsmen and the smiths, one thousand, all of them strong and fit for war.

17 The king of Babylon made his uncle, Mattaniah, king in his place, and changed his name to Zedekiah.

---

7. Hobbs, *Second Kings*, 345. See *BDB* 17–18.

Jehoiachin in the Narratives Concerning the Davidic Kings

Background of the 2 Kings account

Before investigating the implications of Jehoiachin's march into captivity, it is useful to trace the 2 Kings 21–24 account of the last five Davidic kings who ruled on the throne of Judah and Jerusalem. This allows us to develop the portrait of Jehoiachin in contrast to the portraits of the kings who ruled before and after his short reign. The account of Jehoiachin follows the momentous account of the kings slightly before the end of Judean independence. Israel and Judah experienced shifting fortunes and vassal obligations to the seventh-century suzerains of Assyria, Egypt, and Babylon.

The siege of Samaria by the Assyrian army (2 Kgs 18:9) beginning circa 701 BCE took nearly three years. Sennacherib refused the tribute and sent his generals, "Tartan, the Rabsaris, and the Rabshakeh" (18:17), with a large army from Lachish to forewarn Hezekiah that Jerusalem was the next city to suffer siege. The Rabshakeh accused Hezekiah of relying on Egypt—that "broken reed of a staff." Although the Assyrians were prevented from completing the capture of Jerusalem due to miraculous intervention, Hezekiah was rebuked by Isaiah for revealing the treasure in the temple and in the king's house to the Babylonian emissaries (2 Kgs 20:16–18; Isa 39:5–7):

> Hear the word of the LORD: Behold, the days are coming, when all that is in your house, and that which your fathers have stored up till this day, shall be carried to Babylon; nothing shall be left, says the LORD. And some of your own sons, who are born to you, shall be taken away; and they shall be eunuchs in the palace of the king of Babylon.

The Babylonian emissaries were eyewitnesses to the vast treasure store in the temple and king's palace, magnanimously afforded by Hezekiah.

The vituperative condemnation of Manasseh son of Hezekiah is summarized by Southwell:

> 2 Kgs 21 depicts Manasseh as an evil ruler, reverting from his father's piety to the syncretism of the kings of Israel. . . . Upon his death he was buried not in the royal sepulchers but in the "garden of Uzza." Not even the unparalleled reform of Josiah could stem the effects (of Manasseh's sin—23:26–27; 24:3–4).[8]

---

8. Southwell, "Theology of Manasseh," 4:930–32.

Looking Back for Jehoiachin

The unnamed prophets of 21:10 announced disaster on Jerusalem for Manasseh's sins:

> And I will stretch over Jerusalem the measuring line of Samaria, and the plummet of the house of Ahab; and I will wipe Jerusalem as one wipes a dish, wiping it and turning it upside down. And I will cast off the remnant of my heritage, and give them into the hand of their enemies, and they shall become a prey and a spoil to all their enemies (21:13–14).

Amon son of Manasseh reigned two years in like evil manner and was assassinated by his servants (21:23). Manasseh and Amon were both buried in the garden of Uzza (21:18, 26).

The people of the land (עַם הָאָרֶץ) made Josiah king in Amon's stead (21:24). Josiah's reforms, in accordance with the book of the law found in the temple, are detailed in 22:11–23:24.

Despite Josiah's reform, the theological perspective in 23:26–27 states that Yahweh would not turn from his great wrath provoked by Manasseh's sin. "I will remove Judah also out of my sight, as I have removed Israel, and I will cast off this city which I have chosen, Jerusalem, and the house of which I said, My name shall be there."

In 609, Pharaoh Neco king of Egypt went up to the Euphrates to recoup some of the kingdom of the recently defeated Assyria. King Josiah attempted to delay him and was slain.

The עַם הָאָרֶץ made Jehoahaz king in place of his father Josiah (23:30). He reigned three months and was deposed by Pharaoh Neco. He was taken captive to Egypt, where he died.

Pharaoh Neco installed Eliakim (אֶלְיָקִים) son of Josiah as king (23:34)[9] and changed his name to Jehoiakim (יְהוֹיָקִים), the prerogative of a suzerain upon a vassal king (cf. 2 Kgs 24:17). Neco imposed a tribute of 100 talents of silver and a talent of gold[10] on the land. Jehoiakim

---

9. Chronologically, Jehoiakim succeeded Jehoahaz, not Josiah. Long (*The Forms of OT Literature*, 288) classifies the genre of 23:34 as a report. Although this report is in accordance with normal succession notification, it differs from the norm in that Jehoiakim reigned in place of Jehoahaz (his younger brother, cf. 1 Chr 3:15) who is not named. The author of 2 Kgs may have chosen to account for the succession in this manner due to the brevity of Jehoahaz's reign, the fact that he was a brother instead of a son, or because the appointment was made by the Pharaoh and was not regarded as the ideal succession protocol. It may also have been intended as an intentional slight to the memory of his exiled predecessor Jehoahaz.

10. The LXX has ἑκατὸν τάλαντα χρυσίου, "and one hundred talents of gold." The LXX^L and Syriac reflect ten talents.

Jehoiachin in the Narratives Concerning the Davidic Kings

extracted (נגש implies force or coercion) the silver and gold from the עם הארץ for the assessment (23:35). Second Kings 23:37 reports that Jehoiakim did what was evil in the sight of Yahweh.

The phrase "in his days" (בימיו, 2 Kgs 24:1) frequently prefaces an invasion, revolt, or catastrophe occurring in the land (cf. 1 Kgs 16:34; 21:29; 2 Kgs 8:20; 23:29). Thus here, also: Nebuchadrezzar came to Jerusalem to end the era of Egyptian suzerainty and redirect the tribute to Babylon. Jehoiakim paid Nebuchadrezzar's covenant demands for three years and then rebelled (מרד) in 601/600. Yahweh (per the MT) or Nebuchadrezzar (per the LXX) sent against him and the land of Judah marauding bands of Chaldeans, Arameans, Moabites, and Ammonites in fulfillment of the word of the prophets.[11]

Second Kings 24:6 says that Jehoiakim slept with his fathers, (LXX^{L+} "in the garden of Uzza.")[12]

To sum up the shape of the narrative: Josiah, portrayed as a righteous and reverent king, attempted to obviate the wrath of Yahweh by his thoroughgoing reforms. His death at the hand of Pharaoh Neco occurred when Jehoiachin was seven years old. In precipitate fashion, Jehoahaz was enthroned by the people of the land and, within three months, deposed and taken to Egypt, where he died.

The egregious pronouncements of the prophets of 2 Kings 21:13–14 and 23:26–27 hung like the sword of Damocles over the kingdom of Judah at the verge of the sixth century. Jehoiakim, king of broken covenants, struggled continuously but unsuccessfully for independence from suzerains.

Nebuchadrezzar, champion of Carchemish, had restrained Egypt and planned to crush the covenant-breaker Jehoiakim. However, Jehoiakim died before the retributive Babylonian siege of 598. But even death could not obviate the defiling of his corpse. The LXX^L at 2 Kings 24:6 and LXX at 2 Chronicles 36:8 preserve the note that Jehoiakim was buried (with Manasseh and Amon) in the garden of Uzza. The evil characterization of Jehoiakim was graphically precise in the narrative passages 2 Kings 23:34—24:4 and 2 Chronicles 36:5–8.

---

11. The word of the prophets in 24:2 may refer to the curses pronounced successively against Hezekiah (2 Kgs 20:16–19 // Isa 39:5–8), Manasseh (2 Kgs 21:11–15), Jehoahaz (Jer 22:10–12), Jehoiakim (Jer 7:14–15; 22:13–19; 36:29–31), Jeconiah (Jer 22:24–30), and Zedekiah (Jer 21:3–7; 24:8–10; 34:2–3).

12. Manasseh, Amon, and Jehoiakim (LXX^{L+}) were buried in the garden of Uzza. The implication is that only the most wicked kings were buried there.

Looking Back for Jehoiachin

Jehoiachin was eighteen years old and reigned three months in place of his father Jehoiakim. He initially resisted the siege by the Chaldean generals, but eventually surrendered upon the arrival of the king of Babylon (24:12). With only three months experience as king, and without hope for relief from Egypt, he had little choice. Jehoiachin faced King Nebuchadrezzar personally in 2 Kings 25, but was sent for in 2 Chronicles 36. The Babylonian Chronicle corroborates the capitulation to Nebuchadrezzar. Jehoiachin was redeemed by his release in 2 Kings 25:27–30 and Jeremiah 52:31–34. He was the penultimate Judean king in 2 Kings 25, but merely anticlimactic in 2 Chronicles 36.

Second Kings 24:6–17 by verses: Jehoiachin son of Jehoiakim

24:6–7: The death of the provocateur Jehoiakim occurred prior to the arrival of the Chaldeans. Normal succession from father to son followed shortly before the arrival of the aggrieved suzerain Nebuchadrezzar. After the Babylonians defeated Egypt at Carchemish in 605 BCE, there was nothing to prevent the investiture and reduction of the Judean defenses.

24:8–9: Jehoiachin was eighteen when he became king and he reigned for three months in Jerusalem.[13] (His mother was Nehushta daughter of Elnathan of Jerusalem.) He succeeded Jehoiakim during a time of intense military activity.[14] Nebuchadrezzar had asserted his status as Jehoiakim's suzerain in 24:1. Because Jehoiakim had withheld tribute during a time of decreased Babylonian mobility, Nebuchadrezzar sent the surrounding nations to harass Judah's borders.[15] Egypt was unable to ameliorate the situation for its former vassal because Babylon had defeated Egypt in the decisive battle of Carchemish in 605, a note explained in 24:7. Jehoiachin did evil in the eyes of Yahweh as his father had done.

---

13. 2 Chr 36:9 reports that Jehoiachin was eight years old and reigned three months and ten days. This difference is likely due to haplography of the numeral ten (עשרה). See 2 Chr 36:8–10 discussion.

14. Were there brothers who might have been chosen for the throne in place of Jehoiachin? 1 Chr 3:16 names Jehoiakim's sons as Jeconiah and Zedekiah (not the same as Zedekiah son of Josiah). Jer 36:26 mentions Jerahmeel the king's son (ירחמאל בן המלך), who was probably a court official (Avigad, "Baruch the Scribe," and Lundbom, "Jerahmeel"). So, there was at least one other son of Jehoiakim who went into captivity with Jehoiachin.

15. Gray's assertion that Yahweh is a gloss from 24:3 could possibly be correct, since κύριον is not in the LXX, but the impetus behind Nebuchadrezzar's activity would certainly be credited to Yahweh by the author(s) of Kings.

Jehoiachin in the Narratives Concerning the Davidic Kings

24:10–11: The indication of 24:10 (בעת ההיא עלה) is reminiscent of 24:1 (בימיו עלה). Several years had transpired, but the same threat reappeared. Nebuchadrezzar (with additional forces) came up to Jerusalem, and resistance was futile. The siege began, according to the Babylonian Chronicle, in the month of Kislev (November–December) 598 and ended three months later on the second day of Adar (March) 597.[16]

As the text reports, there was no opportunity for relief as in the deliverance of a century earlier (701). At that time, Hezekiah had attempted to negotiate a settlement with the Assyrians during the siege of Jerusalem (18:13–16). Sennacherib refused three hundred talents of silver and thirty talents of gold. Second Kings 19:35 attributes the miraculous deliverance of Jerusalem to the angel of the LORD who slaughtered 185,000 Assyrians in a single night. Presumably some (fortunate) soldiers returned with Sennacherib before the catastrophe, so the force at its strength during siege numbered more than the modern equivalent of ten European infantry divisions. By the time of the 597 siege of Jerusalem, Yahweh had already condemned Jerusalem to destruction (cf. 2 Kgs 23:27). There would be no relief.

24:12–16: Jehoiachin surrendered in the eighth year of Nebuchadrezzar's reign (note the dating shift to the Babylonian regnal system). The Babylonians carried off all (כל)[17] the treasures of the temple and palace and cut up the vessels[18] of gold which Solomon,[19] king of Israel, had made for the temple, as the LORD had foretold. (The use of the phrase "king of Israel" is filled with pathos—there had not been a king of *Israel and Judah* for 333 years.) None remained except the poorest people of

---

16. For dating, see Kutsch, "Das Jahr der Katastophe." In the interest of simplicity, we refer to Nebuchadrezzar's departure from Babylon in 598 and the exile of Jeconiah occurring 597, rather than the more accurate but untidy 598/597. This is not to minimize the complexity of the dating issue, which is vigorously pursued in the literature.

17. This is possibly hyperbolic language (cf. 2 Kgs 24:13, 14, 16). Not all of Jerusalem was taken into captivity, since there were priests, Levites, and others left in Zedekiah's kingdom. This use of כל could also be the feature "synecdoche of the genus," i.e., universals in place of particulars. Ten thousand captives is at least a representative mark. But tension does exist with the smaller numbers of Jer 52:27–30 (4,600 captives).

18. Did Nebuchadrezzar cut up the treasures, or did he take them intact for later salvage? Was his decision based on punishment of the captives, or was it purely utilitarian or economic? Does this imply a tension with other biblical accounts of the vessels being returned to Jerusalem, e.g., Ezra 8:26–30? See chapter 2.

19. Why would the author(s) of Kings record Solomon's name in 24:13? Could this have been a reference to his contribution to the eventual destruction of the Jerusalem temple?

the land and those whom Nebuchadrezzar left to operate the state in vastly reduced form. Jehoiachin with his royal house and nobility were deported to Babylon, likely in Nebuchadrezzar's train for parading naked into Babylon. The army, artisans, and smiths probably followed with the main body of the Babylonian force.[20]

24:17.   Nebuchadrezzar chose Jehoiachin's uncle Mattaniah as a (puppet) king and changed his name to Zedekiah—the prerogative of a suzerain upon a vassal king in a covenant similar to that which Nebuchadrezzar had imposed upon Jehoiakim (cf. 2 Chr 36:13).

How 2 Kings 24:6–17 informs our understanding of Jehoiachin

Second Kings 24:3–4 states that (Jehoiachin's great-great-grandfather) Manasseh's sins (21:1–18) led to the doom of Jerusalem and the decision of Yahweh to abandon Judah to destruction.

With the international political vagaries of 2 Kings 21–24 as background, and the curses of 21:13–14 and 23:26–27 pending fulfillment, Jehoiakim (his father) was crowned king by Neco and ruled through a series of broken covenants. Jehoiakim struggled continuously for independence from authority. Jehoiachin's father was the covenant breaker par excellence. He successively broke covenant with Yahweh (Jer 22:3–4), with the עם הארץ (Jer 22:13–19), with Pharaoh Neco who installed him on the throne (2 Kgs 24:1), and also with Nebuchadrezzar, his Babylonian overlord (24:1). May and Myers speculate that the עם הארץ may have assassinated Jehoiakim[21] hoping to offset the expected retribution against the city and people by the northern invader.[22]

There is wonderful irony in the account of Jehoiakim's extraction of tribute from the עם הארץ, who had bypassed him in favor of his younger brother Jehoahaz, and his breaking of the Egyptian covenant in favor of a Babylonian one, only to break that one when he felt it was opportune. The pharaoh was ineffective in controlling his vassal or protecting Judah from the incursions of the armies from the north and east. Whether immediately under Babylonian mercenary employ (LXX), or at the behest

---

20. See the discussion "carpenters and sappers" in Hobbs, *Second Kings*, 353.

21. May, "Jehoiachin," 811; Myers, *I and II Chronicles*, 218.

22. The texts of 2 Kgs and Jer regarding Jehoiakim's final settlement are in tension as to whether Jehoiakim was buried with his fathers, in the garden of Uzza, or with "the burial of an ass" (Jer 22:19). See n. 12.

Jehoiachin in the Narratives Concerning the Davidic Kings

of Yahweh (MT), the Chaldean, Syrian, Moabite, and Ammonite raiders made life bitter for Jehoiakim. He was surrounded. To the north were the Assyrian-sponsored Samaritans, the hostile Syrians, and the Babylonians. To the south the constrained Egyptian pharaoh was urging Judean, Arab, and Canaanite insurrection against the Babylonians. The Moabites, Ammonites, and opportunistic Edomites were hostile to Judah's continuation. Jehoiakim died before the retributive Babylonian siege occurred.

The different biblical characterizations of the evil of Jehoahaz, Jehoiakim, Jehoiachin, and Zedekiah are intriguing. Jehoahaz, who had a righteous father and an evil grandfather, did evil as his *fathers* (ככל אשר עשו אבתיו) had done. Likewise, Jehoiakim, who had the same righteous father and evil grandfather, did evil as his *fathers* (ככל אשר אעשה אביו) had done. Jehoiachin, who had an evil father and righteous grandfather, did evil as his *father* (ככל אשר אעשה אביו) had done. Zedekiah, like Jehoahaz and Jehoiakim, with a righteous father, evil grandfather, and evil predecessor (Jehoiachin) did evil as Jehoiakim (ככל אשר עשה יהויקים) had done. The characterizations are very precise and seem to reflect the theological *tendenz* of the narrator of 2 Kings.

This begs the question of how much evil an eighteen-year-old king could do in three months (24:9). The terse nature of the narrative says little, although continuing his father's self-interested abuse of the people might have been at the root of the charge. The evil (הרע) could likewise have been idolatry, although Jeremiah's prophetic tone towards Jehoiachin was routinely sympathetic, instructive, and pathetic in contrast to the caustic prophecies addressed to Jehoiakim.[23] As far as the editor(s) of 2 Kings was concerned, Judah had gone beyond the point of forgiveness. Nothing would prevent the young king's exile to Babylon; it had been foretold from the days of Hezekiah (2 Kgs 20:16–18; Isa 39:5–7).

Jehoiachin surrendered (ויצא) to the king of Babylon (24:12). After the introductory formula, this is the only verb with Jehoiachin as subject. All remaining verbs describe what other kings were doing, i.e., Nebuchadrezzar, Neco, and even Solomon. This seems to indicate that all the initiative was external to Jehoiachin; indeed, he had very little choice.

Recapping the critical issues of this pericope, we see that Jehoiakim's death and Jehoiachin's accession occurred during a time of Egyptian constraint due to Babylonian hegemony. The siege of Jerusalem in 597 had a

---

23. See the discussion in chapter 2.

different outcome than the one in 701. Jehoiachin surrendered and was transported to Babylon with his wives, wealth, and talent.

2 CHRONICLES 36:8-10 JEHOIACHIN'S AGE, REIGN AND EXILE WITH THE TEMPLE VESSELS

Having surveyed the longest and most complete pericope regarding Jehoiachin, it is appropriate to examine the Chronicler's shorter account and highlight the differences. Notably, there is a different age (from the MT) and duration of Jehoiachin's reign (MT and LXX), probably due to a misplaced numeral. The Chronicler says that Nebuchadrezzar sent for Jehoiachin instead of personally attending to the siege of Jerusalem. Lastly, the Chronicler states that Zedekiah was the brother (MT) of Jehoiachin rather than his uncle (LXX) as indicated in 2 Kings 24. This pericope also highlights the abominations of Jehoiakim.

Reconstructed text of 2 Chronicles 36:8–10

⁸ ויתר דברי יהויקים ותעבתיו אשר עשה והנמצא עליו הנם
כתובים על ספר מלכי ישראל ויהודה וימלך יהויכין בנו
תחתיו ⁹ -a- בן שמונה [עשרה] שנה יהויכין במלכו -b a- ושלשה
חדשים מלך -b- בירושלם ויעש הרע בעיני יהוה ¹⁰ ולתשובת
השנה שלח המלך נבוכדנאצר ויבאהו בבלה עם כלי חמדת
בית יהוה וימלך את צדקיהו -a- אחי אביו -a- על יהודה וירושלם

Text notes

9a-a: MT has בן שמונה שנים יהויכין במלכו, "Jehoiachin was *eight* years old when he became king." The LXX has υἱὸς ὀκτωκαίδεκα ἐτῶν Ιεχονιας ἐν τῷ βασιλεύειν αὐτόν, "Jeconiah was *eighteen* years old when he began to reign." MT 2 Kings 24:8 has בן שמנה עשרה שנה יהויכין במלכו, "Jehoiachin was *eighteen* years old when he became king" (LXX agrees). First Esdras 1:43 has ὅτε γάρ ἀνεδείχθη ἦν ἐτῶν δέκα ὀκτώ, "for when he was made king he was *eighteen* years old." Dillard[24] and Curtis[25] relocate the עשרה from the duration of his reign

---

24. Dillard, *2 Chronicles*, 296.
25. Curtis and Madsen, *A Critical and Exegetical Commentary on the Books of*

to reflect Jehoiachin's age as eighteen as a misplaced corrector's gloss. Williamson,[26] Japhet,[27] Myers,[28] and Curtis[29] agree that the age should be *eighteen*.[30] This textual decision may eliminate what may have been an important alternate tradition, i.e., that Jehoiachin was indeed a very young king. However, based on the likelihood of a misplaced numeral עשרה, emend Jehoiachin's age to eighteen.

9b-b: MT has ושלשה חדשים ועשרת ימים מלך, "and he ruled three months and ten days." The LXX has καὶ τρίμηνον καὶ δέκα ἡμέρας, "three months and ten days." The MT of 2 Kings 24:8 has ושלשה חדשים מלך, "and he ruled three months." 1 Esdras 1:42 has μῆνας τρεῖς καὶ ἡμέρας δέκα, "three months and ten days." Curtis says the addition of ימי was necessary to make the text intelligible after עשרה.[31] Along with the majority of commentators, delete ימי as a hypercorrection and relocate עשרה (see preceding text note).

10a-a: MT has אחיו, "his brother." The LXX has ἀδελφὸν τοῦ πατρὸς αὐτοῦ, "his father's brother." MT 2 Kings 24:17 has דדו, "his uncle." Perhaps the Chronicler understood אחיו in the broader sense of "kinsman" or אחי was omitted accidentally. Emend to reflect: אחי אביו.

Translation of 2 Chronicles 36:8–10

8Now the rest of the acts of Jehoiakim and the abominations that he did, and what was found against him, are written in the Book of the Kings of Israel and Judah; and his son Jehoiachin succeeded him. 9Jehoiachin was eighteen years old when he became king, and he reigned three months in Jerusalem. He did evil in the sight of the LORD. 10In the spring of the year, King Nebuchadrezzar sent and brought him to Babylon with

---

Chronicles, 522.

26. Williamson, *1 and 2 Chronicles*, 414.

27. Japhet, *I and II Chronicles*, 1067.

28. Myers, *I and II Chronicles*, 218.

29. Curtis and Madsen, *A Critical and Exegetical Commentary on the Books of Chronicles*, 521.

30. But see Bertheau, *Commentary on the Book of Chronicles*, who regards *eight* as original. Benzinger, *Die Bücher der Chronik*, believes *eight* as well as *ten days* for the period of the reign are correct vestiges of the Chronicler's *Vorlage*.

31. Curtis and Madsen, *A Critical and Exegetical Commentary on the Books of Chronicles*, 522.

the precious vessels of the house of the LORD, and he made his uncle Zedekiah king over Judah and Jerusalem.

Background of 2 Chronicles 36:8–10

The Chronicler chose to report the last four kings of Judah differently from the history of 2 Kings 23–24. Second Chronicles follows the sequence of 2 Kings, but some materials are omitted and others selected for reporting in order to reflect a different understanding of the events immediately preceding the exile. The Chronicler reports in twenty-three verses what occupies fifty-seven verses of 2 Kings 23–25, less than half the scope by any method of measurement.[32] The Chronicler's account reflects a dual emphasis: (1) the exile with tribute of each of the last four kings, and (2) the temple despoliation and eventual destruction. Unlike the narrative in 2 Kings, 2 Chronicles does not report the names of the queen mothers or the deaths of the kings. Upon the kings' exile from the land of Judah, there is no report about their subsequent status. Although 2 Kings 25:27–30 and the close parallel in Jeremiah 52:31–34 report Jehoiachin's release from the Babylonian prison, 2 Chronicles ends with Cyrus's edict, probably because it is the beginning of the return from exile in a foreign land to the land of the covenant. The Chronicler does not catalog the extensive deportations under Nebuchadrezzar (e.g., the king, queen mother, wives, etc.), or the change of name from Mattaniah to Zedekiah. Jehoiachin is reportedly only eight years of age with a reign of three months and ten days, although this is a probable misplaced numeral (text notes 9a-a, 9b-b, and 2 Kgs 24:8). The temple vessels are removed in three phases: "some" of the vessels were taken during Jehoiakim's installation (2 Chr 36:7), "precious" vessels were taken during Jehoiachin's surrender (36:10), and "all the vessels great and small" were taken during Zedekiah's deportation (36:18).[33] Each of these factors evidences supplementary reporting by the Chronicler regarding these four kings.

---

32. Japhet, *I and II Chronicles*, 1061.

33. Kalimi and Purvis, "King Jehoiachin," 455. "In the Chronicler's editorial work he abbreviated the account of Jehoiachin's reign. He excluded a great deal, added nothing, and altered slightly but significantly, most notably in regard to the removal of the sacred vessels. In so doing, the Chronicler was able to stress, however subtly, the significance of the vessels' being in Babylon to await their return to Jerusalem—an important theme also in Ezra 1–6."

Jehoiachin in the Narratives Concerning the Davidic Kings

The Chronicler's reporting of the fates of the last four Judean kings informs our understanding of Jehoiachin son of Jehoiakim. These kings are Jehoahaz son of Josiah (three months, 609), Jehoiakim son of Josiah (eleven years, 609–598), Jehoiachin (three months, 597), and Zedekiah son of Josiah (eleven years, 597–586). They are separately treated.

Jehoahaz

The עם הארץ elevated the twenty-three-year-old Jehoahaz to the throne instead of his brother Jehoiakim, who was two years older. His reign of three months is briefly noted in 36:1–4 (cf. 2 Kgs 23:30b–34). Jehoahaz is the object of others' activities in this pericope. He is installed by the עם הארץ, deposed by Neco, and taken to Egypt. The only verb in which he is active is the formulaic description of his age and reign. Surprisingly, the Chronicler does not characterize his reign as he did for the three subsequent kings. The LXX reflects this same lack of characterization. The omission may imply that the Chronicler regarded his exile to Egypt as an undeserved circumstance, a tragic follow-through of Josiah's untimely death at the hands of Pharaoh Neco. The Chronicler depicts Jehoahaz as a pathetic and impotent king, hastily installed on his father Josiah's throne, but just as hastily deposed by a foreign sovereign.

Jehoahaz was the first of the four final kings to suffer exile and imposition of tribute on the land (2 Chr 36:3, 7, 10, 18). The עם הארץ may have paid the tribute imposed by Neco, or it could have been levied from the temple or palace treasury. This dual theme of exile and tribute tends to draw the parallel between Jehoahaz and the denuding of the temple and its eventual destruction.

Unlike the 2 Kings 25:27–30 report of the release of Jehoiachin, there is no optimistic report on any of the last kings in 2 Chronicles 36. Jehoahaz is the only one whose conduct is uncharacterized, therefore, the only one of the four to deserve the reader/hearer's sympathy. As with the three kings who succeeded him, there was no notice of his death or his mother's name. In these verses, there is no mention of a change of name as with Eliakim/Jehoiakim and Mattaniah/Zedekiah. However, he is probably identical with Shallum, the king lamented by Jeremiah (Jer 22:11; cf. 1 Chr 3:15).

Looking Back for Jehoiachin

Jehoiakim

Pharaoh Neco made Eliakim king in place of Jehoahaz and changed his name to Jehoiakim (2 Chr 36:5–8; 2 Kgs 23:34—24:6a). Jehoiakim was much more active in his reign than his younger brother had been. He is described as doing evil, performing abominations, and the unspecified "what was found against him" (עליו הנמצא—*nip'al* participle).[34]

In 2 Kings 24:1, the phrase בימיו, "in his days," implies that the invasion of Nebuchadrezzar and the marauding bands were directed against Judah and Jerusalem. But in 2 Chronicles 36:6, Nebuchadrezzar came up (עליו) "against him," i.e., against Jehoiakim alone. There is no indication that Nebuchadrezzar was punishing the עם הארץ or the kingdom of Judah, but only its king Jehoiakim. We would not go so far as Japhet in concluding that 2 Kings 24:1–6 and the Chronicler's view are deliberately exclusive.[35] Although the 2 Chronicles 36:6 account reports the binding in bronze fetters not otherwise specified in 2 Kings 24:1–6, we attribute this to the different editorial emphasis of the Chronicler from the editor(s) of Kings. Second Kings reports that Jehoiakim served Nebuchadrezzar for three years. This would have followed the Babylonian defeat of the Egyptians at Carchemish in 605. "Some commentators suggest that Jehoiakim was not actually taken to Babylon at this time, but only bound and threatened so as to bring him into submission. This is certainly a possible interpretation of the Hebrew expression used here."[36] "Though the Old Testament would be the only record of such an event, it is by no means impossible that Jehoiakim was 'personally required to go to Babylon to take part in the victory celebrations as a conquered and vassal king . . . as had Manasseh in the days of Esarhaddon (33:11).'"[37] He returned to Judah to reign until his death (2 Kgs does not report Jehoiakim's exile).

The Chronicler attests that King Nebuchadrezzar bound Jehoiakim with bronze fetters to take him to Babylon. This sounds very much like

---

34. NJD White, "Jehoiakim" in *ABD*, p. II:559 cites Jerome (on 2 Chr 36:8), "'that which was found against him' to refer to heathenish marks (forbidden by Lev 19:28) discovered on his dead body. The legend mentioned by Thenius on 2 Kgs 24:1 that the name of the demon *Chodonazer* was found on his skin is merely due to a manuscript confusion of this note with that on 2 Chr 36:10, where Jerome explains the name *Nabu-chodonosor*."

35. Japhet, *I and II Chronicles*, 1066.

36. Williamson, *1 and 2 Chronicles*, 413.

37. Wiseman, *Notes on Some Problems in the Book of Daniel*, 18.

the account concerning Jehoiachin his son in 2 Kings 24:10–11. Although it is not clear, it strikes us that there may be a link between the 2 Kings report of the name of Jehoiakim's wife Nehushta (נחשתא), and the fetters (נחשתים) of 2 Chronicles 36:6. Carrying forward the dual theme of exile and tribute, the Chronicler reported that Nebuchadrezzar also carried some vessels of the LORD to his palace in Babylon. "The rest of the acts of Jehoiakim . . . all that he did" in 2 Kings 24:5 becomes in 2 Chronicles 36:8 "the abominations that he did, and what was found against him." Japhet thinks "abominations" refer to Jeremiah's reproof (Jer 22:17) and "what was found against him" refers to Jeremiah 36:29ff.[38]

Jehoiachin

The Chronicler's report of Jehoiachin is rendered in 2 Chronicles 36:9–10 (cf. 2 Kgs 24:6b–17). The Chronicler's tradition does not reflect the limitation imposed by Babylon on Egypt as in 2 Kings 24:7. "2 Kgs 24:8–16 is compacted into one sentence: It is the king alone—no one of his family, entourage, or the people of Judah—who is affected by this act."[39] "The spring of the year" is a normal description of the time of military campaigns. Nebuchadrezzar sent and brought Jehoiachin to Babylon along with precious vessels of the LORD. He made his (father's) brother Zedekiah king over Judah and Jerusalem.

Zedekiah

Zedekiah is the last Judean king reported in 2 Chronicles 36:11–14 (cf. 2 Kgs 24:17—25:7). He was twenty-one years old and reigned eleven years in Jerusalem, doing evil in the sight of the LORD. In a Chronicles-unique report, Zedekiah did not humble himself before Jeremiah, who spoke from the LORD (but see Jer 37:2). He further rebelled against King Nebuchadrezzar, who made him swear an oath by God. This is interpreted by the phrase, "he stiffened his neck and hardened his heart against the LORD" (2 Chr 36:13). All the leading priests and people were reported as exceedingly unfaithful, following the abominations of the nations, polluting the house of the LORD that he had consecrated in Jerusalem.

---

38. Japhet, *I and II Chronicles*, 1067.
39. Ibid.

Looking Back for Jehoiachin

2 Chronicles 36:8–10 by verses

36:8–9: We will not belabor the point of the age and duration of Jehoiachin's reign. With this emendation to the MT based upon LXX variants and passages in 2 Kings 24 and 1 Esdras 1:43, and the proper relationship to Zedekiah, the sole difficulty is Nebuchadrezzar's location during the siege.

36:10: The Babylonian Chronicle specifies that Nebuchadrezzar departed from Babylon in Kislev, marched to the land of *Hatti* (Palestine), took the city, captured the king (*Yaukin*—Jehoiachin), imposed heavy tribute, appointed a king of his choice (Zedekiah), and took captives back to Babylon. The Chronicler's reporting is distant from the events of Jehoiachin's exile, perhaps explaining the variation in the relationship, i.e., Zedekiah was Jehoiachin's *father's* brother, not his brother.

How 2 Chronicles 36:8–10 informs our understanding of Jehoiachin

According to the reconstructed text, Jehoiachin was eighteen years old (not eight) and reigned three months. There is no indication of the name of the queen mother (although see discussion of the suggestion of נחשתים/נחשתא above). There is no amplification of the other categories of exile as enumerated in 2 Kings. Jehoiachin faced King Nebuchadrezzar and siege personally in 2 Kings, but was *sent* for in 2 Chronicles 36. This suggests a subsequent and distant reporting.

"Brother" Zedekiah may possibly relate to the second son of Jehoiakim from 1 Chronicles 3:16. This would make the account parallel to the Jehoahaz/Jehoiakim succession. Japhet's conclusion that Zedekiah son of Jehoiakim became king after Jehoiachin is interesting, but unconvincing.[40] There is evidence of *brother* Zedekiah in 2 Chronicles 36:10, but it is more likely that *father's* brother (אחי אביו) was original and omitted by *lapsus oculi*.

Due to the Chronicler's abridged narrative, Jehoiachin is anticlimactic. The Chronicler did not seem to be interested in the fate of any of the last four kings; rather, it is the Edict of Cyrus that brightens the rapid-fire descending spiral of 2 Chronicles 36:1–21. There is no expressed hope for the return of the golden age of David's throne.

---

40. Ibid., 98–99.

Jehoiachin in the Narratives Concerning the Davidic Kings

Recapitulating the issues of the Chronicler's report, we saw that Jehoiachin was eighteen years old upon accession (LXX emendation to MT), reigned three months in an evil reign, and was sent for by Nebuchadrezzar from Babylon. Zedekiah son of Josiah was Jehoiachin's uncle—not in the direct line of succession—and was relegated to struggling status by the inferior bureaucracy remaining in Judah and Jerusalem after the exile of Jehoiachin.

2 KINGS 25:27–30: IN THE THIRTY-SEVENTH YEAR OF HIS EXILE, JEHOIACHIN WAS RELEASED FROM PRISON

The demise of Judah and of the final four Davidic kings is recounted in 2 Kings 24 and 25 as well as 2 Chronicles 36. Second Kings 25 begins with Zedekiah's foolish rebellion against Babylon and the resultant siege of Jerusalem by Nebuchadrezzar and the Babylonian army. The rebellion was crushed by the cruel dispatch of Zedekiah's sons, family, nobles, and eyes. The destruction and dismantlement of the city was total. The appointment of Gedaliah as governor (25:22) lasted only a few months until his assassination. The assassins fled to Egypt, carrying Jeremiah and Baruch with them. After these dispiriting events, there is a surprising upturn, twenty-five years after the last account of Judean royalty (25:26). Nebuchadrezzar's successor freed the Judean king Jehoiachin from prison in the thirty-seventh year of his captivity. Moreover, he seated him preferentially above the other captive kings. He spoke kindly to him, changed his clothes and gave him a regular allowance. Jehoiachin ate with the king of Babylon for the rest of his life.

Reconstructed Text of 2 Kings 25:27–30

27 ויהי בשלשים ושבע שנה לגלות יהויכין מלך יהודה בשנים עשר חדש בעשרים ושבעה לחדש נשא אויל מרדך מלך בבל בשנת ᵇ מלכו את ראש יהויכין מלך יהודה ᶜ מבית כלא
28 וידבר אתו טבות ויתן את כסאו ᵃ⁻ מעל כסא ⁻ᵃ המלכים אשר אתו בבבל 29 ושנא ᵃ את בגדי כלאו ואכל ᵇ⁻ לחם תמיד לפניו ⁻ᵇ כל ימי חייו 30 וארחתו ארחת תמיד נתנה לו מאת ᵃ המלך ᵇ דבר יום ביומו ᶜ ⁻ᵈ כל ימי חיו ⁻ᵈ

Looking Back for Jehoiachin

Text notes[41]

27a: One Medieval Hebrew manuscript has וּשְׁמֹנֶה, Targum[Jon] and Jeremiah 52:31 וַחֲמִשָּׁה, LXX Jer = τετράδι.

27b: Probably read with Jeremiah מַלְכוֹ.[42] LXX = ἐν τῷ ἐνιαυτῷ τῆς βασιλείας αὐτοῦ.

27c: Perhaps insert with few manuscripts, LXX, Syriac, Targum, and Jeremiah וַיֹּצֵא אֹתוֹ.[43]

28a-a: Possibly read with Jeremiah 52:33 מִמַּעַל לְכִסֵּא ?מִמַּעַל לְכִסֵּא

29a: Jeremiah 52:33 וְשִׁנָּה.

29b-b: Jeremiah 52:33 inverts the order.

30a: LXX ἐξ οἴκου = מִבֵּית.

30b: Syriac as Jeremiah 52:34, מֶלֶךְ בָּבֶל.

30c: Jeremiah + עַד יוֹם מוֹתוֹ, so read and delete 30d-d.

30d-d: Same as 30c.

Translation of 2 Kings 25:27–30

27 And in the thirty-seventh year of the exile of Jehoiachin king of Judah, in the twelfth month, on the twenty-seventh day of the month, Evil-merodach, king of Babylon, in his accession year, pardoned Jehoiachin king of Judah (and released him) from prison. 28He spoke kindly to him

---

41. See also the reconstructed text of Jer 52:31–34 and side-by-side comparison, as well as these important works: Auld, *Kings Without Privilege*; Talmon, "Case of Faulty Harmonization"; Person, "2 Kings 24:18—25:30 and Jeremiah 52"; and Murray, "Of All the Years the Hopes—or Fears?"

42. Hughes, *The Secrets of the Times*, 157: "The precise day of Jehoiachin's release from prison is also of little chronological importance, but greater significance attaches to the question of whether he was released 'in the year of [Evil-merodach's] accession' (בִּשְׁנַת מַלְכוֹ) or 'in the year of [Evil-merodach's] reign' (בִּשְׁנַת מָלְכוֹ / מָלְכֻתוֹ). A number of scholars have, for chronological reasons, preferred the second possibility, which they interpret as meaning 'in the first year of his reign.' But this is hardly a legitimate interpretation: מָלְכֻתוֹ בִּשְׁנַת or בִּשְׁנַת מָלְכוֹ, can no more be taken to mean 'in the first year of his reign' or 'in (any other) year of his reign.' The only interpretation along these lines which is linguistically possible is that Evil-merodach released Jehoiachin 'in the only year of his reign'—and that is contradicted by the historical fact that Evil-merodach reigned for two years (in addition to his accession year). We therefore have no option but to translate בִּשְׁנַת מַלְכוֹ as 'in the year of his accession' and to reject בִּשְׁנַת מָלְכֻתוֹ as historically meaningless."

43. Burney, *Notes on the Hebrew Text of the Book of Kings*, 127, 369–70, regarding the text of 2 Kgs 25:27, מִבֵּית כֶּלֶא—LXX[L], Syriac are probably correct in reading וַיֹּצֵא אֹתוֹ מִבֵּית כֶּלֶא as in Jer.

and set his throne above those of the kings who were with him in Babylon. 29He changed his prison clothes and ate bread regularly before him all the days of his life. 30He was given a permanent allowance from the king, daily for life.

Background of the 2 Kings account

Before investigating this account, it is useful to sketch the background in 2 Kings 25 as it relates to Jehoiachin's exile. Jehoiachin's uncle, Zedekiah, reigned for eleven years in Jerusalem after the exile of 597. When the Babylonian army breached the city wall in 586, Zedekiah fled toward Jericho. He was captured and taken to Riblah, where Nebuchadrezzar pronounced sentence. His sons and nobles were executed, his eyes were gouged out, and he was transported to Babylon, where he died (Jer 52:11).

Seitz observes, "2 Kgs 25:1–7, from all traditions available, is a compressed . . . example of what happens when a king does not 'give himself up to the King of Babylon' together with his royal family, as did Jehoiachin (2 Kgs 24:12)."[44] Seitz continues, "The narrative of 2 Kings 25 seeks to stress that [Jehoiachin's] original act of submission in 597 BC ultimately found its true purpose in 562."[45]

The Babylonian king Amel-marduk (562–560) succeeded his father Nebuchadrezzar.[46] The MT spelling of the name as Evil-merodach may have been a stylistic device since it means "Fool of Marduk." His motivation for the release is not specified in the biblical account.[47] He placed Jehoiachin's seat above those of the other captive kings in Babylon. The

---

44. Seitz, *Theology in Conflict*, 212.

45. Ibid., 220.

46. Amel-marduk ruled two years and was assassinated by Neriglissar, who succeeded him on the throne of Babylon. G. Jones, *1 and 2 Kings*, 2:649, suggests that "the release was a part of a general amnesty at the beginning of a new reign. Evidence from Mari and from an Assyrian letter to Esarhaddon suggests that this was a normal practice in Mesopotamia." Cf. Gray, *I and II Kings*, 773; Zenger, "Die deuteronomistische Interpretation," 18ff.

47. Clements, *Jeremiah, Interpretation*, 271–22, suggests Amel-marduk released Jehoiachin "to bolster his own position. His throne was decidedly insecure, and he may well have sought to gain support by an act of clemency towards a notable royal person held in Babylon." We find this unconvincing. Jehoiachin's release was more likely an act of largesse than of self-interest.

Looking Back for Jehoiachin

Unger Prism[48] dating from circa 570 suggests these might include the kings of Tyre, Gaza, Sidon, Arvad, and Ashdod.

Four inscribed cuneiform documents (dated to 592, Nebuchadrezzar's thirteenth year), discovered at the site of ancient Babylon, not far from the Ishtar Gate, provide an explicit reference to "*Ya'ukinu* king of the land of *Yahudi*," and a list of the rations from the royal storehouse apportioned to him and his five sons. These tablets published by Weidner underscore the biblical record in 2 Kings.[49] Tadmor observes that "the daily rations issued to Jehoiachin after his release are not those issued to him in Nebuchadrezzar's thirteenth year, but were a new issue some thirty years later."[50]

Bright speculates that Jehoiachin was not in prison at least as late as 592.[51] The very fact that Jehoiachin was only eighteen when exiled, yet had five sons during his captivity (seven in 1 Chr 3:16–17), suggests that his wives were together with him. The generous supply of oil and grain recounted in the Weidner tablets indicates a sizeable family surrounded Jehoiachin. Becking observes that the provisions recounted in these tablets are evidence that the Babylonian court adopted the custom known from Assyrian inscriptions: that prisoners had a right to life, to receive footwear, and to live with their wives.[52]

Although beyond the narrow scope of this narrative investigation of Jehoiachin,[53] it is appropriate to observe that this pericope and its parallel

---

48. Unger, *Theologische Literaturzeitung*, 50; idem, *ZAW* 44 (1926): 314 ff.

49. Weidner, "Jojachin, König von Juda," 2:923–35, reports the quantity as "½ PI for Ya'ukinu . . . king of Yahudi and ½ SILA for the five sons of Ya'ukinu." Cf. *ANET*, 308; Wiseman, *Peoples of Old Testament Times*, 84–86.

50. Tadmor and Cogan, *II Kings*, 329.

51. Bright, *History of Israel*, 369.

52. Becking, "Jehojachin's Amnesty, Salvation for Israel?" 284. See further Saggs, "Assyrian Prisoners of War and the Right to Live," 85–93. See also the fascinating rabbinical traditions surveyed in chapter 5.

53. The discussion will resume in future chapters. We hold an optimistic view of Jeconiah's kingship.

Jehoiachin in the Narratives Concerning the Davidic Kings

in Jeremiah 52:31–34 have occasioned widespread comment. See the summaries of Seitz[54] and Long[55] for additional discussion.

Davidson[56] and Provan,[57] along with Jones,[58] see this as an optimistic record. It sits in vivid contrast to the widespread destruction, devastation, and disorder characterized by the fall of Jerusalem, the assassination of Gedaliah, and flight to Egypt of the assassins in 2 Kings 25:1–26. The exiles in Babylon could only have viewed the restoration and rehabilitation of Jehoiachin in his thirty-seventh year of captivity as a positive sign. In the midst of captivity, Jehoiachin was released. Certainly, Jehoiachin's state after release was far better than that before release. It was certainly more positive than the punishment meted out to Zedekiah—the king without sons or eyes who had been paraded (wretched, pitiful, poor, blind, and naked) to Babylon in 586 after the razing of the capital city.

---

54. Seitz, *Theology in Conflict*, 196, regarding 2 Kgs 25:27–30: "This unit has been the subject of much discussion." See especially von Rad, *Studien*, 63–64; *Theology*, 334–47; Noth, *The Deuteronomistic History*, 98; Gray, *I and II Kings*, 42; Cross, *Canaanite Myth and Hebrew Epic*, 277; Wolff, "The Kerygma of the Deuteronomistic Historical Work," 83–100; Zenger, 'Die deuteronomistische Interpretation,' 16–30; Baltzer, "Das Ende des Staates Juda und die Messias-Frage," 3–43; Pohlmann, 'Erwägungen zum Schlußkapitel des deuteronomistischen Geschichtswerkes," 94–109.

55. Long, *Problem of the Etiological Narrative*, 289: ". . . scholars debate the purposes for which the books of Kings and the Dtr history were written . . . along the lines of pessimism and despair or of optimism and hope. Noth [*Deuteronomistic History*, 97], thinking of a single exilic author, exemplifies the former option . . . von Rad [*Old Testament Theology I*, 343] exemplifies the opposite opinion. . . . Interpreters align themselves more or less with one of these two points of view. Most recent critics continue to express something like von Rad's optimism, which for a Christian reader may preserve an opening for messianic sensibilities. Begg ("Jehoiachin's Release") suggested that the text answered the question, 'Can things go well for the Judean survivors under Babylon's rule?' with a yes. Survival while ruled by Babylonian conquerors seems to have been a matter of political debate among the Judeans. It is reflected not only in the Gedaliah incident (and in the parallel version in Jer 40), but also in Jer 27:12–15, 16–22. Thus Begg's suggestion has real merit."

56. Davidson, *Jeremiah II with Lamentations*, 165: "It has been well said that in this chapter we find history bearing its silent witness to the truth of the prophetic word."

57. Provan, *1 and 2 Kings*, 277, wrote "It is left to Josiah's grandson, Jehoiachin, to offer us such hope as we can find for the future of the Davidic 'lamp,' as the lights go out all over Judah."

58. D. Jones reports, "The release of Jehoiachin provides a glimmer of hope . . . no other event had this positive symbolic force before the rise of Cyrus . . ." (549).

Looking Back for Jehoiachin

2 Kings 25:27–30 by verses

25:27: Both the MT and LXX of 2 Kings 24:27 agree on the timing of the release, i.e., the thirty-seventh year of Jehoiachin's exile, the twelfth month, twenty-*seventh* day of the month (but see Jer 52:31). This unusually precise dating reflects the specificity of 2 Kings 25:1, Nebuchadrezzar's siege of Jerusalem (his ninth year, tenth month, tenth day); and 2 Kings 25:8, the day Jerusalem burned (nineteenth year, fifth month, seventh day). "The general dating of invasions and attacks by foreigners into Judah and against Jerusalem, such as 'in his days' (בימיו, e.g., 2 Kgs 24:1) now gives way to an exactness not seen before in Kings."[59]

"Lift up the head" (נשא . . . את ראש) is a gesture of rehabilitation (Gen 40:13; Job 10:15; Ps 110:7; 140:9) as "subduing" the head, or crown, is a gesture of humiliation (Jer 2:16; 13:18–19).

25:28: The king of Babylon spoke kindly to him. His seat was set in preference to those of the other kings with him. Whether this was accompanied with additional favor is unknown. The use of "spoke kindly" (דבר טוב) could imply covenant language and the possibility of restoration to the throne.

25:29: He was reclothed in garments appropriate for an audience with the king of Babylon.

25:30: He was provided a daily allowance and ate at the king's table for the rest of his life (דבר יום ביומו, literally, "A matter of a day in its day," so RSV, "every day a portion.") The idiom is not infrequent, being used, e.g., of the daily allowance of Daniel and his friends (Dan 1:5), of the manna gathered by the people (Exod 16:4), and of the daily burden imposed by the Egyptian taskmasters (Exod 5:13, 19). Second Kings does not report Jehoiachin's death. Perhaps he was still alive when the account was composed.

How 2 Kings 25:27–30 informs our understanding of Jehoiachin[60]

Reviewing the critical issues of 2 Kings 25:27–30, we noted that there was a surprise ending to the account of the downfall of the Davidic kings and Jerusalem: the last surviving king, Jehoiachin, was released from the Babylonian prison when he was fifty-five years old. The Weidner tablet confirmed that Yaukin (Jehoiachin) was provided a ration for his large

---

59. Hobbs, *Second Kings*, 368.
60. See the section on Jer 52:31–34.

family near the Ishtar Gate in Babylon. The Unger Prism names the other captive kings in Babylon with him.

JEREMIAH 52:31-34 PARALLEL ACCOUNT OF JEHOIACHIN'S RELEASE FROM PRISON AND DEATH

We turn now to the close parallel account of Jehoiachin's release from prison. There are minor date variances in this account. Jeremiah also adds the indication that Jehoiachin did die in Babylon, something unrecounted in 2 Kings 25:27–30. Although this death of the remaining Davidide should have stamped "closed" on the line of kings, the optimistic account portends that Yahweh was indeed doing something different (cf. Jer 33:14–26).

Reconstructed text of Jeremiah 52:31–34

³¹ ויהי בשלשים ושבע שנה לגלות יהויכן^a מלך יהודה
בשנים עשר חדש בעשרים וחמשה^b לחדש נשא אויל מרדך
מלך בבל בשנת מלכתו^c את ראש יהויכין^a מלך יהודה^d
ויצא אותו מבית הכלוא^{e 32} וידבר אתו טבות ויתן את
כסאו ממעל לכסא^a המלכים אשר אתו בבבל ³³ ושנה
את בגדי כלאו ואכל לחם לפניו תמיד כל ימי חיו^a
³⁴ וארחתו ארחת תמיד נתנה לו ^{a-} מאת ^{-a} מלך בבל דבר יום
ביומו ^{b-} עד יום מותו ^{-b c-} כל ימי חייו ^{-c}

Text notes

31a: LXX Ιωακιμ. See text note at Jeremiah 37:1b-b.
31b: Second Kings 25:27 ושבעה, LXX^{Jer} τετράδι.
31c: Read with LXX, as 2 Kings 25, מלכו.
31d: LXX^{B+} καὶ ἔκειρεν αὐτόν, cf. Genesis 41:14.
31e: Occurs only here and in Jeremiah 37:4; Kethib = הַכְּלִיא, Qere = הַכְּלוּא. Perhaps this form is a variant of the more common בית כלא as in 2 Kings 17:4; 25:27.
32a: A few manuscripts, LXX, and 2 Kings 25:28, as Qere, so read.
33a: QMss חייו.
34a-a: Second Kings 25:30, המלך.
34b-b: Absent from a few manuscripts and 2 Kings 25.

Looking Back for Jehoiachin

34c-c: Absent from LXX*.

Translation of Jeremiah 52:31–34

31 And in the thirty-seventh year of the exile of Jehoiachin king of Judah, in the twelfth month, on the twenty-fifth day of the month, Evil-merodach, king of Babylon, in his accession year, pardoned Jehoiachin king of Judah and released him from prison. 32 He spoke kindly to him and set his throne above those of the kings who were with him in Babylon. 33 So he changed his prison clothes and ate bread regularly before him all the days of his life. 34 He was given a daily permanent allowance from the king, for life, until the day he died.

Background of the Jeremiah account

Keown observes that Jeremiah 52:31–34 "provides a word of hope that may also be significant as part of the larger Jeremianic message; . . . borrowing an existing account of Jerusalem's fall may well provide more 'convincing' evidence of prophetic fulfillment than that produced by an editorial summary."[61] Carroll calls attention to the contrasting symmetry between the references to Zedekiah and Jehoiachin in this final chapter of Jeremiah.[62] It is difficult to imagine a more horrific punishment than that of Zedekiah. Had he been summarily executed, it would have ended his mutilated and tortured existence. In contrast to Zedekiah's fate, Jehoiachin was treated relatively well, although we do not know the conditions of the captivity or the prison. The fact that Jehoiachin lived to be fifty-five upon his release from prison (exiled at eighteen, released in his thirty-seventh year) suggests that he was well treated during captivity.[63]

The shorter text of 2 Kings 25:27–30 probably indicates that it was written earlier (see the text comparison).[64] It is difficult to imagine why the author(s) of the 2 Kings 25 account would have abbreviated the

---

61. Keown, Scalise, and Smothers, *Jeremiah 26–52*, 383.

62. Carroll, *The Book of Jeremiah*, 871.

63. Chapter 5 will investigate the rehabilitation of Jehoiachin by Josephus and the rabbinical literature.

64. According to the reconstructed texts, 2 Kgs 25:27–30 is 23 consonants shorter than Jer 52:31–34. This counts the longer *Kethib* spellings, the Jer additions (ויצא אותו and עד יום מותו), and the likely editorial changes.

Jehoiachin in the Narratives Concerning the Davidic Kings

account of Jeremiah had it been extant. The flow of Jeremiah 52 seems to be better (see text notes), suggesting the 2 Kings account was improved by the final redactor of the prophetic book.

Bright provides a probable rationale for the appending of 2 Kings 25 to Jeremiah 52:

> Perhaps the editor felt that an account of the fall of Jerusalem, the event that brought vindication to Jeremiah's lifelong announcement of the divine judgment, would furnish a fitting conclusion to the book because it would allow history itself to give its silent witness to the truth of the prophetic word. Perhaps, too, he saw in the account of the release of Jehoiachin from prison with which the chapter closes some hint, some foreshadowing of the hoped-for future which Jeremiah, at the bidding of his God, had promised beyond the tragedy. In its present context the chapter seems to say: the divine word both has been fulfilled—and will be fulfilled![65]

Malamat, addressing the status of Zedekiah in Jerusalem while Jehoiachin lived, provides an interesting portrayal of Jehoiachin's status during the Babylonian captivity:

> Although Zedekiah was duly and properly installed as king by Nebuchadrezzar, his exiled nephew, Jehoiachin, was not divested of his royalty, but enjoyed special status at the Babylonian court. . . . [H]e may have been regarded as titular head of the Jewish Diaspora in Babylonia. Other exiled kings at the Babylonian court also retained their royal titles, and were perhaps to be used, *inter alia*, as a trump card against the new rulers appointed by Nebuchadrezzar.[66]

At three sites (Tell Beit Mirsim, Beth-shemesh, and Ramat Rahel) wine jug handles were found with the impression *l'lyqm n'r ywkn*, commonly thought to mean, "to Eliakim steward of *Yaukin*."[67] Albright believed these seals meant that Jehoiachin was the legitimate king of Judah while he was in exile.[68] The Weidner tablets record the rations of oil and

---

65. Bright, *History of Israel*, 370.
66. Malamat, "The Last Years," 213.
67. On the Eliakim seals as an indication of Jehoiachin's status in exile as official king of Judah, see Albright, "The Seal of Eliakim"; and May, "Three Hebrew Seals." For reservations about this conclusion, see Liver, "Jehoiachin"; and Malamat, "The Twilight of Judah," 37.
68. Albright, "The Seal of Eliakim," 77.

grains given to *King Yaukin* and his five sons. These inscriptions witness to the historicity of the biblical record.

Jeremiah 52:31–34 by verses

52:31: Hughes suggests that the original figure preserved in the LXX, "'the twenty-fourth day of the month' may explain the variation in 2 Kgs 25:27 'twenty-seventh' (ושבעה עשרים) as a corruption of 'twenty-fourth' (עשרים וארבה). The other variant, 'twenty-fifth' (עשרים וחמשה) in MT's text of Jer 52:31, may be explained as a partial assimilation of '745' (שבע מאות ארבעים וחמה) in the preceding verse."[69] Although possible, this does not really address which day is the precise day of the audience. As a speculative proposal, the LXX^{Jer} twenty-fourth day, as the earliest day, could be the day Jehoiachin was notified; the twenty-fifth, a day later, could be the day he was released (and shaved, LXX^B); while the twenty-seventh (MT^{2Kgs}) could have been the day of the audience.

52:32–33: Holladay says:

> One is left uncertain whose life is referred to in "all the days of his life," and since Evil-merodach died after only two years' reign, one wonders what became of Jehoiachin if the implication is "all the days of Evil-merodach's life" (as Cornill and Rudolph hold), if the Jewish king outlived the Babylonian one. "Until the day of his death" may be ambiguous as well, though the phrase would more likely be heard as "until the day of Jehoiachin's death."[70]

How Jeremiah 52:31–34 informs our understanding of Jehoiachin

Many questions remain regarding these two pericopes: Why did Evil-merodach release Jehoiachin? What is the significance of the new clothing? Why does Jeremiah 52:34 report the death while 2 Kings 25 does not? As with the precise date of the audience, we can only suggest likely answers. Clements's contention that Evil-merodach strengthened his position by the "clemency towards a notable royal person held in Babylon" is unlikely.[71] Clemency would tend to destabilize rather than strengthen

---

69. Hughes, *Secrets of the Times*, 157.
70. Holladay, *Jeremiah 2*, 443.
71. Clements, *Jeremiah, Interpretation*, 271–72.

Jehoiachin in the Narratives Concerning the Davidic Kings

a new ruler's power (cf. 1 Kgs 2:19–25). Jehoiachin had been in prison for thirty-seven years while Nebuchadrezzar reigned. Neither Jehoiachin nor Judah was significant in the international politics of Babylon in 562. Upon his coronation, the new king might have granted amnesty in accordance with Mesopotamian precedents,[72] but why would he have assigned precedence to the Judean king?

The reclothing suggests the normal protocol of royal audiences. As Joseph was shaved and reclothed (Gen 41:14) before he met the pharaoh, so Jehoiachin put aside his prison garb and was given an appropriate outfit. It is unlikely that his own royal robe, which he wore when he bowed before Nebuchadrezzar, would still be available. He was probably given a Babylonian caftan to accompany his exalted seat above the other kings captive with him.

Jeremiah 52:34 refers to the death of Jehoiachin (עד יום מותו). This, along with the other Jeremiah additions, suggests that the 2 Kings passage was earlier. Most commentators agree. Perhaps the appending of the king's coda from 2 Kings 25:27–30 to Jeremiah 52 happened after the death of Jehoiachin, or perhaps the redactors wanted to underscore that Jeremiah's prophecies were fulfilled (Jer 22:26; 24:5; 28:6, 16; 29:8, 9; 36:30, 31).

---

72. G. Jones, *1 and 2 Kings*, 649; Becking, "Jehoiachin's Amnesty, Salvation for Israel?" 92.

Looking Back for Jehoiachin

Side-by-side comparison of 2 Kings 25:27–30 and Jeremiah 52:31–34

2 Kings 25:27–30	Jeremiah 52:31–34
27 ויהי בשלשים ושבע שנה לגלות יהויכין מלך יהודה בשנים עשר חדש בעשרים ושבעה לחדש נשא אויל מרדך מלך בבל בשנת מלכו את ראש יהויכין מלך יהודה מבית כלא 28 וידבר אתו טבות ויתן את כסאו מעל כסא המלכים אשר אתו בבבל 29 ושנא את בגדי כלאו ואכל לחם תמיד לפניו כל ימי חייו 30 וארחתו ארחת תמיד נתנה לו מאת המלך דבר יום ביומו כל ימי חיו	31 ויהי בשלשים ושבע שנה לגלות יהויכין מלך יהודה בשנים עשר חדש בעשרים וחמשה לחדש נשא אויל מרדך מלך בבל בשנת מלכתו את ראש יהויכין מלך יהודה ויצא אותו מבית הכליא 32 וידבר אתו טבות ויתן את כסאו ממעל לכסא המלכים אשר אתו בבבל 33 ושנה את בגדי כלאו ואכל לחם לפניו תמיד כל ימי חיו 34 וארחתו ארחת תמיד נתנה לו מאת מלך בבל דבר יום ביומו עד יום מותו כל ימי חייו
Comments 2 Kings 25 27 ושבעה = (2)7th מלכו = his reign 29 inverted order in Jeremiah 52:33 חייו but חיו in Jeremiah 52:33 30 המלך = the king חיו but חייו in Jeremiah 52:34	*Comments Jeremiah 52* 31 וחמשה = (2)5th מלכתו = his accession ויצא אותו = and he brought him (Jer+) 34 מלך בבל = king of Babylon (Jer+) עד יום מותו = till day he died (Jer+)[A]

A. See Person, "II Kings 24:18–25, 30 and Jeremiah 52," 174–205, for the retroverted Hebrew texts of LXX[2 Kgs] and LXX[Jer].

How Jeremiah 52:31–34 informs our understanding of Jehoiachin

Is it likely that the texts of 2 Kings 25 and Jeremiah 52 imply that the king of Babylon released Jehoiachin merely as a fulfilment of Mesopotamian precedents? We suspect there is more to this account than accession year amnesty. Indeed, the elevation of king Jehoiachin's throne above those confined with him is much more than clemency. We encamp with von Rad's optimism, with those who believe Yahweh was looking after the "good figs" (Jer 24), while holding in healthy respect the skepticism of Noth, Cogan, and Tadmor.

Jeremiah 52:31–34, possibly picked up from 2 Kings 25:27–30 with minor additions, was used by the editors to emphasize the fulfillment of the prophecies in the Book of Jeremiah. The accounts suggest the rehabilitation of Jehoiachin prior to his death. We defer conclusions on the meaning of the release until after investigating the prophecies in Jeremiah to determine the further story of Jehoiachin (Jer 36:30, 31; 22:26; 24:5; 28:6, 16; 29:8, 9).

The king's coda occurs twenty-five years after the fall of Jerusalem and the exile of Zedekiah. The upturn in fortunes of the exiles at their captive king's exaltation began to portend a new work on their behalf. Chronicles ends on the high note of Cyrus's edict, which permitted return to Judah and Jerusalem. The expectation of the exiles for restoration must have been accelerated by their prophets (cf. Jer 27–29) and anticipated by Jeremiah.

Reviewing the critical issues, we conclude that King Jehoiachin died in Babylon after being released from prison in the thirty-seventh year of his captivity at age fifty-five. Whether or not this was an accession-year amnesty, it was probably in the first year of Amel-marduk's reign as Nebuchadrezzar's successor. However, precedence over captive kings implies much more. This very favorable news at the end of 2 Kings 25 and Jeremiah 52 could be compared to the upbeat news of the edict of Cyrus at the end of 2 Chronicles 36. This positive turn on the downcast fortunes of the exiles begs the question, "What about Jehoiachin's offspring?" This will be investigated in chapters 2 and 3.

CHAPTER 1 CONCLUSION

The reconstructed text of 2 Kings 24:6–17 provides the outline for the years from Jehoiachin's birth to Jehoiakim and Nehushta (616) through the exile in 597. It specifies that Jehoiachin was eighteen years old when he acceded to the throne of his covenant-breaking father. Second Kings 24:9 provides the nuanced formula for his reign: "he did evil in the sight of the LORD, according to all that his father had done." This characterization was specific to his reign in contrast to the other kings of Judah. Nebuchadrezzar personally attended the siege of Jerusalem, prompting the surrender in March 597 of Jehoiachin, his mother, wives, servants, captains, officials, craftsmen, and smiths. The Babylonian Chronicle confirms that this occurred in Nebuchadrezzar's eighth year.

Although 24:13–16 uses כֹּל repeatedly, we propose that this was synecdoche, for not *all* the treasures or *all* the people of Jerusalem were

Looking Back for Jehoiachin

exiled, but rather ten thousand—a representative number that included most of the bureaucracy, nobility, and the royal household.

We reviewed the context of 2 Kings 21–24 so that the portraits of Jehoiachin might be compared with the portraits of kings from Hezekiah to Zedekiah. The dimension of the international powers Nebuchadrezzar and Neco dwarfs these portraits. Without the possibility of relief from Egypt due to Babylonian dominance, Judah was isolated. The curses pronounced against the kings from Hezekiah to Jehoiakim (excluding Josiah) found their initial fulfillment in 597 when Jehoiachin marched into Babylonian captivity. Nebuchadrezzar did not destroy Jerusalem, but left Zedekiah as (puppet) king in reduced circumstances.

The Chronicler introduced interesting details (exile and tribute) in his portraits of the final four kings. We determined that a misplaced numeral עשרה led to the confusion of Jehoiachin's age and the duration of his reign. We did not emend the notice of 36:10 that Nebuchadrezzar *sent* for Jehoiachin rather than harmonize it with 2 Kings 24:10–11 and the Babylonian Chronicle. We determined that Zedekiah was Jehoiachin's uncle (אבי אחי) instead of his brother (אחיו).

We temporarily pass by the years 597–563 (addressed in chapters 2 and 3) to focus on the king's coda, the final pericopes in 2 Kings and Jeremiah. Although considered separately, we concluded that Jehoiachin was released from prison in the thirty-seventh year of his exile (562). We endorsed Seitz's opinion that Jehoiachin's submission in 597 found its true purpose in 562. Inscriptional evidence (Weidner tablets, Unger prism, Eliakim seal impressions) underpins the historicity of the release of Jehoiachin. The minor date variations in Jeremiah 52:31 are not as significant as the death notice in 52:33 of Jehoiachin, which adds his epitaph. Neriglissar assassinated Evil-merodach in 560, so it is probable that Jehoiachin's death was near that date.

Despite Jehoiachin's death in Babylon, we believe the two pericopes paint an optimistic portrait of the last living king of Judah. The release of Jehoiachin at the end of 2 Kings and Jeremiah, combined with the edict of Cyrus at the terminus of 2 Chronicles 36, portends a departure from the calamity of the exile. The questions of the offspring and legacy of Jehoiachin are deferred until chapters 2 through 5.

CHAPTER 2

Jeremiah's Prophecies: Jeconiah in Babylon

WITH THIS CHAPTER, WE move from the narratives concerning Jehoiachin to the prophecies regarding Jeconiah/Coniah. We investigate eight pericopes in the book of Jeremiah. The first two passages are not addressed by name to this king, but certainly predict his exile, i.e., Jeremiah 36:30–31 and 13:18–19.[1] The remaining six passages concerned Jeconiah (or Coniah), son of Jehoiakim, after his exile, i.e., 22:24–30; 24:1–3; 27:19–22; 28:1–4; 29:1–3; and 37:1–2—what we have termed "afterthoughts"—that served as signposts warning of what was to happen if and when the curses of Jeconiah came to fulfillment on Jerusalem and Judah.

JEREMIAH 36:30–31 TO JEHOIAKIM: "NONE TO SIT UPON THE THRONE OF DAVID"

As we will see, the tone of Jeremiah 36:30–31 is condemnatory. The command to speak to king Jehoiakim (36:29) follows the infamous burning of Jeremiah's scroll (36:20–26) and is preceded by the introductory formula כה אמר יהוה, "Thus says the LORD." This confrontational judgment speech predicted that Jehoiakim would have no successor to sit on the throne of David and, furthermore, that his corpse would be defiled and dishonored. The prophecy specifies the cause of this punishment: neither

---

1. The Book of Jeremiah is not chronological.

the king, his son, nor his servants had been obedient to the word which the LORD had spoken. The punishment for ignoring the LORD was about to be visited (פקד) upon Jehoiakim, Jeconiah, Judah, and Jerusalem.

Reconstructed Text Jeremiah 36:30–31

³⁰ לכן כה אמר יהוה על יהויקים מלך יהודה לא יהיה לו
יושב על כסא דוד ונבלתו תהיה משלכת לחרב ביום
ולקרח בלילה ³¹ ופקדתי עליו ועל זרעו ועל עבדיו
ᵃ את עונם והבאתי עליהם ועל ישבי ירושלם
ואל ᵇ איש יהודה את כל הרעה אשר דברתי
אליהם ולא שמעו

Text notes

31a : MT has את עונם, "their iniquity," which is not in the LXX. פקד frequently uses a direct object marker את and substantive, hence the MT. However, the Greek use of ἐπισκέψομαι, a first singular future middle indicative, could also take an object such as "(their) iniquity," yet there is none. Whether the LXX was translating a shorter *Vorlage* or the object was erroneously deleted cannot be determined. In the absence of compelling evidence, we retain the MT in parenthesis and italicize *for their iniquity* in the translation. See verse-by-verse discussion of . . . פקד על.

31b: MT has איש יהודה, "men of Judah,"[2] whereas LXX has γῆν Ιουδα "land of Judah." The MT parallel ישבי ירושלם would commend the use of איש יהודה, but the LXX use of γῆν Ιουδα, could be appropriate; i.e., "inhabitants of Jerusalem" would still be a near parallel with "land of Judah." In Jeremiah, the phrase "men of Judah and inhabitants of Jerusalem" occurs in 4:3, 4; 11:2, 9; 17:25; 18:11; 32:32; and 35:13. The phrase "land of Judah" occurs in 31:23 and 37:1, both in spatial contexts where איש would be impossible. Based on word usage, retain MT.

Translation of Jeremiah 36:30–31

30 Therefore, Thus says Yahweh concerning Jehoiakim, king of Judah: "He shall not have anyone to sit on the throne of David; and his corpse

---

2. The noun is a collective in parallel to "the residents of Jerusalem," (ישבי ירושלם).

Jeremiah's Prophecies: Jeconiah in Babylon

will be cast out to the heat by day and the frost by night. 31 Moreover, I will punish him and his offspring and his servants *for their iniquity* and I will bring upon the inhabitants of Jerusalem and the people of Judah all the calamity that I spoke concerning them, but they would not listen."

Background of the Jeremiah 36:30–31 account

Jeremiah 36 is in three sections: vv. 1–8, commission to dictate a scroll; vv. 9–26, three readings of the scroll; and vv. 27–32, conclusion. The concluding section reflects the commission (v. 27 with time indication and formula, v. 28 commission to Jeremiah, v. 32 execution of the commission).

The MT establishes that the events of Jeremiah 36 happened in the fourth and fifth years of Jehoiakim's reign, 605/604 BCE, or, according to the LXX, in the eighth year, 601. In 605, the Babylonians defeated the Egyptians initially at Carchemish on the Euphrates and subsequently and finally at Hamath in central Syria. Egypt was reduced to a local power and Babylon eclipsed Assyria as the dominant power over the Levant. By 604, the Babylonian and Chaldean army had reduced Ashkelon and most of the Philistine plain and sent the residents to captivity in Babylon. With Babylon threatening, Jehoiakim changed his allegiance to become a vassal of Nebuchadrezzar. He paid the tribute to maintain the vassal status of Judah until 601. Jeremiah 36:9 indicates the people of Judah fasted before Yahweh, possibly due to the siege of Ashkelon in December of 604.

Yahweh's prophet Jeremiah pronounced the words of Yahweh (דברי יהוה) in oral and written form concerning Jehoiakim. Jeremiah 26:1 states that Jeremiah had preached in the temple at the beginning of Jehoiakim's reign (609). That seems to have been a reprise of the temple sermon of Jeremiah 7:1–15, where Jeremiah warned the people that, if they would not listen to the word of Yahweh, the temple would become like the tabernacle at Shiloh. The reaction was not positive: only Ahikam ben Shaphan's intervention saved Jeremiah's life at that time. This possibly accounts for the exclusion of Jeremiah from the temple (Jer 36:5). Uriah ben Shemaiah prophesied in similar fashion until Jehoiakim murdered him and threw his corpse into the burial place for the common people (26:20–23). The confrontation at the temple recounted in Jeremiah 26 was reprised in Jeremiah 36 at the reading of Jeremiah's scroll. Baruch read the scroll publicly, imploring the people to repent or perish.

35

Looking Back for Jehoiachin

The officials heard of Baruch's scroll from a grandson of Shaphan (36:11–12). Baruch was then escorted to the secretary's chamber where he read the scroll a second time. The alarmed officials, anticipating the reaction of Jehoiakim, told Baruch (and Jeremiah) to hide.

The officials indicated there was a message, then retrieved the scroll at the king's command. As the scroll was read, Jehoiakim cut it apart and cast it into the fire. As the text records, the officials warned the king regarding effrontery against the word of the Lord, but neither he nor his advisors paid heed. Indeed, not content with burning the scroll, Jehoiakim sent men to arrest Baruch and Jeremiah. This bid to silence the prophet and his amanuensis was ultimately unsuccessful, for Jeremiah redictated the scroll and added to the previously recorded material (36:32).

See Isbell[3] for an excellent discussion of his proposal that 2 Kings 22–23 is the foil for understanding Jeremiah 36. Jehoiakim's actions are best understood in contrast to those of his father Josiah. Quoting Keown:

> The similarities include: the rare use of a written scroll to deliver a divine message, the prophetic claim of authority ("thus says the Lord" oracular introduction), the concern for "evil" (רעה) specifically noted in both passages, and the call for reform.
>
> The crucial distinctions: Both episodes involve "tearing" on the part of the king. Josiah "tears" his garments ... Jehoiakim ... "tears" the sections of the scroll from the whole and casts them into the fire. "Burning" (שרף) is important to both episodes. Josiah burns altars in an attempt at reform; Jehoiakim attempts to invalidate the message by burning the scroll. Josiah "heard" the word of the Lord, while Jehoiakim pointedly does not "hear." Finally, the end result is that God "hears" Josiah, but the outcome for Jehoiakim and Judah is another matter, as Jer 36:30–31 clearly indicates.[4]

This passage provides a clear explanation for the exile. Holladay observes:

> The nation of Judah was fasting for a word from Yahweh. Jeremiah had dictated an answer nearly a year earlier. Baruch pronounced the word from Yahweh for the people, for the secretaries, for the king (and his heir!) and his officials. Jehoiakim

---

3. Isbell, "II Kings 22:3–23:24 and Jer 36: A Stylistic Comparison," in JSOT 8 [1978] 33–45.

4. Keown, Scalise, and Smothers, *Jeremiah 26–52*, 203.

Jeremiah 36:30–31 by verses

36:30: The לָכֵן at the outset of the verse directs the reader to the immediate context—Jeremiah 36:27–32, i.e., the conclusion to the burning of Jeremiah's scroll. The prophecy attributed Jehoiakim's punishment to his disobedience concerning the word of the Lord. The threatened change in Davidic succession was profound. No longer would a ruling Davidic king have a son to sit on David's throne, even though there was a living heir. The additional curse upon the king's person, that his corpse would be cast out, reflected disdain on the ruling monarch. This curse was a graphic repudiation of the honor normally accorded to Davidic rulers.

36:31: The verse predicts the punishments that followed in 597 and 586.

> פָּקַד—The negative meaning *punish* is most often construed with the collocation פָּקַד עַל, where the preposition indicates the object of divine displeasure. The verb can also bear the meaning punish with an unmarked object, or with the object indicated by an independent pronoun or a pronominal suffix. The reasons for the punishment are commonly indicated by אֵת or left unmarked.[6]

The presence of פָּקַד עַל indicates that the object of Yahweh's displeasure in this verse is Jehoiakim, his son (זַרְעוֹ—Jeconiah), and his servants (עֲבָדָיו).

How Jeremiah 36:30–31 informs our understanding of Jeconiah

The excoriation of Jehoiakim is harsh and brutal. Although Jehoiakim's son Jeconiah was capable and awaiting accession to the throne of David, Jeremiah prophesied that Jehoiakim would not have a son to sit on that throne.[7] This antisuccession pronouncement in 604 (MT) or 601 (LXX)

---

5. Holladay, *Jeremiah II*, 262.
6. Williams, "פָּקַד" in *NIDOTTE* 3:659–60.
7. Although Jeconiah reigned ninety to one hundred days, the reign was during the siege of Jerusalem and would certainly not constitute a normal reign. See discussion of Jer 22:24–30.

came true in 598 when Nebuchadrezzar departed from Babylon to crush the rebellion. (One can only imagine Jeconiah's reaction when he recalled this curse at the death of his father Jehoiakim.)

Summarizing Jeremiah 36:30–31, there is tension in the final disposition of Jehoiakim's corpse. The options included burial in the tombs of the kings, burial of an ass, and burial in the garden of Uzza. Certainly, the association of the latter two options would suit his evil doing. Given the impending siege of Jerusalem and the notation of 2 Kings 25 and 2 Chronicles 36 that Jehoiakim did not live beyond 598, we can only presume Jeconiah's accession to the throne was in unusual circumstances. His departure into exile three months later and his replacement by his uncle Zedekiah seemed to substantiate the prophetic record of Jeremiah 36:30–31. There is no direct evidence that Jehoiakim's body was cast out, but the conditions of siege would suggest that he did not enjoy a mourning period or honorific burial. The calamity pronounced personally against Jehoiakim and his advisors seems to have been visited upon his son Jeconiah, and more fully upon Zedekiah at the destruction of Jerusalem in 586.

Jeremiah 13:18–19 to the king and queen mother: "All Judah is taken into exile"

This pericope is set within the context of the enacted sermon of the spoiled linen waistcloth, culminating in the pronouncement, "Thus says Yahweh: 'Even so will I spoil the pride of Judah and the great pride of Jerusalem'" (13:9). Jeremiah 13:15–16 and 20–27 concern "the LORD's flock" and its impending destruction. Jeremiah 13:18–19 was isolated for review because of the royal addressees.

The young king Jeconiah was exiled at the age of eighteen—an earlier age than any of his predecessors. A reign cut short was looming from the outset of Jeremiah's prophecies regarding Jeconiah (cf. 36:30–31; 22:30). In 13:18–19, the addressees are nonspecific, namely "the king and the queen mother" (לַמֶּלֶךְ וְלַגְּבִירָה). Although any of the last four kings of Judah could be considered the addressees, the most probable recipients were Jeconiah and his mother Nehushta. This is suggested by the prominence of Nehushta in the narrative of 2 Kings 24:6–19, the queen mother (גְּבִירָה) exiled with Jeconiah. The indication that the cities of the South (Negev) had been shut up without relief argues for a date later than that of Jehoahaz's reign. The language of 13:19 ("All Judah ... entirely taken into exile") is probably hyperbole, although it would become increasingly certain from 597 and historically true within eleven years after Jeconiah's exile.

Reconstructed text of Jeremiah 13:18–19

¹⁸ אמר למלך ^b ולגבירה ^a
השפילו שבו כי ירד ^c מראשותיכם אטרת תפארתכם
¹⁹ ערי הנגב סגרו ואין פתח ^a הגלת יהודה כלה ^b הגלת שלומים ^{-b}

Text notes

18a: MT אמר reflects a singular spokesman, whereas the LXX εἴπατε is plural. Lundbom's argument is apt: "Either singular or plural will do, although plural is more prevalent in Jeremianic poetry."[8] Without additional evidence, retain MT.

18b: MT is ולגבירה, "and the queen mother," whereas the LXX has καὶ τοῖς δυναστεύουσιν, "and the princes" which retroverts to ולגבורים, a slight deviation between the masculine plural and the feminine singular. Either is possible.

18c: MT has מראשותיכם, "your head-pieces/ornaments." LXX has ἀπὸ κεφαλῆς ὑμῶν, "from your heads." Some commentators emend to מראשיכם. Most arrive at this same translation with Dahood[9] without emending the MT.

19a: MT has הגלת, "(Judah) is taken into exile," a *hop'al* perfect feminine singular to match the subject "Judah."[10]

---

8. Lundbom *AB*, 680: "The *qal* imperative singular of אמר occurs only once elsewhere in (Jeremiah's) prose (in) 18:11, whereas the plural appears seven times in the poetry (4:5; 31:7,10; 46:14; 48:17, 19 [feminine]; 50:2) and is once duplicated in a superscription (4:5)."

9. Dahood, "Two Textual Notes on Jeremiah," (CBQ 23 [1961] 462).

10. Lundbom *AB*, 682, suggests that this is "prophetic perfect; also hyperbole, in this instance to impress upon the king and queen mother that the cause is already lost." Holladay, *Jeremiah II*, 408, believes a ה has dropped out of the expected הגלתה (see Esth 2:6). No proposed explanation is entirely satisfactory.

19b-b: MT has הגלת שלומים, a feminine singular verb and masculine plural adverb. The versions and Amos 1:6, 9 read גלות שלמה.[11] LXX has ἀποικίαν τελείαν.

Translation of Jeremiah 13:18–19

18Say to the king and queen mother,
"Take a lowly seat,
For your beautiful crowns
Have fallen from your heads."
19The cities of the south are shut up;
And there is none to open.
All Judah is taken into exile,
Entirely taken into exile.

Background of the Jeremiah 13:18–19 account

The king and queen mother are not identified here, but Jeconiah and his mother Nehushta, widow of Jehoiakim (cf. 29:2; 2 Kgs 24:8, 12, 15), are the most likely candidates for many reasons. The queen mother is named with Jeconiah prominently in Jeremiah 29:2— the only other occurrence of גבירה in the book. Jeremiah 22:26 and 2 Kings 24:15 specify that Nehushta went into exile with Jeconiah. No other passages note this association. Although Jehoiakim suffered raiding parties after withholding tribute (2 Kgs 24:2), there is no evidence that the Negev was lost during his reign. Jeremiah 36:30–31 is dated either to 605/604 (MT) or 601 (LXX). It is unlikely that Jehoiakim would be named in that pericope and left unnamed here. Zedekiah was addressed personally and by name on many occasions, and there seems to be no reason for the indefinite address למלך when Jeremiah had routinely spoken directly to Zedekiah. For these reasons, we conjecture that 13:18–19 was spoken to Jeconiah and his mother Nehushta. After Jeconiah's departure, the imminence of exile was readily apparent, and the humbling of Judah had already begun.

Jeremiah exhorted the young king and his mother to humble themselves in light of the coming exile. Since they went into captivity in 597, this prophecy must have been spoken during his three-month reign.

---

11. GKC, para. 118q and 124d.

Jeremiah's Prophecies: Jeconiah in Babylon

Since Jeconiah was only eighteen years old at accession, some suppose that his mother directed his activities; there is no concrete evidence to support this.¹² (Jeconiah would have been better served by Yahweh's spokesman Jeremiah than the wife of his dead father.)

Jeremiah 13:18–19 by verses

13:18: This is a prophecy of humiliation. Rulers sitting in the dust without crowns implies submission to another authority. The antecedent prophecy 36:30 should have caused Jeconiah to recoil from arrogance on the throne of David. Jeconiah's ninety- to one-hundred-day reign does not equate to the normal reign of a monarch. Shallum's similarly abbreviated reign was but a moment on the Tishr-Tishri calendar. (This verse should have dashed Jeconiah's expectations of regnal success.)

If our proposal is correct that this pericope was addressed to Jeconiah and Nehushta, then Jeremiah's exclusion from the throne room and temple (Jer 36:5) was probably still in effect. The imperative אֱמֹר is unusual in Jeremiah. Even if he were permitted access, Jeremiah's message was not going to get a favorable hearing if the recipient were Jehoiakim, but perhaps slightly more so if presented to Jeconiah. The message was clear: "Humble yourselves (before the Lord) and sit (not on the throne of David) in the dust (the position of servants) before your crowns tumble off your heads (into the hands of your enemies)!"

The prophecy with its attendant humiliation would have been both unwelcome and portentous. This command to step down and to sit humbly in the dust is in like measure to the other pronouncements of Jeremiah to Jeconiah.

If the LXX, καὶ τοῖ δυναστεύουσιν, "and the princes," is correct, there might still be no difference to the addressees, since the impending exile had been indicated. The LXX plus at Jeremiah 13:20 lists Jerusalem as the subject of the feminine verb "lift up your eyes." If the MT is preferred, the subject of 13:20 would be the queen mother. Lundbom¹³ draws the pericope unusually from 13:18–20 despite the *setumah* after 13:19. He makes this demarcation based on the inference of Jeremiah

---

12. However, see Andreasen, "The Role of the Gebira," 192, who opines that Nehushta "represented a political point of view that saved city and land but made political prisoners of the entire court," and Ben-Barak, "The Status and Right of the Gebira," 23–34.

13. Lundbom, *AB*, 679.

3:2, where the same feminine singular imperative verbs (נשׂא and ראה), like the *Kethib* of 13:20, are used with eyes (עיני). This would certainly be the more difficult reading. *BHS* commends *Kethib*. If this is correct and the *Kethib* is original, then this is further evidence the addressees are Jeconiah and Nehushta rather than Jehoiakim and Zebidah (2 Kgs 23:36).

13:19: The poetic couplet "The cities of the south are shut up / And there is none to open" may be a reference to the usurpation of the king's royal prerogative (cf. Job 12:14; Isa 22:22 and 45:1), to raids upon southern territory (2 Kgs 24:2), or to an opportunistic encroachment by the Edomites. Whichever of these disasters it represented, the circumstances were to get far worse in the coming months. The unusual adverbial use of שלמים in 13:19 occasioned speculation among interpreters. Rashi interpreted this as "She (Judah) was exiled peacefully." Perhaps this has merit, for it seems to accord with the 597 exile. Kimchi rendered it: "She was exiled completely." Most commentators and English versions favor the latter treatment.

How Jeremiah 13:18–19 informs our understanding of Jeconiah

Jeremiah, either through Baruch (Jer 36:5) or through a delegation, transmitted to the king and the queen mother (or the princes) the LORD's warning. Although we cannot be certain who the prophecy was addressed to, we believe along with most commentators that they were Jeconiah and his mother Nehushta, the widow of king Jehoiakim. Duhm believed they were Jehoiakim and his mother Zebidah. However, the tone of the pericope does not reflect the caustic relations existing between Jeremiah and Jehoiakim (22:13–23; 26:20–23; 36:30–31). The tone seems rather to be directive, sympathetic, announcing the coming judgment, more likely addressed to the teenage king than Jehoiakim.

There is irony and pathos in the plea to step down and sit in the dust either actually or symbolically. When Josiah heard the scroll read (possibly Deut 28:36–37?), he humbled himself, tore his clothing, and repented in sackcloth and ashes. Perhaps Jeremiah hoped for such a response from the addressees of 13:18–19. This would have been the appropriate posture for the monarch before Yahweh in view of the inevitable maelstrom.

Jeremiah urged the king to come down from David's throne before it was too late. Perhaps this word had the desired effect on Jeconiah (2

Kgs 24:12). Similar words to Zedekiah did not seem to have the same propitious outcome (2 Kgs 25:4–7).

The full power of Babylonian hegemony was about to descend upon Judah and Jerusalem. Certainly the Davidic crown worn by Jeconiah became the conqueror's prize of war (cf. Ezek 16:12; Zech 9:16).

Summarizing Jeremiah 13:18–19, we noted the context, which directed humility instead of arrogance. To amplify this counsel, Jeremiah enacted the sermon of the ruined linen waistcloth. We conjecture that, although the recipients (למלך ולגבירה) were indefinite, the prophecy was intended to be for Jeconiah and Nehushta. With Josiah as an exemplar, the prophet appealed to the king and queen mother to humility, not arrogance. (Perhaps this counsel was recalled by Jeconiah when Nebuchadrezzar appeared at the gates of Jerusalem with the Chaldean force.)

From the two pericopes spoken before Jeconiah's exile, we turn to the afterthoughts,[14] beginning with the most poignant regarding Coniah's destination.

JEREMIAH 22:24–30 CONIAH, YAHWEH'S CAST-OUT SIGNET (חוֹתָם): DISHONORED AND עֲרִירִי

The pericopes we have examined thus far say little about Jeconiah other than that he did evil in the eyes of the LORD. He was only one of the kings in the descending spiral toward the destruction of Jerusalem and Judah. (Jeconiah would have heard the curse of Jeremiah 36:30 which excluded him, as Jehoiakim's זֶרַע, from the throne of David. Likely he also heard the words of 13:18–19.)

His variable names (Jehoiachin in the narratives, Coniah in two Jeremianic prophecies, and Jeconiah in the afterthoughts) seemed to foreshadow the change of fortunes of the king whose names meant "May Yahweh establish/uphold." It was not apparent that Yahweh was upholding him in 598.

We now address the most detailed and poignant prophecy concerning Jeconiah in Jeremiah's "book of books." Jeremiah 22:24–30 may have been spoken immediately after Jeconiah's departure into exile, judging

---

14. By *afterthoughts*, we mean that the preponderance of the texts that use Jeconiah (Jer 24:1–3; 28:1–4; 29:1–3) and Coniah (22:24–30; 37:1–2) appear to coincide with his exile and not with his brief reign. The "king's coda" (2 Kgs 25:27–30; Jer 52:31–34) reflects the name Jehoiachin and appears to be based on the historian's narrative rather than the prophecies before his exile.

Looking Back for Jehoiachin

from the longing to return of 22:27. Certainly 22:24–30 was spoken before the remaining pericopes in this chapter (24:1–3; 27:19–22; 28:1–4; 29:1–3; 37:1–2).

Supplemented by the oath (חי אני) and oracular (נאם יהוה) formulas, the prophecy conceded that Coniah had been the metaphorical signet upon Yahweh's right hand, i.e., seated on the throne of David; but asserted that he was to be plucked off the hand (metaphorically the throne) and given into the hands of those whom he feared, namely, the Chaldeans. He was then to be hurled (טול) into a land where neither he nor his mother had been born. There he would die, even though he was desperately homesick (this does seem to replay the theme of Deut 28:36). In the poetic verses (Jer 22:28–30), the pathetic state of the young king is tragically relayed: "Is this man a despised, broken pot, a vessel no one cares for?" The earth was summoned as witness to the word of the LORD, namely, that this man Coniah would not be recorded as king of Judah, but as "childless," or "stripped of honor." The echoes of Jeremiah 36:30 resound here. None of Coniah's descendants would be king of Judah.

Stark tragedy overwhelmed the eighteen-year-old king who could not resist the Babylonian reprisal set in motion by his father's violation of the suzerainty treaty. The prose oracle and poetry imply that King Coniah might once have been regarded as valuable as Yahweh's own signet, as the reigning king of Jerusalem, or as a treasured vessel. But the word of the LORD now having been spoken, all that glittering value was refuse. Condemned to dethronement, captivity, and the absolute knowledge that his children, marching to captivity with him, would never accede to the throne, Coniah was cast out and hurled into Babylon to die.

Coniah was the penultimate figure in the decaying plunge into exile which marked the end of the kings in Judah. Four hundred years of regnal traditions were about to fade into hopeful reminiscences. He, too, would be simply an afterthought. Like the kingdom of Israel one hundred and twenty-five years previously, the kingdom of Jerusalem and Judah was about to be removed from the land of promise and relocated to a foreign land.

Reconstructed text of Jeremiah 22:24–30

24 [a] חי אני נאם יהוה כי אם יהיה כניהו בן יהויקים מלך יהודה
חותם על יד ימיני כי משם אתקנך 25 ונתתיך ביד מבקשי נפשך

Jeremiah's Prophecies: Jeconiah in Babylon

וּבְיַד אֲשֶׁר אַתָּה יָגוֹר מִפְּנֵיהֶם <>ᵃ בְּיַד הַכַּשְׂדִּים ²⁶ וְהֵטַלְתִּי אֹתְךָ
וְאֶת־אִמְּךָ אֲשֶׁר יְלָדַתְךָ עַל ᵃ אֶרֶץ ᵃ-<> אֲשֶׁר לֹא יְלַדְתֶּם שָׁם וְשָׁם
תָּמוּתוּ ²⁷ וְעַל הָאָרֶץ אֲשֶׁר הֵם מְנַשְּׂאִים אֶת נַפְשָׁם לָשׁוּב <>ᵃ לֹא
יָשׁוּבוּ ᵃ ²⁸ נִבְזֶה בָנְיָהוּ כִּכְלִי אֵין חֵפֶץ בּוֹ
ᵇ כִּי הוּטַל וְהֻשְׁלַךְ עַל אֶרֶץ אֲשֶׁר לֹא יָדָע
ᵃ ²⁹ אֶרֶץ אֶרֶץ אֶרֶץ שִׁמְעִי דְּבַר יְהוָה
ᵃ ³⁰ כְּתֹב <>ᵇ אֶת הָאִישׁ הַזֶּה עֲרִירִי
ᶜ כִּי לֹא יִצְלַח מִזַּרְעוֹ אִישׁ יֹשֵׁב
עַל כִּסֵּא דָוִד מֹשֵׁל עוֹד בִּיהוּדָה

Text notes

24a: Note the efforts of Wells[15], Janzen,[16] and Tov[17] to explain the fuller MT tradition.

25a: The MT adds the phrase "into the hand of Nebuchadrezzar king of Babylon," a mechanical expansion by "Editor II." See Tov.

26a-a: The MT reflects a definite article and the adjective (הָאָרֶץ אַחֶרֶת), "another land," whereas the LXX has "land" (γῆν). McKane[18] points out that הָאָרֶץ can be translated by εἰς γῆν as in v. 28. אַחֶרֶת looks like the characteristically fuller tradition of the MT. Delete the definite article and the adjective.

27a: The MT has the infinitive construct and particles to specify what the king and his mother longed for, i.e., "(to return) there . . . there (they shall not return)." The second adverb (שָׁמָּה) is possibly emphatic, if the first adverb is original. The LXX does not have these particles. Emend to reflect shorter LXX.

28a: This verse is difficult in both MT and LXX, so the reconstruction is approximate. See Holladay,[19] who believes the MT of vv. 28–30 preserves a better tradition.

---

15. Wells, "Indications of Late Reinterpretation," 405–20, esp. 414–15. The MT changes are "a modest, disciplined reinterpretation of the Jeremianic tradition . . . [incorporating] assonances, changes of letters, increased use of particles, and sharper allusions to related texts . . . preference for three-fold expressions and a tendency to add or expand names or titles," 406.

16. Janzen, *Studies in the Text of Jeremiah*, 406.

17. Tov, "Some Aspects of the Textual and Literary History of the Book of Jeremiah," 145–167.

18. McKane, *A Critical and Exegetical Commentary on Jeremiah*, 545.

19. Holladay's MT preference: "LXX suffered by haplography or deliberate omission of synonyms" (608).

28b: The MT's tradition reflects the interrogative "why?" and the nouns "he and his seed," thereby expanding the questions of the first half of this verse and inflecting all successive verbs as plurals. The conjunction ὅτι in the LXX is translated with causal force, i.e., "Coniah is dishonored because he is hurled out."

29a: The LXX tradition has only two iterations of "earth," where the MT has 3. This predilection for twofold LXX and threefold MT holds true in Jeremiah 7:4 ("the temple of the Lord") but not in Isaiah 6:3 ("Holy, holy, holy, Lord God of hosts"). Retain.

30a: The MT formula "Thus says the Lord" is lacking in the LXX. Delete.

30b: וכתבו in MT, singular in LXX. Emend to כתב.

30c: The LXX hapax phrase ἐκκήρυκτον ἄνθρωπον could be variously translated "an outcast man," "a banished man," or "a man stripped." The MT ערירי translated "childless" (see also Gen 15:2 and Lev 20:20–21) may reflect the nuance of the LXX "stripped of all honor." Routinely, the LXX translates "childless" as ἄτεκνος; see discussion in verse-by-verse.

30c: The MT preserves the tradition גבר לא יצלח בימיו, that Coniah would not prosper in his lifetime. The LXX does not reflect this sentiment. Delete.

Translation of Jeremiah 22:24–30

24As I live, declares Yahweh, Coniah son of Jehoiakim king of Judah shall no longer be the signet *ring* on my right hand; surely from there I have plucked you off 25and I have given you into the hands of those who seek your life, before whom you are afraid, into the hand of the Chaldeans. 26And furthermore I have hurled you and the mother who bore you to a land where neither of you were born, and there you both shall die. 27But to the land to which their souls long to return, they shall never return.

28Coniah is dishonored like a vessel in which there is no delight;
for he is hurled out and cast to a land that he does not know.
29 O land, land, land, hear the word of the Lord:
30 "Record this man, 'Childless,' for none of his offspring
will reign on the throne of David or ever rule in Judah."

Jeremiah's Prophecies: Jeconiah in Babylon

Background of the Jeremiah 22:24–30 account

The parameters for blessings upon Davidic kings were announced in 22:3—maintain justice and righteousness, defend the oppressed, outlaw lawlessness and bloodshed; "then through the gates of this palace shall enter kings of David's line who sit upon his throne" (22:4). If these parameters were transgressed, the calamity "this palace shall become a ruin" would accrue (22:5).

Jeremiah 22:10–12 was a redirection of lament from the dead king Josiah to the king to be exiled to death—Shallum. Also known as Jehoahaz (2 Kgs 23:30–33; 2 Chr 36:1–4), he was appointed by עם הארץ to be king at the loss of Josiah. He reigned three months before being exiled to Egypt in 609. This lament was spoken during the lifetime of Jeconiah, approximately eleven years before he (briefly) ascended the throne.

Jeremiah 22:13–19 is a polemic against Jehoiakim's extravagant lifestyle, oppression of his laborers, and unrighteousness (in violation of 22:3). This invective culminates with the prediction that he would remain unburied and unlamented—a possible allusion to burial in the garden of Uzza.[20] Jehoiakim died (or was killed) shortly before the siege in 598.

Jeremiah 22:20–23 is an address to "you who dwell in Lebanon, nestled among cedars," possibly a generic reference to the kings of Judah living in the House of Lebanon.[21]

Jeremiah 22:24–30 is the indictment of Coniah to be explored shortly. According to this pericope, neither Coniah nor any of his sons would prosper in life or rule in Jerusalem.

Jeremiah 23:1–2 is a polemic against the shepherds (leaders) who failed to tend their flocks. The reference to צמח צדיק "righteous Branch" (23:5) is paronomasia, a play on Zedekiah's name צדקיהו. This prophecy announces the reign of the "righteous Branch" as the Davidic king who would fulfill all the stipulations of 23:5. Whoever that individual was to be, 22:24–30 established he would not be Coniah's offspring.

---

20. See discussion of Jer 36:30–31.

21. See also the discussion in Chapter Four of this dissertation regarding "Lebanon" in Ezek 17.

Looking Back for Jehoiachin

Jeremiah 22:24–30 by verses

22:24: The wide variety of translations for כִּי אִם demonstrates its difficulty: RSV: "though Coniah . . . were the signet ring on my right hand, yet I would tear you off;" Bright: ". . . even were you (Coniah) the signet ring on my right hand, I would snatch you off;"[22] Holladay: "Coniah . . . shall never be the signet-ring on my right hand. Yes, from there I would pull you off!"[23] McKane: "Coniah . . . shall no longer be a signet ring on my right hand. I will pull you off from my finger (O Coniah)!"[24] Thompson: "Coniah ben Jehoiakim king of Judah shall not be the signet ring on my right hand. Yes, Coniah, I will pull you off."[25] Note also the unique TEV rendering: "The LORD said to King Jehoiachin, son of King Jehoiakim of Judah, "As surely as I am the living God, even if you were the signet ring on my right hand, I would pull you off." The choice of "no longer" in our translation concedes Coniah's one-time status as Yahweh's earthly regent, but now asserts his fate as a plucked-off signet.

"Plucked you off" is one possible translation. Others: RSV/NRSV/Carroll "tear you off," NIV/TEV/NCV/Holladay/McKane/Thompson "pull you off," NAC "snatch you from it."

How often does Yahweh invoke "As I live"? In addition to the occurrences in Ezekiel,[26] there are four occurrences of the phrase חַי אָנִי נְאֻם יהוה (an irrevocable oath curse—see also Deut 33:40) and a fifth similar to it: (1) Numbers 14:28 (cf. 14:21), Yahweh's oath against Israel for refusing to obey; (2) Isaiah 49:18, Yahweh swears to Zion she shall have her children; (3) Zephanaiah 2:9, Yahweh's oath that Moab shall be as Sodom and Ammon shall be as Gomorrah; and (4) this pericope, Jeremiah 22:24. In each of these four instances, Yahweh makes a certifying oath that the condition would occur as prophesied. (5) Jeremiah 46:18: "As I live, says the King, whose name is the LORD of hosts" (חַי אָנִי נְאֻם הַמֶּלֶךְ יהוה צְבָאוֹת), a warning to Egypt to prepare for

---

22. Bright, *Jeremiah*, Anchor Bible 21 (Garden City, NY: Doubleday, 1965)

23. Holladay, *Jeremiah I*, #.

24. McKane, *Jermiah 1–25*, International Critical Commentary (Edinburgh: T&T Clark, 2000), #.

25. Thompson, *The Book of Jeremiah*, 483: ". . . in an oath כִּי אִם may be understood as an 'unthinkable' condition implying an (unstated) drastic apodosis, hence negatively: 'Coniah will never be the signet ring. . . .'"

26. In the oath phrases in Ezekiel, there are variations in the word order, insertion of אֲדֹנָי, or intervening clauses between the words of the oath in these passages: 5:11; 14:16, 18, 20; 16:48; 17:16; 18:3; 20:3, 31, 33; 33:11, 27; 34:8; 35:6, 11.

Jeremiah's Prophecies: Jeconiah in Babylon

exile, for Nebuchadrezzar would surely come and destroy Egypt. The LXX oath form is longer: (ζῶ ἐγώ λέγει κύριος ὁ θεός). The oath form was employed very selectively in order to underline the solemn pronouncement that followed.

The reference to Yahweh's hands is an anthropomorphism. His signet is "Thus says the LORD" or "Oracle of Yahweh." He could not be deprived of his signet, but his earthly regent could be deposed if disobedient to the covenant (Jer 22:3–4; Deut 28:36). There was a vast difference between the hand of Yahweh and the *hand* of the Chaldeans.

22:25: Instead of reigning from the throne, Coniah was given into the hands of those seeking his life (MT plus, "into the hands of Nebuchadrezzar") and the hands of the Chaldeans. Although Yahweh symbolically plucked Coniah off and handed him to those whom he feared, they did not kill him. Coniah was safe in Babylon because Yahweh was watching over him to achieve his purposes (see discussion in Jer 24:1–3 and 29:1–3). The window for delivery of the oracle was brief—certainly not before his accession, and not long after Jeconiah's march through the Ishtar Gate—all within a space of three to four months.

22:26: He was to be hurled with his mother to die. The imagery of being hurled into a different land than that of their birth would be violent and repulsive. To be outside the covenant land of Israel was figuratively to be outside of Yahweh's covenant (Deut 28:36). That his descendants were to be excluded from the land as well as the throne (Jer 22:27) was egregious. (One hopes Coniah's response was more contrite than that of Hezekiah when he learned of the fate to be actuated upon his offspring.)

22:27: Craigie opines based on the retrospective longing of Coniah and his mother for their homeland that the oracle should be translated as prophetic perfect. He concludes that Coniah had gone into captivity at the time of the prophecy, explaining that 22:24–27 is parallel to the oracle against Shallum in 22:11–12.[27] Yahweh removed Shallum into an exile until death. Jeremiah proclaimed an exile until death for Coniah. As Shallum was lamented and mourned, Coniah was also lamented and mourned. Neither Shallum nor Coniah would ever see Judah again. Both had short reigns of three months. Both succeeded their fathers and were succeeded by an older "brother" (2 Chr 36:4, 10) installed by an invading national sovereign.[28]

---

27. Craigie, *Jeremiah 1–25*, Word Biblical Commentary, Volume 26, editor Bruce Metzger, et.al., 317–19.

28. Jehoahaz died in Egypt and was never remarked upon again. After Jeconiah's

22:28: Craigie further observes: "22:24–30 is a prose-poetic double oracle. The prose oracle (22:24–27) is mostly concerned with the length of the exile, whereas the poetic oracle (22:28–30) is concerned with Coniah's descendants."[29]

The MT has נִבְזֶה, a niphal participle meaning "despised," "despicable," "vile," or "worthless." The LXX has ἠτιμώθη, an aorist passive meaning "dishonored." Although we have retroverted the LXX to a "thinner" reconstructed text, it should be noted that the alliteration and assonance of the MT tradition is better:

העצב נבזה נפוץ האיש הזה
כניהו אם כלי אין חפץ בו

The unusual verb "to hurl" (טול) links the prose passages 22:24–27 and the poetic oracle 22:28–30. It occurs as a *hip'il* perfect in 22:26 "I have hurled you . . ." and as a *hop'al* perfect in 22:28, "He is hurled out." This is a violent action, as in the hurling of a spear (1 Sam 18:11; 20:33). The only other occurrence of the verb in Jeremiah is at 16:13: "I will hurl you (לעם הזה "this people," 16:10) out of this land into a land which neither you nor your fathers have known," an echo of 22:28. A spear is meant to be hurled; people and Davidic kings are not. Jerusalem was to be hurled out into captivity where her people and her king would die in exile.

A *pilpel* participle of טול occurs with Yahweh as subject in Isaiah 22:17. Yahweh was about to hurl away Shebna the steward into a broad land. There, according to Isaiah 22:18, he would die. Interestingly, this pericope shares several words with Jeremiah 22:24–30, e.g., גבר, "fellow"; תמות ושמה שמה , "there you will die . . . there." Isaiah 22:15–19 provides precedent for the hurling that Jeremiah described as the fate of Coniah.

The rhetorical questions of the MT are unanswered, but the implication was that Coniah was *not* a despised pot or an unwanted vessel. Although he was thrown away as a useless vessel on the refuse heap, there were priests, prophets, and people who ardently desired his return from Babylon (28:4). The root of "pot" (עצב) means "something fashioned," an "image," or "idol." That Coniah was only a fashioned image sent to

---

death in Babylon, there are numerous echoes and reflections of his life (to be considered in chapters 3 through 5).

29. OpCit, 319.

serve false gods in Babylon (Deut 28:36) may be implied by the MT.[30] The MT includes Coniah's offspring in the curse of this verse, but the LXX delays that curse until 22:30.

22:29: "O Land, land, land" could alternatively be translated, "Earth, earth, earth" or be punctuated "Land! Land! Land!" (as in McKane).[31] Apparently, the people were trusting in the institutions of the temple and the monarchy instead of trusting fully in Yahweh. Even as the temple was a grand edifice, it was impermanent. The monarchy had rich tradition, but it, too, was transitory. We retain the threefold MT based on the trebled "Temple of the LORD" in the MT of 7:3.

22:30: The MT has כתבו, a *qal* imperative with a range of meaning: "write!" "inscribe!" or "register!" LXX has γράψον, aorist imperative, meaning "write!" "record!" or "compose!" "Record" captures the commandment without specifying exactly what activity is required. The imperative to record Coniah as "childless"[32] may have been an instruction to the scribes enrolling the exiles before leaving for Babylon. This curse was a dramatic reversal of the expected succession.

The remainder of the verse in the MT and the second half of 22:30 in the LXX proscribed Coniah's descendants from sitting on the throne of David. The LXX has ἐκκήρυκτον ἄνθρωπον—"a man stripped." Although this is entirely possible given the Babylonian procedure of denuding captives, "stripped of honor" and "stripped of royalty" are equally possible.

The MT has יצלח with the negative particle, a *qal* imperfect meaning "(not) prosper." The LXX has αὐξηθῇ, an aorist passive subjunctive meaning "grow." The implication of the passage is clear: Coniah would never have any offspring who would rule on the throne of David.

The MT עוד is translated "ever" instead of "still" or "yet" to reflect the impossibility of a descendent of Coniah ruling on the throne of David.

---

30. Holladay, *Jeremiah I*, 610.

31. McKane, *A Critical and Exegetical Commentary on Jeremiah*, 546.

32. Hamilton "ערירי"in *NIDOTTE*, 3:534–35: "childless may be understood non-literally. Coniah was to be called childless (22:30), not because he never fathered any children but because none of his offspring would ever succeed him as king of Judah. Possibly Jeremiah's prophecy was motivated by his conviction that it was not Yahweh's plan to permit a descendant of Coniah to assume the throne of David. When Coniah's grandson Zerubbabel (1 Chr 3:19) returned from the Exile, he returned not as king but as governor in postexilic Jerusalem under the Persian emperor."

Looking Back for Jehoiachin

How Jeremiah 22:24–30 informs our understanding of Coniah

The context of Jeremiah 22:1–30 is key to placing Coniah in the setting of the last four kings of Judah. The specific parameters of 22:3–4 were violated by both Jehoiakim and Zedekiah as well as by the two short-reigning kings Jehoahaz and Coniah. All four were the final contributors to the downward spiral of the Judean monarchy that began in the seventh century.

Both the MT and the LXX (favored in our reconstructed text) lend a poignancy to the account of this king. The imagery of Coniah, a treasured signet, Yahweh's *imprimatur* (a סגלה?), yet now hurled out into Babylon, is a startling and brutal reversal. The handover from Yahweh into the hands of those Coniah feared—LXX and MT, the hands of the Chaldeans; MT plus, the hand of Nebuchadrezzar, king of Babylon—was amplified by the violence of hurling Coniah and his mother into a strange land. Their death had been prophesied, and they surely feared death from the moment Nebuchadrezzar commanded their exile (March 597 per the Babylonian Chronicle). The LXX retroversion, not as expressive as the rhetorical questions of the MT, still arouses the reader/hearer's emotion over the tragedy of their plight. "Coniah is dishonored ... because he is hurled out" (22:28). The young king, though having sons (1 Chr 3:16–19) was recorded as ערירי, for none of his sons would prosper (לא יצלח) or reign on the throne of David.

The negative assurances of 22:28–30 seem to echo the curses upon Hezekiah (2 Kgs 20:16–19) and Jehoiakim (Jer 36:31). The succession protocol was abruptly terminated with Coniah's departure and (his uncle) Zedekiah's accession. The exile of king, queen mother, wives, children, and officials looked like the dead end of the Davidic kingdom.

But another reversal was in the offing.

JEREMIAH 24:1–3: YAHWEH LOOKS AFTER "GOOD FIGS" (JECONIAH) AND "BAD FIGS" (ZEDEKIAH)

Jeremiah stated that the LORD showed him a vision of good and bad figs placed before the temple—the same place Hananiah son of Azzur would break the yoke and predict Jeconiah's return with the temple vessels within two years (28:1–4). The parenthetical time notation in 24:1 interrupts the flow (thus the variation in the English translations), but is necessary to understand the interpretation. This vision, following that of

Jeremiah's Prophecies: Jeconiah in Babylon

22:24–30, sets in stark relief the figs in Babylon and the figs in Jerusalem and Egypt. Given the tenor of Deuteronomy 28:36 that the exiled king would serve wood and stone non-gods and become a byword, it is surprising that Yahweh announced to Jeremiah that Jeconiah and the exiles were the *good* figs.

Reconstructed text of Jeremiah 24:1–3

הראני יהוה והנה שני דודאי תאנים ᵇ מועדים לפני היכל יהוה ᵃ ¹
ᶜ אחרי הגלות נבוכדראצר מלך בבל את ᵈ יכניהו בן יהויקים מלך
יהודה ואת שרי יהודה ואת החרש ואת המסגר ᵉ מירושלם
ויבאם בבל ᶜ⁻² הדוד אחד תאנים טבות מאד כתאני
הבכרות והדוד אחד תאנים רעות מאד אשר לא
תאכלנה מרע ³ ויאמר יהוה אלי מה אתה ראה
ירמיהו ואמר תאנים התאנים הטבות טבות מאד
והרעות רעות מאד אשר לא תאכלנה מרע

Text notes

1a: *BHS* suggests reading כֹּה, "Thus," which might have fallen out by haplography following תשבה at the end of 23:40.

1b: The participle translated "placed" (מוּעָדִים) is somewhat uncertain. Presumably, it is the *hopʿal* of יעד and so means something like "appointed" (cf. Ezek 21:21). Some commentators emend to עמדים, "standing," or מעמדים, "placed." Thomas proposed that the verb results from a metathesis of מודעים, *hopʿal* of ידע.[33] Retain MT.

1c-c: Holladay deletes the parenthetic, syntactically subordinate, temporal clause, stating it is "clearly an editorial insertion designed to explain the historical context."[34] It is evidently present in the LXX *Vorlage*, so if it were an insertion, it was early. We retain the clause, yet invert the order in translation.

1d: The spelling of the name "Jeconiah" (יכניהו) is unique in the OT, but we have already noted the interchangeability and variation of the spelling of these names.

1e—LXX has καὶ τοὺς δεσμώτας, "and the prisoners." The word המסגר may imply locksmiths or goldsmiths. LXX "prisoners" does

---

33. Thomas, D. Winton, "A Note on מוּעָדִים, in Jeremiah 24:1," *JTS* NS 3 (1952) 55.
34. Holladay, *Jeremiah I*, 654–655.

indicate the root סגר. LXX also adds καὶ τοὺς πλουσίους, "and the rich," following this phrase.

Translation of Jeremiah 24:1–3

1After Nebuchadrezzar, king of Babylon, exiled Jeconiah, the son of Jehoiakim, the king of Judah, along with the princes of Judah, the skilled craftsmen, and the smiths from Jerusalem, and brought them to Babylon, Yahweh showed me two baskets of figs placed before the temple of the Lord. 2 The one basket had very good figs, like first-ripe figs, and the other basket had very bad figs that could not be eaten they were so bad.

3Then Yahweh said to me, "What do you see, Jeremiah?" Then I said, "Figs; the good figs are very good, but the bad figs are very bad, which cannot be eaten, they are so bad."

Background of the Jeremiah 24:1–3 account

In Jeremiah 24, the prophet sees a vision of good and bad figs. The surprising interpretation (24:4–10) reverses what one might expect. To be exiled, as Jeconiah was in 22:24–30, was to be cursed—excluded from the land of the covenant. But 24:1, 5 indicates that Jeconiah and the exiles in Babylon were like good figs to Yahweh.

The temporal clause of 24:1, present in the MT and LXX, indicates that the events of chapter 24 took place sometime after the 597 exile. Sufficient time had elapsed so that the horror of the Babylonian siege had dissipated. Life in Jerusalem returned to a semblance of normality. The harsh memories of Chaldean brutality began to soften. Perhaps even talk of withholding tribute to Babylon surfaced. Into this drama Yahweh inserted two baskets of fruit offerings.

Jeremiah 24:1–3 by verses

24:1: The specification of those exiled with Jeconiah, i.e., the princes of Judah, the skilled craftsmen, and the smiths, is an abbreviation of the listing in 2 Kings 24:12–16, which included Jeconiah's mother, his wives, his officials, the chief men of the land, the mighty men of valor, and the

Jeremiah's Prophecies: Jeconiah in Babylon

craftsmen and smiths. The hearers of Jeremiah's vision were familiar with the exile, and further specification was unnecessary.

It is not possible to tell whether the vision had a physical basis or was only a dream. The location "before the temple" suggests that the figs were an offering.

24:2–3: The vision called to mind the offering of the first fruits in a basket before the Lord (Deut 26:10). In one of the baskets, the figs were very good and resembled those that ripen early (Isa 28:4; Hos 9:10; Mic 7:1). The second basket contained rotten figs that could not be eaten. Such offerings were unacceptable to the Lord (Mal 1:6–7). Zedekiah's kingdom was likewise repulsive to Yahweh's eyes, ears, and nose.

How Jeremiah 24:1–3 informs our understanding of Jeconiah

Jeremiah 24:5 announces that Yahweh is the one who drove out the exiles to Babylon.

The dramatic reversal of the horrendous imagery of the cast-out signet begins with 24:1–3 and the interpretation of 24:5–7. But this reversal continues with the interpretation of 24:8–10. Not only were the exiles with Jeconiah to be regarded as "good figs" by Yahweh, but the inhabitants remaining with Zedekiah in Jerusalem were to be regarded as "bad figs." (This unexpected change of fortunes is further reinforced in the letter which Jeremiah was to dispatch to Jeconiah and the exiles in Jeremiah 29:1–3.)

> The reality of two Jewish communities, one in exile and one in Jerusalem, is peculiarly important for this passage. There must have been rivalry and conflict between a community in exile and a community at home. On the face of it, one would imagine that the ones left behind (even if they are not the leading citizens) must have felt themselves fortunate for not having been deported. It must have been obvious to them that they were God's chosen—not only especially loved, but protected and entrusted with God's future. Given that self-understanding, it would be equally obvious to the ones in Judah that the Jews in exile were not in God's favor. Because they were the ones who suffered the punishment of exile, they must be rejected and judged by God.[35]

---

35. Brueggemann, *To Pluck Up, To Tear Down*, 209.

Looking Back for Jehoiachin

In reviewing the highlights of Jeremiah 24:1–3, we determined that 24:1, although parenthetical, is necessary to the vision of good and bad figs. The unique spelling of Jeconiah (יכניהו) does not cause difficulty due to the changes in this king's name in the narratives, prophecies, and afterthoughts. The unexpected announcement that the exiles were the good figs and those in Judah/Egypt were the bad figs must have been extreme. Both the audience in Babylon and those who were to be destroyed in Jerusalem were shocked.

JEREMIAH 27:19–22: THE REMAINING TEMPLE VESSELS TO GO TO BABYLON (LIKE JECONIAH)

Jeremiah 27 concerns the final disposition of the temple vessels and submission to Nebuchadrezzar. The prophecy included the construction of a yoke with straps fitted to Jeremiah's neck to symbolize submission to Babylonian hegemony. The envoys of 27:3–11 were told to instruct their kings to submit to Nebuchadrezzar. Jeremiah 27:9 instructs the kings to ignore the prophets, diviners, dreamers, soothsayers, and sorcerers who counseled rebellion from Nebuchadrezzar; 27:10 indicates that any such counsel is a lie (שקר / ψεύδη).

Jeremiah 27:12–15 is addressed to Zedekiah in the same way. The warning again alludes to the lie (שקר / ἐπὶ ἀδικῷ ψεύδη).

Jeremiah 27:16–22 is addressed to the priests and people of Jerusalem. Once again, the prophets are accused of speaking lies (שקר / ἄδικα). Jeremiah pronounces the challenge, preceded by the dual qualification, "If indeed they are prophets, and if the word of the LORD is with them . . ." let them intercede for the vessels not taken to Babylon.

Jeremiah countermanded the prophets of false hope who counseled against serving the king of Babylon. He appealed to Zedekiah to submit to Nebuchadrezzar (27:12–15). He also appealed to the priests not to listen to the prophets who were saying that the vessels of the LORD's house would soon come back from Babylon. Jeremiah invoked כה אמר יהוה in 27:16 and challenged the prophets who, like him, declared כה אמר יהוה to intercede with the LORD that the vessels left in the house of the LORD might not go to Babylon. This was a direct challenge to these prophets, who, like Hananiah (28:1–4), predicted the end

Jeremiah's Prophecies: Jeconiah in Babylon

of Babylonian hegemony. They were demonstrably wrong then, and their message that Jeconiah would come back within a short time was also perilously audacious. The proof of who truly declared כה אמר יהוה from Yahweh would be attested by what happened to Jeconiah and the nobles. According to Jeremiah's כה אמר יהוה, the remainder of the vessels were to depart.[36]

Reconstructed text of Jeremiah 27:19–22

19 כי כה אמר יהוה <>a <>b-b <>c על יתר הכלים 20 d-d אשר לא לקחם a מלך בבל בגלותו את b יכניה c-c מירושלם בבלה d-d 21 a <> a 22 b-b יובאו נאם יהוה c-c

Text notes

19a: MT adds צבאות.

19b-b: MT adds אל העמדים ועל הים ועל המכנות. The MT explains that the vessels (הכלים) include the pillars, the sea, and the stands remaining at the temple after the Babylonians departed. The LXX does not give any indication regarding the details of הכלים, other than that they were going to Babylon. Tov remarks about the MT expansions in Jeremiah 27:18 and beyond:

> From here to the end of the chapter the MT is greatly expanded. Interestingly enough, except for two significant additions, the expanded text stresses details which were already found in the short text. It is remarkable how well the editor of the MT managed to insert the new elements (sometimes whole sentences) between the existing parts of LXX without introducing significant changes. The author of the additions showed a great interest in the fate of the temple vessels, adding details which are based, among other things, on data mentioned in both Jeremiah and 2 Kings. In the course of his reworking, the editor of MT used the expression הכלים הנותרים (27:18, 21) instead of the similar phrase יתר הכלים found in LXX. These vessels (כלים) were specified as "the vessels left in the house of the Lord" (both LXX and MT) and "the vessels in the house of the king" (MT only). In the second detail, MT contains a little piece of information not

---

36. On this passage and theme, cf. Ackroyd, "The Temple Vessels—A Continuity Theme."

contained in LXX which is probably reliable. In 52:13 ... Nebuchadrezzar took vessels from the "house of the Lord" before it was burnt; he probably acted similarly with regard to the vessels found in the "house of the king."[37]

19c: MT has copulative, i.e., ועל. Tov argues that the preposition is difficult:

> This reconstruction of על in על יתר הכלים ... continues the opening formula כי כה אמר יהוה. The translator started a new sentence with them: καὶ τῶν ἐπιλοίπων σκευῶν (As for the remaining vessels...). His *Vorlage* actually may not have contained the preposition על, even though it is in the full formula כי כה אמר יהוה על occurring in 27:21 and elsewhere in the OT and LXX (cf. 22:6; 23:2, 15; 36:28).[38]

19d-d: MT adds הנותרים בעיר הזאת as an explanatory addition.

20a: MT adds נבוכדנאצר.

20b: *Kethib* spelling is unique יכוניה. It appears to be a combining of כוניה and יכניה. The *Qere* spelling is also found in 28:4 and 29:2 (Esth 2:6; 1 Chr 3:15–16).

20c-c: MT adds בן יהויקים מלך יהודה.[39]

20d-d: MT adds ואת כל חרי יהודה וירושלם as a continuation of the tradition of 29:2 where החרי (the nobles) are mentioned (cf. 39:6 and 2 Kgs 24:14).

21a: MT adds כי כה אמר יהוה צבאות אלהי ישראל על הכלים הנותרים בית יהוה ובית מלך יהודה וירושלם. This sentence reemphasizes the importance of the temple and palace vessels and their location within Jerusalem. It adds no new information to the LXX. Tov's summary is probably correct: "The editor of the MT added so many elements in the preceding two verses that he felt obliged to repeat parts of 27:18–19 by way of *Wiederaufnahme*."[40] In light of Tov's conclusion, we have excised the entirety of verse 21.

22a: MT adds בבלה as an explanatory comment.

22b-b: MT adds ושמה יהיו עד יום פקדי אתם. This, with the following MT plus (22c-c), is the major substantive addition in this

---

37. Tov, "Exegetical Notes on the Hebrew Vorlage," 89.
38. Ibid., 89.
39. See Janzen, *Studies in the Text of Jeremiah*, 139–55, for full data on MT versus LXX proper names.
40. Tov, "Exegetical Notes on the Hebrew Vorlage," 90.

pericope. It seems out of place. The context suggests that only adverse consequences would accrue from the activities of the prophets aligned against Jeremiah. The MT additions (22b-b and 22c-c) allude to a future return to Jerusalem of the vessels. Jeremiah 27:18 and Jeremiah 28 are at odds with this hopeful outcome. The MT editor appears to have had a more optimistic view than that of the (presumed) LXX *Vorlage*.

22c-c: MT adds והעליתים והשיבתים אל המקום הזה. See previous comment.

Translation of Jeremiah 27:19–22

19For thus says the LORD concerning the rest of the vessels 20which the king of Babylon did not take into captivity with Jeconiah from Jerusalem to Babylon: 22*they* shall be carried away; an oracle of the LORD.

Background of the Jeremiah 27:19–22 account

The MT heading of Jeremiah 27:1 is absent from the LXX. The Hebrew sentence: בראשית ממלכת יהויקם בן יאושיהו מלך יהודה היה הדבר הזה אל ירמיה מאת יהוה לאמר ("In the beginning of the reign of Jehoiakim son of Josiah, king of Judah, this word came from the LORD, saying") establishes the timing of the following pronouncements at the beginning of the reign of Jehoiakim. This seems to be an erroneous repetition of the title of 26:1. The beginning of Jehoiakim's reign would be difficult to reconcile with 26:3 and 12, Jeremiah's discussion with the national envoys to Zedekiah, and to Zedekiah himself. It would also be contrary to 26:16–22, Jeremiah's address to the priests and people concerning the vessels not taken with Jeconiah by the king of Babylon. Most commentators read the variant tradition לצדקיהו.

Jeremiah 27:7 and 25:14, which prophesied that Babylon would eventually be punished, are MT additions not present in the LXX. It is unlikely that the LXX translator omitted them from the *Vorlage*. The MT plus of 27:7 "does not conform with its immediate context ... punishment of Babylon itself is not expected (and would) impart a completely different dimension to the text."[41]

---

41. Tov, "Exegetical Notes on the Hebrew Vorlage," 84–85. He continues: "The translator could conceivably have omitted this verse prophesying submission to the grandson of Nebuchadrezzar because, to our knowledge, Nebuchadrezzar did not

Jeremiah 27:19–22 by verses

27:19–20: This is the first pericope we have encountered in Jeremiah with significant differences between the MT and LXX. The reconstructed text, based primarily on the shorter LXX, concerns the "rest of the vessels" which were not taken by Nebuchadrezzar with Jeconiah.

27:21: This verse is absent from the reconstructed text. If the LXX is the better reading, as Tov has demonstrated, the prophesied return of the vessels seems to be superfluous.

27:22: The vessels were to be carried away. The MT plus is out of place.

How Jeremiah 27:19–22 informs our understanding of Jeconiah

We agree, in this case at least, with Tov, that the LXX is preferable to the MT. Jeremiah 27:3, 12, 16–22 indicate that the yoke sign-prophecy took place during the reign of Zedekiah. Malamat places this "conference" in Jerusalem in Zedekiah's fourth year, Tishri 594–Tishri 593.[42]

Although we prefer the reading of the LXX over the MT in this chapter, this choice is not without difficulties. For example, the lack of 27:13 in the Greek causes a break in continuity between the words spoken by Jeremiah in 27:12 and the lies spoken by the prophets in 27:14.

Jeremiah 27:19–22 in the LXX is a pessimistic account of the remaining vessels. Yahweh had determined that they would go to Babylon regardless of the prayers of those who acted as prophets and claimed to prophesy the words of the LORD (27:18).

The MT report concerning the vessels is far more optimistic than that of the LXX, and our reconstructed text. Jeremiah 27:19 provides the inventory of the rest of the vessels that were left in Jerusalem. Jeremiah 27:20 adds proper names, titles, patronyms, and the nobles to the list of

---

have a grandson who ruled. However, since we cannot ascribe such developed historical motivations to the translator elsewhere in Jeremiah, it is doubtful that they should be ascribed to him here. For the same reason it is also unlikely that the translator would have omitted this verse as disagreeing with the idea of an exile lasting seventy years, foretold in Jer 29:10. Since the translator probably did not omit this verse, it must have been lacking in his Vorlage, as suggested, too, by our general view of the shorter text of the LXX."

42. Abraham Malamat, "The Twilight of Judah: In the Egyptian-Babylonian Maelstrom" in *The History of Biblical Israel: Major Problems and Minor Issues* (Leiden: Brill, 2004), 311–312.

exiles. Verse 21 specifies that the vessels included those from the house of the Lord and the house of the king; 27:22 adds the hopeful phrase "they shall . . . remain there until the day when I give attention to them . . . then I will bring them back and restore them to this place." These MT pluses do not directly change the status of Jeconiah from 24:5–7. They do, however, extend Yahweh's "good figs" watchcare to the vessels.

The prophets and diviners who counseled resistance to Nebuchadrezzar were predicting an eclipse of Babylonian power. This hopeful counsel was rendered moot by the destruction of Jerusalem in 586 (Jer 52). These tragic events validated Jeremiah's counsel to submit to Nebuchadrezzar. The prophecy of Jeremiah 27 must have caused confusion in Jerusalem. Imagine the hearer's dilemma: whether to believe the hopeful words of many sages and trust in the inviolability of the city, or to align themselves with the doom prophecies of Jeremiah.

Whether Jeconiah heard reports of Jeremiah's prophecies or not is moot. There were those in Babylon who predicted a quick end to the exile (29:8–9). Jeconiah longed for his homeland (22:27), but, confined as he was in the capital city of the Babylonian empire, the prospects for release must have seemed exceedingly remote.

JEREMIAH 28:1–4: HANANIAH PREDICTS, "JECONIAH AND THE VESSELS TO RETURN IN TWO YEARS"

This pericope begins in the same year as 27:1 (בשנה ההיא), 594, the year Jeremiah announced the temple vessels would go to Babylon (27:19–22). The prophet Hananiah son of Azzur, from Gibeon, spoke to Jeremiah with the phrase כה אמר יהוה. He claimed that Yahweh had broken the yoke of the king of Babylon, and, within two years, the vessels, Jeconiah, and all the exiles would return. Jeremiah's response was half-hearted: "May the Lord do so." But he augmented the amen with a caution for the prophet deigning to speak כה אמר יהוה . . . שלום. Undeterred, Hananiah broke the yoke from Jeremiah's neck, and, using the messenger formula, announced, "Even so will I break the yoke of Nebuchadrezzar . . . within two years." According to 28:16–17, Jeremiah predicted Hananiah's death within a year. The temple vessels, Jeconiah, and the nobles remained in Babylon. Hananiah died for his boldness in speaking כה אמר יהוה.

Looking Back for Jehoiachin

Reconstructed text of Jeremiah 28:1–4

¹ ויהי <>ᵃ ᵇ-בשנה הרבעית לצדקיה-ᵇ מלך יהודה בחדש החמישי אמר אלי חנניה בן עזור ᶜהנביאᶜ אשר מגבעון בבית יהוה לעיני הכהנים וכל העם לאמר ² כה אמר יהוה <>ᵃ לאמר שברתי את על מלך בבל ³ בעוד שנתים ימים אני משיב אל המקום הזה את <>ᵃ כלי בית יהוה ⁴ ᵇ<>ᵇ ואת יכניה <>ᵃ ואת ᵇ גלות יהודה <>ᶜ כי אשבר את על מלך בבל

Text notes

1a: MT adds בשנה ההיא בראשית ממלכת, which appears to be a conflate text.⁴³

1b-b: The preposition ל prefixed to Zedekiah; בשנה הרבעית repositioned (see 1a).

1c: LXX specifies that Hananiah was a false prophet, ὁ ψευδοπροφήτης.

2a: MT adds צבאות אלהי ישראל.

3a: MT adds כל, not in LXX.⁴⁴

3b: MT adds אשר לקח נבוכדנאצר מלך בבל מן המקום הזה ויביאם בבל, a gloss from 27:20. See also 2 Chronicles 36:7.

4a: MT adds בן יהויקים מלך יהודה, typical of clarifying patronym and title.

4b: MT adds כל. See 3a.

4c: MT adds הבאים בבלה אני משיב אל המקום הזה נאם יהוה, from Jeremiah 28:3.

Translation of Jeremiah 28:1–4

1 And in the fourth year of Zedekiah king of Judah, in the fifth month, Hananiah son of Azzur the prophet from Gibeon spoke to me in the house of the LORD in the presence of the priests and all the people,

---

43. Janzen, *Studies in the Text of Jeremiah*, 15: "MT of 28:1 is clearly a conflation of two variant traditions . . . : בשנה ההיא B and ל בשנה הרבעית A conflating to ויהי בראשית צדקיהו מלך יהודה ממלכת."

44. Janzen, *Studies in the Text of Jeremiah*, 67, concludes regarding כל and πᾶς in Jer: "in most instances the plus (whether in MT or LXX) is secondary, and has arisen from adjacent or parallel context."

saying, 2"Thus says Yahweh: I have broken the yoke of the king of Babylon. 3Within two full years, I will bring back to this place the vessels of the house of the LORD 4and Jeconiah and the exiles of Judah, for I have broken the yoke of the king of Babylon."

Background of the Jeremiah 28:1–4 account

Jeremiah 28 continues the sign prophecy of Jeremiah 27 with an encounter between Jeremiah and one of the leading prophets in the temple precincts in July/August 594. This confrontation may have come about as a result of the aborted rebellion against Nebuchadrezzar in Babylon in December 595/January 594.[45] Hananiah was probably a well-known prophetic figure, judging from the definite article (הנביא) and the mention of his hometown. Gibeon, five and a half kilometers northwest of Jeremiah's home Anathoth in Benjamin, was "a priest's inheritance, and thus two priest-prophets stood publicly opposed in a time of religious and political tension."[46]

The confrontation between rival prophets in the temple about the exile of Jeconiah to Babylon was of enormous importance to the observers. This was not a theoretical debate between religious clerics. The implications cut to the continuation of the Judean state. Hananiah's appeal to the faithfulness of Yahweh, who would surely protect Jerusalem and the vessels of *this house*, were significant. Jeremiah's unpopular stance for capitulation to the Babylonian and Chaldean forces had been unwavering.

The specificity of Hananiah's death in September/October 594 (28:17) speaks for its historicity.

> The denouement of the incident (28:12–17) is likewise interesting. Hananiah (28:16) is sentenced to death. This accords perfectly with the thought expressed in Deut 18:20 that to prophesy falsely in the name of Yahweh, as Hananiah had done, was to commit a capital crime. We may recall that Jeremiah's enemies had tried to execute him, because they believed that *he* had prophesied falsely. In this case, however, the sentence

---

45. The Babylonian Chronicle (British Museum 21946, rev. 21–22): "In the tenth year the king of Akkad was in his own land; from the month of Kislev to the month of Tebet there was rebellion in Akkad . . . with arms he slew many of his own army. His own hand captured his enemy." See Wiseman, *Chronicles*, 72–73, and compare Malamat, "The Twilight of Judah in the Egyptian-Babylonian Maelstrom," 36.

46. White, "Jehoiachim," 106.

was to be executed by no human hands, but by Yahweh himself. There is no reason whatever to doubt that Hananiah, borne down—we may suppose—by this awful curse, actually did die as 28:17 states: the incident would scarcely have been recorded otherwise.[47]

Jeremiah 28:1–4 by verses

28:1: At the same site where Jeremiah saw the vision of the good and bad figs, he was confronted by a rival prophet, Hananiah son of Azzur of Gibeon. This was to be a public test of who had Yahweh's authority to declare כה אמר יהוה.

28:2 Hananiah claimed to speak for Yahweh, "I have broken the yoke...."

28:3 The MT is more specific that (all) the vessels... which Nebuchadrezzar took away from this place and carried to Babylon would be returned.

28:4 MT plus.

How Jeremiah 28:1–4 informs our understanding of Jeconiah

Jeconiah had been taken prisoner to Babylon by Nebuchadrezzar in 597. If the dating of 28:1 is correct as reconstructed, Jeconiah had been incarcerated in some form for nearly four and one half years. The abortive rebellion in Akkad may have led to a tightening of controls upon the exiled king, but there is no definite way of knowing. Bright rightly points out that Jeconiah had previously been treated with some measure of leniency. Jeconiah's exile as the legitimate king of Judah should have kept pressure on Zedekiah to maintain his vassal status as required by the suzerainty covenant.

Hananiah's prophecy that the exiled king would be returned within two years with the vessels of the temple would certainly have been provocative in the presence of the temple priests and within Zedekiah's court. This would compromise the puppet reign of Zedekiah and end the gains of the Levites and priests remaining in Jerusalem after the departure of Jeconiah and the 597 exiles. This would be a startling reversal, something

47. Bright, *Jeremiah*, 203.

that only Yahweh was capable of performing. Jeremiah's cautionary proviso brought to mind the curse of Deuteronomy 18:20.

The ordering of the prophecy, i.e., vessels first, and then the king, suggests that the temple vessels were of primary interest to Hananiah rather than the return of the king, prophets, priests, and people of Judah. It is reasonable to suppose that these insurrectionist ideas ("I have broken the yoke of the king of Babylon") would have incurred the disfavor of the Babylonian and Chaldean forces.

On the other hand, those forces would have viewed Jeremiah's consistent policy of capitulation to the Babylonian suzerainty of Nebuchadrezzar positively. The confrontation was one of intensive interest; however, Hananiah's apparent victory over Jeremiah was short-lived. The tug-of-war between Hananiah (with his false-hope minions) and the defeatist-prophet Jeremiah was intense. The outcome would indicate who truly spoke כה אמר יהוה. The death of Hananiah ended his short-exile prophecy and set the course for Jeremiah's letter to the exiles.

JEREMIAH 29:1–3: JEREMIAH'S LETTER TO (JECONIAH) BABYLON: "BUILD AND MULTIPLY"

There is a similarity in the listing of exiles of Jeremiah 29:1–3 and that of 24:1–4 (cf. 2 Kgs 24:6–17). In the Jeremiah 24:1–4 vision of good and bad figs, Yahweh assured Jeremiah that he would be looking after the good figs in exile, but would also tend to the bad figs remaining in Jerusalem. This surprising announcement of fortunes is now written down and sent from Jerusalem to Babylon with two diplomatic couriers. The catalog of exiles in 29:2 is more complete than any other Jeremiah list and emphasizes the remaining elders among the exiles, priests, (false) prophets, and all the people of the exile. The list is not as intrusive as the parenthetic date and time indications had been in 24:1b. It is likely that the letter was hand-delivered by Elasah ben Shaphan and Gemariah ben Hilkiah to the elders, priests, and prophets in Babylon. Although there is no notice of the temple vessels in the correspondence, this concern could not have been too far below the surface. Jeremiah 29:4 indicates that Yahweh had sent the exiles to Babylon, and 29:15–17 establishes that Zedekiah and the remaining residents are like loathsome figs so bad that they could not be eaten (as in 24:2–3). Jeremiah 29:2 has the verb יצא, indicating that Jeconiah voluntarily went out to Nebuchadrezzar in accordance with 2

Looking Back for Jehoiachin

Kings 24:12. Just as the LXX of 28:1–4 labels Hananiah a false prophet (ψευδοπροφήτης), so the prophets in Babylon are called false prophets (ψευδοπροφήτας).

Reconstructed text of Jeremiah 29:1–3

1 ואלה דברי הספר אשר שלח ירמיה ᵃ מירושלם
אל ᵇ זקני הגולה ואל הכהנים ואל הנביאים
ואל כל העם ᶜ<>ᶜ 2 אחרי צאת יכניה המלך
והגבירה והסריסים ᵃ⁻ שרי יהודה וירושלם
והחרש והמסגר ⁻ᵃ מירושלם 3 ביד אלעשה
בן שפן וגמריה בן חלקיה אשר שלח
צדקיה מלך יהודה אל מלך בבל בבלה לאמר

Text notes

1a: Omit הנביא with the LXX.
1b: Omit יתר with the LXX.
1c: Omit אשר הגלה נבוכדנאצר מירושלם בבלה with the LXX.
2a-a: LXX has only καὶ παντός ἐλευθέρου, "and all free *people*."

Translation of Jeremiah 29:1–3

1These are the words of the document which Jeremiah sent from Jerusalem to the elders among the exiles, to the priests, to the prophets, and to all the people 2(after the departure of Jeconiah the king, the queen mother, the palace officials, royal officials of Judah and Jerusalem, the craftsmen, and the smiths from Jerusalem) 3by the hand of Elasah son of Shaphan and Gemariah son of Hilkiah whom Zedekiah king of Judah sent to Babylon, to the king of Babylon, saying:

Jeremiah 29:1–3 by verses

29:1: ספר is a general word for any kind of document; it is used in 3:8 for a "bill (of divorce)" and in 25:13 for the (second) scroll of Jeremiah. Here (and in 29:25 and 29), it refers to a "letter."

Jeremiah's Prophecies: Jeconiah in Babylon

29:2: This parenthetical date indication identifies the exiles in 29:1 as persons deported in 597 with Jeconiah and his court (2 Kgs 24:12–15). Jeremiah 24:1 shares the same date formula, minus the queen mother and palace officials, and similar content.

29:3: "The envoys were . . . both from priestly families that played an important part in Josiah's reform. They were friendly toward Jeremiah and may even have had sympathy with his preaching (26:24; 36:10, 25; etc.)."[48] Perhaps the envoys were sent to Babylon to reassure Nebuchadrezzar of Zedekiah's loyalty after the Jerusalem conference mentioned in 27:3.

How Jeremiah 29:1–3 informs our understanding of Jeconiah

This letter provides substance to the "good figs" metaphor of Jeconiah's exile from Jeremiah 24. Because of the similarity of categories, it is important to read both chapters together. Compare also 29:16–19, where Zedekiah and the people remaining in Jerusalem were to be chastised by Yahweh. The unexpected favor that Yahweh was to show to King Jeconiah and the exiles in Babylon, announced initially in 24:1–3 and amplified by this letter, helps to explain why this otherwise insignificant Davidic king recurs so often in the prophecies and afterthoughts. It was not that Jeconiah had done anything significant—his only biblical significance is that Yahweh chose to favor him.

Reviewing the prophecy, we note that this letter sent to the exiles and King Jeconiah is similar in content to the prophetic vision of 24:1–3. The elders, priests, and prophets received this correspondence from the diplomatic couriers sent by Zedekiah to Babylon. They may have been supportive of Jeremiah's message and preaching.

JEREMIAH 37:1–2: ZEDEKIAH TO REIGN IN JUDAH IN PLACE OF THE EXILED CONIAH

We turn now to the pericope 37:1–2, normally seen as an introduction to the Zedekiah accounts, which specifies that Zedekiah reigned in place of Coniah and was castigated with his servants and the הארץ עם for failing to obey the LORD's word spoken by Jeremiah.

---

48. Ibid., 30–31

Looking Back for Jehoiachin

Reconstructed text of Jeremiah 37:1–2

וַיִּמְלָךְ מֶלֶךְ ᵃ צִדְקִיָּהוּ בֶן יֹאשִׁיָּהוּ תַּחַת ᵇ⁻ כָּנְיָהוּ בֶן ᵇ יְהוֹיָקִים ¹
אֲשֶׁר הִמְלִיךְ נְבוּכַדְרֶאצַּר ᶜ⁻<>⁻ᶜ ᵈ⁻ בְּאֶרֶץ יְהוּדָה ⁻ᵈ ² וְלֹא שָׁמַע הוּא
וַעֲבָדָיו וְעַם הָאָרֶץ אֶל דִּבְרֵי יְהוָה אֲשֶׁר דִּבֶּר בְּיַד יִרְמְיָהוּ <>ᵃ

Text notes

1a: Bright omits "as king" (מֶלֶךְ) with LXX—apparently a dittography, or perhaps to be read הַמֶּלֶךְ and translated, "And King Zedekiah . . . reigned."[49]

1b-b: Lacking in LXX, which has ἀντὶ Ιωακιμ "instead of Jehoiakim." Keown observes that "this changes the basic thrust of the verse: in LXX, it is Jehoiakim, not his son, whom Nebuchadrezzar displaced."[50] He fails to account for the frequent substitution in LXX of Ιωακιμ for Ιεχονιας, e.g., 2 Kings 24:8, 12, 15; 25:27, 29; Jeremiah 52:31, 33; Ezekiel 1:2; 1 Esdras 1:43. Ιεχονιας occurs in 1 Chronicles 3:16, 17; 2 Chronicles 36:8, 9; Esther 2:6; Jeremiah 24:1; 27:20; 28:4; 29:2; Baruch 1:3, 9; 1 Esdras 1:9, 34. Retain MT.

1c-c: Lacking in LXX, which has only the proper name Ναβουχοδονοσορ. Delete.

1d-d: Lacking in LXX, which has (βασιλεύειν) τοῦ Ιουδα, "(to reign) over Judah." Retain but italicize *the land* in the translation.

2a: הנביא is lacking in LXX, which has only the proper name Ιερεμιου.

Translation of Jeremiah 37:1–2

1Zedekiah son of Josiah, whom Nebuchadrezzar made king in *the land of* Judah, reigned in place of Coniah son of Jehoiakim. 2But neither he, nor his servants, nor the people of the land listened to the words of the Lord, which he spoke through Jeremiah.

---

49. Ibid., 220. See also Janzen, *Studies in the Text of Jeremiah*, 155.
50. Keown, Scalise, and Smothers, *Jeremiah 26–52*, 212.

Jeremiah's Prophecies: Jeconiah in Babylon

Background to the Jeremiah 37:1–2 account

The events of Jeremiah 37 took place when the Babylonian siege of Jerusalem was briefly interrupted because of the approach of an Egyptian army (37:5), probably in the late spring or early summer of 588.[51] This was a show of force by the pharaoh against the Chaldeans, designed to draw them away from Jerusalem. It was marginally successful without inflicting serious losses upon the Egyptians. It also gained a temporary reprieve for Zedekiah. "From a purely historical standpoint, it is difficult to reconstruct events leading up to the fall of Jerusalem. There are no Babylonian records comparable to what exists for the events of 597."[52] Malamat calls the Egyptian assistance "too frail to be of any real consequence."[53] Spalinger says, "The feint by Egypt into Palestine in 588 was a small affair."[54]

Jeremiah 37:1–2 provides a superscription (presumably) written by Baruch. It serves to link the account of Jeremiah 36, Jehoiakim's reign, to the reign of Zedekiah recounted in Jeremiah 37–39, and to the larger scribal chronicle. Most commentators agree with the unity of (at least) Jeremiah 37–43. Not all accept Baruch as author.[55]

Jones believes that the Jeremiah tradition is dependent upon the 2 Kings 24–25 report rather than the reverse.[56] He cites Jeremiah 37:1–2 as his reference point, alleging annalistic introduction of 37:1 (a summary of the fuller 2 Kgs 24:17), the reference to Coniah instead of Jehoiachin (a form found otherwise only in Jer 22:24, 28), and an appraisal of the king in place of the stereotyped judgment of 2 Kings 24:18–20. We agree that this is most likely.

Lachish Ostracon III, dated approximately to the time of the events of Jeremiah 37 (perhaps in the autumn of 589 or 588, shortly before Nebuchadrezzar's invasion), records: "It has been reported to your servant,

---

51. Thompson, *The Book of Jeremiah*, 630.

52. Seitz, *Theology in Conflict*, 254–55. For reconstructions, see Malamat, "Twilight," 140–41; Idem., "The Last Years of the Kingdom of Judah," 218–19; Freedy and Redford, "The Dates in Ezekiel," 470–72, 480ff.; Katzenstein, *A History of Tyre*, 317ff.; Spalinger, "Egypt and Babylonia," 232ff.; Greenberg, "Ezekiel 17 and the Policy of Psammetichus II," 308ff.

53. Malamat, "The Last Years of the Kingdom of Judah," 219.

54. Spalinger, "Egypt and Babylonia," 232.

55. See the helpful summary in Keown, Scalise, and Smothers, *Jeremiah 26–52*, 211ff.

56. D. Jones, *Jeremiah*, 451. See also Bright, *Jeremiah*, 222.

Looking Back for Jehoiachin

that the army commander Coniah (כוניהו), the son of Elnathan, has arrived on his way down into Egypt."⁵⁷ This may reflect the Judean effort to solicit Egyptian military assistance—although it ultimately proved futile.

Jeremiah 37:1–2 by verses

37:1: Four points are worthy of note. Firstly, Zedekiah is identified as the son of Josiah (cf. 1 Chr 3:15—not the son of Jehoiakim, 3:16).⁵⁸ Secondly, Nebuchadrezzar made Zedekiah king of Judah (*hip'il* perfect of מלך). Third, Zedekiah reigned in place of Coniah, although the LXX says in place of Ιωακιμ. This could be due to the widespread substitution of Ιωακιμ; see text note 1b-b. Lastly, the name Coniah appears in place of Jehoiachin only in Jeremiah 22:24, 28, and 37:1. The variation between the three names (Coniah, Jeconiah, and Jehoiachin) seems to be neither problematic nor significant.

37:2: Zedekiah did not listen to the words of the Lord which Jeremiah spoke; see 37:15, 20; 38:3, 14, 17–18, 23; and 39:4. His servants did not obey the commands; see 37:13–17; 38:14; and 39:4. Nor did the עם הארץ listen to the words; see 34:19; 44:21; 2 Kings 25:3, 19, 22. McConville says, "The issue is whether the king will listen to Jeremiah's announcement that the city must fall and lessen the force of the disaster by surrendering; the message referred to in 37:2 was first introduced in 21:1–10."⁵⁹ Seitz, trenchantly observes, "[T]he complete disobedience of king and people is anticipated from the opening scene (37:1–2)."⁶⁰

Zedekiah in contrast to Jehoiakim

The obvious contrast between the arrogant Jehoiakim (Jer 36) and weak-willed Zedekiah (Jer 37–39) is evident. Whereas Jeremiah excoriated Jehoiakim for a multitude of heinous offenses, Zedekiah was upbraided as a pitiable and incompetent king. He was, in the words of Keown, "not fully negative, but consistently weak. It may be a more damning characterization . . . for here is one portrayed as knowing the truth on many occasions

---

57. Gibson, *Textbook of Syrian Semitic Inscriptions*, 32.

58. For defense of Zedekiah as Jehoiachin's brother see Japhet, *I & II Chronicles*, 1068.

59. McConville "Jeremiah," 699.

60. Seitz, *Theology in Conflict*, 220.

when he refused to act upon it."⁶¹ Carroll's evaluation: "Zedekiah ... and his followers are known as those who 'would not listen to the word of the LORD.' Nothing more need be known about Zedekiah. He is suitably identified."⁶²

Zedekiah in contrast to Jeconiah

Eight contrasting points between Zedekiah and Jeconiah are worth examining.

First, as indicated in 37:1, Nebuchadrezzar king of Babylon made (*hip'il* perfect מלך) Zedekiah king of Judah. This would be a grievous affront to the independent-minded Judeans—cf. Jehoiakim, whom Pharaoh made (*hip'il* imperfect מלך) king to the distaste of the עם הארץ. Jeconiah succeeded Jehoiakim by primogeniture (1 Chr 3:16).

Second, Zedekiah resisted the siege of the city. He did not listen to the word of Yahweh from Jeremiah, though it was consistently delivered. Zedekiah was scourged by Nebuchadrezzar for his resistance (39:6–7; 52:9–11). Jeconiah surrendered with his family, nobles, and treasures. If 13:18 was addressed to Jeconiah, he obeyed and humbled himself. Whether that prophecy was addressed to him or not, his demeanor before Nebuchadrezzar was submissive (2 Kgs 24:12).

Third, the consequence of Zedekiah's resistance was the destruction of Jerusalem (Jer 39:8; 52:12–13). Jerusalem was spared destruction for an additional eleven years when Jeconiah and his entourage surrendered in 597 (2 Kgs 24:18).

Fourth, Zedekiah suffered tremendously as a result of his (in-)actions. He fled for his life, but was captured (Jer 39:4; 52:9). He was sentenced and watched as his sons and nobles were slaughtered (39:5–6; 52:9–10). Then, his eyes were put out and he was transported in chains to Babylon. Jeconiah, on the other hand, did not suffer extraordinarily as a result of his surrender (2 Kgs 24:12). He, along with his wives, mother, and nobles, were transported to Babylon and lived in some measure of comfort. He enjoyed the consolation extended by Yahweh in the land where Jeremiah pronounced them to be "good figs" (Jer 24).

---

61. Keown, Scalise, and Somers, *Jeremiah 26–52*, 214.
62. Carroll, *The Book of Jeremiah*, 671.

Fifth, Zedekiah died in Babylon in humiliation (52:11). Jeconiah died after being favored by Nebuchadrezzar's successor Amel-marduk (52:31–34; 2 Kgs 25:27–30).

Sixth, Zedekiah was left to rule over Judah's depleted populace and kingdom: the poorest of the land.[63] *Aiding* him in his reign were the pro-Egyptian advisors who counseled resistance to Babylon. Jeremiah (nicknamed מגור מסביב [Jer 20:10]), was his constant nemesis, predicting that, unless he surrendered, the Chaldeans would "burn the city with fire."[64] Jeconiah, as prisoner, retained his family and the title "King of *Jehudi*" while in Babylon (see Weidner Tablets). Ezekiel and the well-regarded exiles were there in Babylon with him.

Seventh, Zedekiah was the recipient of the disfavor of Yahweh announced by both Jeremiah and Ezekiel. Ezekiel 12:10–13 reads:

> Say to them, "Thus says the Lord GOD: This oracle concerns the prince in Jerusalem and all the house of Israel who are in it." Say, "I am a sign for you: as I have done, so shall it be done to them; they shall go into exile, into captivity." And the prince who is among them shall lift his baggage upon his shoulder in the dark, and shall go forth; he shall dig through the wall and go out through it; he shall cover his face, that he may not see the land with his eyes. And I will spread my net over him, and he shall be taken in my snare; and I will bring him to Babylon in the land of the Chaldeans, yet he shall not see it; and he shall die there.

Jeconiah did not turn out to be the "despised, broken pot, a vessel no one cares for" (Jer 22:28). He was cast into a foreign land, but his exile was not the end of his story.

Eighth, the dates associated with Zedekiah's reign (597–586) were merely a hiatus. The fall of Jerusalem and end of the Judean kingdom occurred during his reign. By contrast, the onset of Jeconiah's exile is the start of a new era: the Babylonian captivity, recorded initially in Ezekiel 1:2. Even though Zedekiah, "the *prince*," still sat on the throne in Jerusalem, he was not accorded the deference such a position should have accorded.[65]

---

63. See Carter, *The Emergence of Yehud in the Persian Period*.

64. Jer 21:10–12; 32:29; 34:2, 22; 37:8, 10; and 38:18 all predict the conflagration of Jerusalem.

65. Matt 1 commemorates the exile during Jeconiah's, not Zedekiah's, reign. See discussion in chapter 5.

Jeremiah's Prophecies: Jeconiah in Babylon

The prophetic date from which Ezekiel reckoned the years of exile was 597, when Jeconiah's long imprisonment began and when the nobility, priests, and craftsmen of Judah, transplanted to a foreign home, began their term of submission to Nebuchadrezzar. This captive nation still had a recognized king and a prophesied future. Both Jeremiah and Ezekiel regarded Zedekiah not as Yahweh's anointed, but as the one whom Nebuchadrezzar "had made king" (Jer 37:1; Ezek 17:16), "the king that sits upon the throne of David" (Jer 29:16). The last "real" king of Judah was Jeconiah.[66]

Reviewing the critical issues, we concluded that Jeremiah 37:1–2 was a summary introduction to the Zedekiah accounts. He and his counsellors were disobedient to the word of the LORD spoken by Jeremiah. That would lead inexorably to the disaster of 586.

CHAPTER 2 CONCLUSION

The tone of Jeremiah's prophecy in 36:30–31 is condemnatory. The Hebrew and Greek texts are notably consistent. Following Jehoiakim's effrontery in burning the scroll, Jeremiah said there was to be no successor for Jehoiakim on the throne. Furthermore, Jehoiakim's corpse would be defiled. Yahweh was to punish (פָּקַד) Jehoiakim, Jeconiah, Judah, and Jerusalem. Whether with the burial of an ass or in the garden of Uzza, Jehoiakim's final demise is uncertain. The punitive excursion of the Chaldean force suggests Jeconiah's accession to the throne was not a normal one. No longer, according to 36:30–31, would a ruling Davidic king have a son to sit on David's throne, even though there was a living heir. This momentous prophecy, addressed to Jehoiakim, should have sounded a note of despair and fear in Jeconiah.

The tone of 13:18–19 is pathetic and instructive. We concluded it was spoken to Jeconiah and Nehushta. Jeremiah still may have been excluded from the throne room (36:5), thus indicating the imperative אֱמֹר (command to Baruch?) to speak to the king and queen mother. Jeconiah's surrender to Nebuchadrezzar may have had its inspiration here.

Jeremiah 22:24–30 is the key prophecy given to Jeconiah/Coniah. He had once been, but was no longer to remain, the signet on Yahweh's

---

66. Berridge, "Jehoiachin," 3:662, opines, "[T]he messianic promise contained in Ezek 17:22–24 may refer to the descendents of Jeconiah." This will be examined in chapter 4.

hand. He was plucked off and handed off to those whom he feared. He and his mother were hurled (טול) into a foreign land to die. He was recorded as "childless" (ערירי), for none of his offspring would prosper or reign on the throne of David. Four hundred years of regnal traditions were about to end as the lights flickered all over Judah. The reconstructed text favors the shorter LXX here and in most of the following Jeremiah afterthoughts.

The vision of good and bad figs begins the reversal of expectations. The time notation of 24:1 aids in understanding the interpretation given by Yahweh to Jeremiah in 24:6–10. Jeconiah and the exiles in Babylon were to be regarded by Yahweh as very good figs, an announcement only Yahweh could accomplish, despite the audacious pronouncements of Hananiah and his ψευδοπροφήτης. Zedekiah and the nobles remaining in Jerusalem were to be regarded as figs so loathsome they could not be eaten. The specifications of exiles is an abbreviated listing of 2 Kings 24:12–16.

Jeremiah, the authoritative spokesman of Yahweh, declared in 27:19–22 that the remaining temple vessels would go, like Jeconiah, to Babylon. The prophets who counseled resistance to the suzerainty of Babylon were exposed by Jeremiah. The optimism of the MT is unwarranted here.

Jeremiah 28:1–4 is the prediction of the prophet Hananiah that Jeconiah and the temple vessels were to be returned within two years. The initial confrontation between the prophets from Gibeon and Anathoth seemed to favor the former, who symbolically broke the latter's yoke. But his life and prophecy were cut short and the broken wooden yoke was refashioned of iron.

Jeremiah 37:1–2 is the castigation of Zedekiah and his servants for failing to obey the word of the LORD spoken by Jeremiah. An Egyptian show of force from the south of Jerusalem caused the Babylonians to lift the siege temporarily in 588. The Lachish Ostracon III is useful in reconstructing the appeal of the Judean official Coniahu to the Egyptians. This final pericope allows us to contrast the portraits of the final four Judean kings to one another. Zedekiah is appropriately painted as the king who would not listen to the LORD. Although Jeconiah was described accurately in 2 Kings 24:9 as evil, he submitted to Nebuchadrezzar in accordance with the counsel of Jeremiah 13:18–19 and gained a reprieve for himself and the city of Jerusalem.

CHAPTER 3

Jehoiachin in Other Prophetic and Narrative Literature

INTRODUCTION

HERETOFORE, WE HAVE SEEN in chapter 1 a series of four narratives that established the major outlines for Jehoiachin's life. This young prince was elevated to kingship during a harrowing period, was besieged, and surrendered to Nebuchadrezzar, king of Babylon. Nebuchadrezzar took him, his family, and most of the temple vessels to Babylon. He was replaced by his uncle Zedekiah—the last king before the final capitulation of Judah and Jerusalem in 586 BCE.

In chapter 2, we examined eight prophecies in the book of Jeremiah. Two were spoken in prediction before the exile of Jeconiah, and six were afterthoughts, the pivotal prophecy being Jeremiah 22:24–30, which specified that Coniah was to be cast out as a signet, hurled into captivity to die in Babylon. The other prophecies predicted the carrying away of the remainder of the temple vessels, the (demonstrably false) prophecy of Hananiah, and the enacted sermon maintaining that Jeconiah and the exiles were the good figs that Yahweh was going to watch over while Zedekiah and the citizens remaining in Jerusalem were to be regarded as bad figs. Jeremiah sent correspondence to the elders, priests, and prophets who, with Jeconiah, were to settle down in Babylon and prepare for a lengthy exile. The final pericope explained that none of the "bad figs" obeyed the words of the LORD spoken by Jeremiah.

At the end of his life, Jehoiachin was freed from prison, elevated to prominence over the other captive kings in Babylon, and privileged to dine with the son of the great King Nebuchadrezzar. The ongoing echoes of this goodwill effort (2 Kgs 25, Jer 52) resound in the prophecies and narratives in four additional locations of the Hebrew literature.

In this chapter, we will study sequentially the dating of Ezekiel's oracles from the exile of Jehoiachin (Ezek 1:1–3); then the generations following Jeconiah's captivity (1 Chr 3:16–19); the reversal of Jeremiah 22:24–30 in the return, like a signet, of Zerubbabel, Coniah's grandson (Hag 2:20–23); and the activity of Mordecai traced back to Jeconiah's exile (Esth 2:5–7).

EZEKIEL 1:1–3: EZEKIEL IN BABYLON IN THE FIFTH THROUGH TWENTY-SEVENTH YEAR OF THE EXILE OF JEHOIACHIN

Ezekiel 1:1–3 describes the date of a divine vision by the priest Ezekiel. This is said to have occurred in the "thirtieth year," without further explanation of the reference. Speculation abounds about the referent of this statement. Does the thirtieth year refer to the priest/prophet's age? Was it the year of the compilation of the prophetic book of Ezekiel? Does the year of the discovery of the law scroll in the temple under King Josiah explain the reference? Rowley provides the best summation: "I know of no wholly satisfactory solution."[1]

In addition to the uncertainty of the thirtieth year, many scholars opine that Ezekiel 1:2, 3 is a gloss. The change in personal pronoun from first person in 1:1, 4ff. to third person in 1:2–3 is the basis for this conjecture. Those who, by implication, denigrate the verses as a spurious insertion of a redactor overstate the freedom of such an editor. "The function of an editor is to assemble the tradition, connect its parts and provide literary coherency—not provide wholesale composition or improvisation."[2] For this reason, recognizing that 1:2–3 may be a gloss does not invalidate its contribution to the dating of Ezekiel. Furthermore, it relates the

---

1. Rowley, *Men of God*, 202.
2. Freedy and Redford, "The Dates in Ezekiel," 462.

Jehoiachin in Other Prophetic and Narrative Literature

opening vision to the dating system in use throughout the book of Ezekiel.[3] Therefore, these verses are not spurious, but rather part of the text.

The Babylonians referred to Jehoiachin (*Yaukin*) as King of the Jews (*Yehudu*) even after the appointment of Zedekiah as king in Jerusalem. Ezekiel calls the exiled Jehoiachin "king" (מלך) but refers to Zedekiah as "prince" (נשיא).[4]

In this pericope, we will explore the implications of the dating of Ezekiel 1:1–3, the naming of Jehoiachin (יויכין), and the link to the exile (הגולה).

Reconstructed Text of Ezekiel 1:1–3

1 ויהי בשלשים שנה ברביעי בחמשה לחדש ואני בתוך הגולה
על נהר כבר נפתחו השמים ואראה מראות אלהים 2 בחמשה
לחדש היא השנה החמישית לגלות המלך יויכין היה‍ᵃ ᵃ 3
דבר יהוה אל יחזקאל בן בוזי הכהן בארץ כשדים על
נהר כבר ותהי עלי ᵇ יד יהוה

Text notes

2a: The LXX has Ιωακιμ, an occasional substitution for Jehoiachin. See discussion in chapter 2, especially Jeremiah 37:1–2, text note 1b-b.

3a-a: The MT reads הָיֹה הָיָה, a probable dittography.

3b: MT שם is not reflected in the LXX, which further supports עלי not עליו.

Translation of Ezekiel 1:1–3

1In the thirtieth year, in the fourth month, on the fifth of the month, while I was among the exiles by the Kebar Canal, the heavens opened, and I saw visions of God. 2This was in the fifth year of the exile of King Jehoiachin. 3The word of the LORD came to Ezekiel son of Buzi the priest in the land of Chaldea by the Kebar Canal. The hand of Yahweh was on me *there*.

---

3. Ezekiel's prophecy continues in the sixth (Ezek 8:1), seventh (20:1), ninth (24:1), tenth (29:1), eleventh (26:1; 30:20; 31:1), twelfth (32:1, 17; 33:21), twenty-fifth (40:1), and twenty-seventh (29:17) years.

4. See the excellent discussion by Duguid, *Ezekiel and the Leaders of Israel*, 10–57.

Looking Back for Jehoiachin

Background of the Ezekiel 1:1–3 account

Additional resonance accrues to the "afterthoughts" of Jeremiah in Jerusalem (24:1–3; 27:19–22; 28:1–4; 29:1–3; 37:1–2) in this set of verses. After Jehoiachin left for Babylon, many of the Jeremiah prophecies, like aftershocks following a major earthquake, continued to resound in the capital city until it, too, fell, and the prophecies were fulfilled with all their terrible implications of calamity, captivity, and exile. But Ezekiel, in captivity in Babylon with Jehoiachin, dated his book to the beginning of that exile. These opening verses set the dating reference point for the entire book of Ezekiel.

Ezekiel's prophecy started in the mysterious thirtieth year, which seems to coincide with the fifth year of the exile of Jehoiachin, specifically, 593. Ezekiel's prophecies concerning Jehoiachin continued to sound like afterthoughts, i.e., Jehoiachin provided an essential dating schema, but did not figure prominently in the prophecies of the book of Ezekiel.[5] As the focus of life in Babylon displaced the activities of the Jerusalem temple and the "good figs" adjusted to life outside Judah, Ezekiel's prophecies took on more significance for the exiles. He seldom addressed those remaining in Jerusalem: *Prince* Zedekiah, priests, and people who were unimportant to life in exile.

We will see in chapter 4 that Ezekiel 17 and 19 speak much more positively about Jehoiachin than Zedekiah, but more favorably still of the reconstituted Davidic monarchy that would be reestablished in the future kingdom.

Whether Ezekiel 1:2–3 are an intrusion is not critical to understanding this book. The first half of Ezekiel is primarily about what was occurring during the years before the final destruction of Jerusalem, so the dating is essentially accurate, even if it appears as a gloss.

Ezekiel 1:1–3 by verses

1:1: The "thirtieth year" (בשלשים שנה) has an uncertain referent. Origen suggested it was the priest Ezekiel's age when he saw the divine visions. It has additionally been offered as the date for composition of the book and as a marker for the midpoint of a fifty-year Jubilee cycle passed in the five elapsed years of the exile of Jehoiachin. Another proposal is the time

---

5. See chapter 4, especially the discussion of Ezek 17 and 19.

Jehoiachin in Other Prophetic and Narrative Literature

elapsed since the finding of the law in the temple during Josiah's reign. All these opinions are interesting, but none is ultimately persuasive. The thirtieth year, whatever it otherwise specified, is tied to the divine vision of 1:4ff.

Freedy and Redford[6] established that the dates in Ezekiel (and related passages in Kings and Jeremiah) constitute (1) a homogenous system grounded in the historical reality of the captivity of 597; (2) a correlative system, synchronizing completely with the dating systems in Jeremiah and 2 Kings; and (3) an explicative system, facilitating the interpretation of several passages to which dates are attached. If they are correct, as seems probable, the dating of the passages in Ezekiel is authentic and consistent. The link between the three initial verses of Ezekiel 1 and the rest of Ezekiel is demonstrated.

The prophet was in the midst of the exiles from Judah near the banks of the Kebar Canal (3:15, 23; 43:3). Allen observes that, based on Psalm 137:1–2 and Acts 16:13, this was a likely place of worship, the cleansing presence of water serving to mitigate the uncleanness of a foreign land (Amos 7:17).[7]

1:2: The exile (הגולה) was such a significant milestone in Jewish self-understanding that it required a new marker. The exile of King Jehoiachin and ten thousand captives in 597 was not marked by referring to the reign of Zedekiah. The exiles in Babylon would not consider that Jehoiachin's "reign" was continuing while he was imprisoned in Babylon. Although he was the "legitimate" king of Judah and Jerusalem, whereas Zedekiah was a regent, he did not have a kingdom. His uncle Zedekiah was prince-regent appointed by Nebuchadrezzar, apparently subject to recall if he violated his oath of allegiance to Babylon.

In 2 Kings 24 and 25, the author shifts the dating system to reflect the system of the Babylonians, e.g., from the erstwhile Hebrew Tishri-Tishri regnal year to the Chaldean/Babylonian Nisan-Nisan regnal year. This accounts for the difficulties in understanding the correlation of dates between Ezekiel, the deuteronomistic history, and Jeremiah. King Jehoiachin's fifth year of exile is the equivalent of June/July 593. This comports well with dated passages in Ezekiel.[8] Parker and Dubberstein's calendrical

---

6. Freedy and Redford, "The Dates in Ezekiel," 462.

7. Allen, *Ezekiel 1–19*, 22.

8. Ezek 8:1; 20:1; 24:1; 26:1; 29:1, 17; 30:20; 31:1; 32:17; 33:21; 40:1—in the fifth to twenty-seventh years of the exile.

reconstruction of Nebuchadrezzar's reign date it more precisely as 31 July 593.[9]

The fifth day of the fifth year of the exile was specific to the exile of Jehoiachin in 597, not the subsequent exile of Zedekiah in 586 or a previous one under Jehoiakim in 605 (Dan 1:1–2). The further indication that this was the exile of *King* Jehoiachin is significant. Ezekiel was writing this account in Babylon. The use of מלך in captivity must have been suggested as appropriate by some usage within the (גלה) community. It also provides a basis for the contention that Zedekiah was only a regent and that Jehoiachin was still the king of Jerusalem and Judah, although confined to Babylon, thus without a kingdom. At least Ezekiel considered Jehoiachin the legitimate king of Judah and Zedekiah only a prince (נשיא). Ezekiel uses the term מלך to refer to Yahweh once, Jehoiachin twice, Nebuchadrezzar thirteen times, Pharaoh six times, the king of Tyre once, and the coming King David three times. He refers to Zedekiah consistently as prince (נשיא) in excoriating language in 12:10–13 and 17:13–21, and with lament in 19:5–9.

1:3: According to the text, Ezekiel's initial divine visions were received in Babylon in the vicinity of the Kebar Canal. That he was living there and not in Jerusalem gives him a unique vantage point for associating with the exiles. He was not reciting his own view of the situation, but rather reporting "the word of the Lord" and that "the hand of Yahweh was on him (MT; LXX 'me') there."

How Ezekiel 1:1–3 informs our understanding of Jehoiachin

The dating of Ezekiel's prophecy is keyed to the departure into exile of the last legitimate king of Judah—Jehoiachin son of Jehoiakim. This reinforces the significance of the exiles of 597 over those of any previous exile (605, during Jehoiakim's third year, Dan 1:1–2) or the subsequent exiles of 586 during Zedekiah's eleventh year.

The letter written by Jeremiah to those in exile with King Jeconiah (Jer 29) was surely read with this understanding among the exiles in Babylon. Jeconiah was the putative king of the Jews, but without a kingdom. Had the prophecy concerning Coniah not prospering in his lifetime (Jer 22:30) come literally true? As far as the book of Ezekiel reports, Jehoiachin only enjoys the title *king* without the kingdom.

---

9. Parker and Dubberstein, *Babylonian Chronology*, 28.

Jehoiachin in Other Prophetic and Narrative Literature

The spelling of Jehoiachin's name (יֹויָכִין) in Ezekiel 1:2 is unique. It is a minor variation of the spelling used by Jeremiah and the author(s) of 2 Kings. Although not significant in itself, it is interesting that this king's names vary so much from a fixed form. There are at least six different spellings in Hebrew for the same king, e.g., יְהוֹיָכִין ,יְהוֹיָכִן (with and without the hireq yodh, both in the same verse, Jer 52:31), כָּנְיָהוּ, יְכָנְיָהוּ ,יְכָנְיָה, and יוֹיָכִין.

The title "King Jehoiachin" used in the land of the Babylonians for the ruler of the Jewish people has real significance. The inscriptional evidence suggests this was the view of the Babylonians.[10]

By way of review, we have seen that this pericope is the first indication of a scheme of dating in Ezekiel that continues throughout the book from the baseline of Jehoiachin's exile. Jeremiah 52 and 2 Kings 25 fill in the detail that the release was in the thirty-seventh year. There was, therefore, a gap of ten years at the end of Jehoiachin's captivity upon which Ezekiel does not comment. His final vision (40:1) was fourteen years after the fall of Jerusalem and described the future temple. The entire sequence of divine judgments on Israel (Ezek 1–24), nations (25–32), and restoration (33–48) were synchronized with Jehoiachin's exile. He was still alive after the final prophecy in Ezekiel. Not only was his exile a defining moment in the history of Israel (and Ezekiel's prophecy), but Jehoiachin's longevity preserved the promise of potential restoration of the Davidic line on a restored Judean throne.

The next pericopes in this chapter will investigate Jeconiah's grandson Zerubbabel son of *Pedaiah* in 1 Chronicles 3:16–19, but Zerubbabel son of *Shealtiel* in Haggai. The link between Jeremiah 22:24 of the cast-out signet (החותם) and Zerubbabel returning to Jerusalem like a signet (כחותם) in Haggai 2:23 will be investigated. Finally the mention in Esther 2:5–6 of the exile of Mordecai's great-grandfather Kish with Jeconiah in 597 is discussed.

---

10. See the inscriptions discussion in the introduction.

Looking Back for Jehoiachin

1 CHRONICLES 3:15–19: SONS BORN TO JECONIAH, THE CAPTIVE (האסר)

Introduction

In this pericope, we peruse the lineage of Davidic kings starting with Josiah, the relationship between Jeconiah and Zedekiah, the meaning of אסר, and the paternity of Zerubbabel.

There are numerous divergences of the 1 Chronicles 3 account when compared to 2 Kings 24, 25, and Jeremiah: (1) Who was Johanan and did he ever rule in Judah? (2) Who was Shallum? Was he to be identified as Jehoahaz? (3) How should ובנו in 1 Chronicles 3:16 be translated? (4) What is the meaning of אסר in 3:17? If it is not the proper name Assir, and is correctly translated "prisoner," then what happened to the definite article? (5) If Assir is the name of Jeconiah's firstborn son, then there should have been another generation between him and Shealtiel; therefore, Zerubbabel is the great-grandson of Jeconiah. (6) Who was Zerubbabel's father—Shealtiel or Pedaiah? (7) Who was Shelomith, and why was she included in the name list? Was this a reflection of Tamar in 3:9? This list of uncertainties cannot be finally resolved, but proposals are advanced in the discussion.[11]

Reconstructed text of 1 Chronicles 3:15–19

15 ובני יאשיהו הבכור יוחנן [a] השני יהויקים השלשי צדקיהו
הרביעי שלום 16 ובני יהויקים יכניה בנו צדקיה בנו 17 ובני
יכניה אסר שאלתיאל בנו 18 ומלכירם ופדיה ושנאצר יקמיה
הושמע ונדביה 19 ובני פדיה [a] זרבבל ושמעי ובן [b] זרבבל
משלם וחנניה ושלמית אחותם

Text notes

15a: The LXX[L] reflects Ιωαχαζ, "Joahaz," whereas other LXX mss reflect Ιωαναν.

16a: Note that the MT spelling of Zedekiah (צדקיה) is different than 3:15, צדקיהו.

---

11. Not considered germaine to the dissertation is the scholarly conundrum of equating Sheshbazzar of Ezra 1:7, 11ff with Shenazzar. See especially Japhet, *I & II Chronicles* for additional discussion.

Jehoiachin in Other Prophetic and Narrative Literature

19a: LXX has Σαλαθιηλ, Salathiel.
19b: LXX has υἱοι, sons.

Translation of 1 Chronicles 3:15–19

15And the sons of Josiah were Johanan the firstborn, Jehoiakim second, Zedekiah third, and Shallum fourth. 16And the successors of Jehoiakim were Jeconiah and Zedekiah. 17The sons of Jeconiah the captive were Shealtiel (his son) 18and Malchiram, Pedaiah, Shenazzar, Jekamiah, Hoshama, and Nebadiah. 19 The sons of Pedaiah were Zerubbabel and Shimei. The sons of Zerubbabel were Meshullam, Hananiah, and their sister Shelomith.

Background to the 1 Chronicles 3:15–19 account

First Chronicles 1–9 is the principal section of name lists in Chronicles. This section covers the time from before the flood (1:1–23) to the return from the exile (9:1–3). The focus of the genealogical record in 1 Chronicles 3 is the house of David extending from David to the return from exile under Zerubbabel. The twin emphases of throne and temple[12] show continuity and bind the name lists to the people of Israel and Judah through the generations. The turning points of exile (הגולה) and restoration are nearly ignored—only Jeconiah the Captive (אסר) indicates the significance of the exile, and there is no obvious indication that Zerubbabel is the leader of the restoration.

First Chronicles 3:15 is a natural starting point for the pericope with the interruption of the narrative flow of the genealogy with the phrase (ובני יאשיהו) "and the sons of Josiah." The Chronicler makes definitive breaks in the flow of the name lists in 3:1, 10, 15, 19, and 24. The relatively contained pericope of 3:15–19, from the sons of Josiah to the sons of Pedaiah, relates to Jeconiah. The listing of "Shelomith their sister" makes a clean break at 3:19.[13]

12. Wilcock, "1 and 2 Chronicles," 388.
13. The pericope continues beyond where we decided to terminate our investigation with 3:20–21: "And Hashubah, Ohel, Berechiah, Asadiah, and Jushab-hesed, five. The sons of Hananiah: Pelatiah and Jeshaiah, his son Rephaiah, his son Arnan, his son Obadiah, his son Shecaniah." These verses extend the Chronicler's account of the Davidic genealogy beyond our immediate interest in Jeconiah, an additional seven to twelve generations, a period of 140 to 280 years.

1 Chronicles 3:15–19 by verses

3:15: The Chronicler reports the sons of Josiah in a slightly different order than 2 Kings 23 and 24 and substitutes the name Johanan for Jehoahaz. The correction to Jehoahaz in the Lucianic Greek is an attempt to reconcile this difference. Japhet opines that the son of Josiah named Shallum, mentioned in Jeremiah 22:10–12, is also named Jehoahaz.[14] Without further information, it is difficult to reconcile the accounts.

3:16: A possible implication of different spellings of the name Zedekiah is that there were two Zedekiahs: the son of Josiah who ruled after Jeconiah, and an otherwise unknown son of Jehoiakim. The Chronicler's accounts are internally consistent, but general considerations still make a better case for the tradition of Kings. "Although the consistency of the Chronicler's view counts strongly in its favor, . . . Kings was much closer to the events than Chronicles, and no reason has been shown why the author of Kings should change the original affiliation of the last king of Judah."[15]

The issue revolves around the Chronicler's reporting of Zedekiah's relationship to Jeconiah; i.e., was the successor to Jeconiah as king in Jerusalem his uncle (Kings and Jeremiah), brother (2 Chr 36:10), or possibly even son (1 Chr 3:16)? First Chronicles 3:15 states that Zedekiah was the third son of Josiah. First Chronicles 3:16 seems to imply that the sons of Jehoiakim were Jeconiah and Zedekiah, or possibly that Zedekiah was the son of Jeconiah if בנו ("his son") is taken in a literal fashion. The NIV translates this verse, "The *successors* of Jehoiakim: Jeconiah his son, and Zedekiah." Second Kings 24:17 says that Mattaniah/Zedekiah son of Josiah became king after Jeconiah. Second Chronicles 36:10 reports that Nebuchadrezzar made Jehoiachin's *brother* Zedekiah king in his place. Jeremiah 1:3 and 37:1 state that Zedekiah was the son of Josiah. The Hebrew spelling of Zedekiah in 3:15 (צדקיהו) and 3:16 (צדקיה) imply that there were at least two different individuals with similar names within the family.

3:17: The verse makes a delineation between Shealtiel and the other sons of Jeconiah in 3:18. In this pericope alone, the singular בן "son" is followed by more than one son in 3:20, 21, and 23; the plural בני "sons"

---

14. Japhet, *I & II Chronicles*, 97.
15. Ibid., 98–99.

Jehoiachin in Other Prophetic and Narrative Literature

here (MT) and 3:19, 22b, 24; and the plural by only a single son in 3:22. Note also the unusual use of the plural בְּנֵי four times in 3:21b.[16]

The meaning of (אַסִּר/ἀσιρ) is difficult. Is this the otherwise unknown name of Jeconiah's firstborn son, or a substantive describing his status as prisoner? Williamson suggests that the RSV's translation "the captive" represents a slight, and correct, emendation of the MT (אַסִּר).[17] אַסִּר seems to be a substantive missing the definite article "[the] prisoner" that reasonably accounts for Jeconiah's status for thirty-seven years as a prisoner in Babylon. However, Japhet's contention that 3:17 is parallel to 3:10 and Assir is the son of Jeconiah is also possible. Assir is a perfectly acceptable Hebrew name occurring in Exodus 6:24 and 1 Chronicles 6:22, 23, and 37 (MT 6:7, 8, 22).

Regarding the genealogy in this verse, Japhet says,

> The list does not provide a full genealogy of the house of David ... the Davidic dynasty maintained a clear line of succession for many generations after the end of the monarchy; probably these Davidic scions held also a certain status within the community—although nothing of this is preserved in our sources.[18]

We concur with Japhet's analysis and posit that this name list was an attempt to preserve a record of the Davidic house well beyond the exile and restoration.

3:18: That Zedekiah's name is not included in this verse implies that he was not a son of Jeconiah, but rather of Josiah and successor on the throne. The name Shenazzar (as well as Zerubbabel in 3:19) is clearly Babylonian while the rest of the names in the genealogy are Hebraic.

3:19: Zerubbabel's father is reported as Shealtiel (שְׁאַלְתִּיאֵל) in Haggai (1:12, 14; 2:2, 23), Ezra (3:2, 8; 5:2), and Nehemiah (12:1), but as Pedaiah (פְּדָיָה) here in 1 Chronicles 3:19. LXX 1 Chronicles 3:19 reads Salathiel (Σαλαθιηλ). Myers opines that "either Shealtiel died early, after which Pedaiah became the head of the family, or the latter may have married the childless widow of the former in accordance with Levirate marriage rules."[19]

---

16. Braun, *First Chronicles*, 49.
17. Williamson, *1 & 2 Chronicles*, 57.
18. Japhet, *1 & II Chronicles*, 99.
19. Myers, *1 Chronicles*, 21.

Japhet is probably correct in presenting Shelomith as "a figure of some standing at the time of the Restoration."[20] Avigad suggests that she was the owner of the seal bearing the inscription "Shelomith, the maidservant (אמה) of Elnathan."[21]

How 1 Chronicles 3:15–19 informs our understanding of Jeconiah

The Chronicler's portrait of Jeconiah differs substantially from that of 2 Kings/Jeremiah. Notable deviations include that his grandson Zerubbabel was the son of Pedaiah instead of Shealtiel; there are structural issues implied regarding ובני and אסר. The Chronicler reports that Jeconiah had seven sons (if Assir is taken to mean "prisoner"). According to Japhet, only two of Josiah's sons were king: Jehoahaz then Jehoiakim.[22] Following Jehoiakim were two of his sons, Jeconiah and Zedekiah the younger.

The issues raised in the Chronicler's work about Jeconiah are significant and cannot be easily dismissed. Japhet is a careful and capable expositor of the value of the Chronicler's tradition. She demonstrated the consistency of that tradition—namely, that it was the son of Jeconiah named Zedekiah who succeeded him on the throne after his exile. However, she favors the accounts of 2 Kings and Jeremiah for historical accuracy. There seems to be no definitive resolution to the dilemma, so we leave the accounts in tension.

It seems more reasonable, although not absolutely persuasive, that Zedekiah son of Josiah succeeded Jeconiah on the throne of David. The consistent reporting of the books of 2 Kings and Jeremiah, as well as the books of Zechariah and Haggai, suggest that the deuteronomistic history is to be favored over that of Chronicles. If this is so, then the successor to Jehoiakim was his son Jeconiah, followed by Zedekiah son of Josiah and consequently Jeconiah's uncle. Furthermore, we see the portrait of Jeconiah fleshed out with his firstborn son Shealtiel and followed by his grandson Zerubbabel as the returning signet (Hag 2:23) to Jerusalem.

The father of Zerubbabel is likewise uncertain. The best explanation we have seen is that advanced by Wilcock[23] and Williamson,[24] that Sheal-

---

20. Japhet, *1 & II Chronicles*, 99
21. Avigad, *Bullae and Seals*, 11, 22.
22. Japhet, *1 & II Chronicles*, 98.
23. Wilcock, "1 and 2 Chronicles," 392.
24. Williamson, *1 and 2 Chronicles*, 221.

tiel died before Zerubbabel was conceived by his (Shealtiel's) younger brother Pedaiah under Levirate marriage customs.

The translation of 3:16, "the successors of Jehoiakim" is correct, although not textually demanded. Were Zedekiah the son of Jeconiah, his name would not be omitted from 3:18.

The substantive "prisoner" appended to Jeconiah's name fits the historical record of 2 Kings 25 and Jeremiah 52. Although unusual, it is possible that the Chronicler used sources that alluded to this status as prisoner of Nebuchadrezzar, and the definite article was misplaced during copying.

Reviewing the name lists of 1 Chronicles 3:15–19, we noted significant differences in the Chronicler's recording from that of 2 Kings 24–25, many of the Jeremiah pericopes, Ezra, Nehemiah, Haggai, and Zechariah. This makes the Chronicler the most discordant voice in the chorus of royal reporters. Sometimes discords are more memorable once the resolution is produced. Unfortunately, there is no simple answer in reconciling the variety of voices. We favor the 2 Kings/Jeremiah unified reporting that Josiah was succeeded by Jehoahaz/Shallum, then Jehoiakim, then (his son) Jeconiah, then (his uncle) Zedekiah. It seems logical to presume אסר is a substantive, not a proper name. It is less of a stretch to maintain the parentage of Zerubbabel must be Shealtiel rather than Pedaiah based on Levirate marriage. Regardless of the patronymic, Zerubbabel is the grandson of Jeconiah if אסר is substantive. The artifacts that link Shelomith to Elnathan are certainly suggestive of the house of David's longevity and importance in the mind of the Chronicler.

In the next pericope, we will investigate the signet likeness between Coniah and Zerubbabel.

HAGGAI 2:20–23: ZERUBBABEL (CONIAH'S GRANDSON) TO BE LIKE A SIGNET (כחותם)

Introduction

This pericope can be confidently dated to December 18, 520 (Hag 2:10, 18), the laying of the foundation stone of the Second Temple. The word of the LORD commands Haggai to speak to Zerubbabel son of Shealtiel, governor of Judah, saying that Yahweh was about to shake the entire created order (represented by the merism "heavens and earth"). Furthermore, in the shaking, the thrones of kingdoms and power of the nations would be overturned, and armaments would be destroyed. Haggai 2:23 especially contains a rich infusion of apocalyptic terms and oaths reflective of the Servant of the Lord (Isa 40–55). Zerubbabel would be taken (לקח) as Yahweh's servant (עבדי) and would be set like a signet (כחותם) on that day (ביום ההיא) because Yahweh had chosen (בחר) him.

This is surprising, because Zerubbabel's grandfather, King Jeconiah, ruled on the Davidic throne in Jerusalem as the earthly regent of Yahweh and was cast off as the signet (חותם) from Yahweh's right hand (Jer 22:28). (Although Zerubbabel was "Governor of Judah" and a Davidide, he was not "ruling again in Judah" [Jer 22:30], but rather given divine reassurance in order to complete the rebuilding of the Second Temple; i.e., he was not king, but entrusted with a highly significant role.)

Reconstructed text of Haggai 2:20–23

²⁰ ויהי דבר יהוה שנית אל חגי בעשרים וארבעה לחדש לאמר ²¹ אמר
אל זרבבל ᵃ פחת יהודה לאמר אני מרעיש את השמים ואת הארץ ᵇ
²² והפכתי כסא ממלכות והשמדתי חזק ממלכות הגוים והפכתי
מרכבה ורכביה וירדו סוסים ורכביהם איש בחרב אחיו
²³ ביום ההוא נאם יהוה צבאות אקחך זרבבל בן שאלתיאל עבדי
נאם יהוה ושמתיך כחותם כי בך בחרתי נאם יהוה צבאות

Text notes

21a: The LXX adds "τὸν τοῦ Σαλαθιηλ," "the son of Salathiel." (See 1:1, 12; 2:2.)

21b: The LXX adds "καὶ τὴν θάλασσαν καὶ τὴν ξηράν" "and the sea and the dry land," an expanded parallelism based on 2:6.

22a: The LXXᴬ adds, καὶ καταστρέψω πᾶσαν τὴν δύναμιν αὐτῶν καὶ καταβαλῶ τὰ ὅρια αὐτῶν καὶ ἐνισχύσω τοὺς ἐκλεκτούς μου, "And I will overthrow their whole power and pull down their frontiers and strengthen my chosen one."[25] This seems to be an expansion in the LXXᴬ not reflected in other Greek manuscripts. See verse-by-verse.

---

25. Wolff, *Haggai: A Commentary*, 98.

Jehoiachin in Other Prophetic and Narrative Literature

Translation of Haggai 2:20–23

20Then the word of the LORD came a second time to Haggai on the twenty-fourth *day* of the month, saying: 21"Speak to Zerubbabel, the governor of Judah, saying: 'I am about to shake the heavens and the earth. 22I will overturn the thrones of the kingdoms and destroy the power of the kingdoms of the nations. I will overthrow the chariot and its rider. I will make *all* horses and riders fall by the sword of their brother. 23On that day,' Yahweh of hosts declares, 'I will take you, Zerubbabel son of Shealtiel my servant,' Yahweh declares, 'and I will set you as a signet *ring*, for I have chosen you,' declares Yahweh of hosts."

Background of the Haggai 2:20–23 account

The book of Haggai, although only two chapters long, relates to an extremely important historical period, lasting five months after Cyrus's 538 decree permitting the restoration of the Jews to Jerusalem. Initial work to rebuild the temple commenced in 536 (Ezra 1–4, especially 3:8), but was halted by adversaries (Ezra 4:24). Haggai and Zechariah arrived in Jerusalem and prodded Zerubbabel and Jeshua son of Jehozadak to commence rebuilding without delay. According to Haggai 1:12–14, the governor, priest, and people responded to the directive. According to the majority view, the laying of the foundation stone of the Second Temple can confidently be dated as December 18, 520 (twelfth-fourth day of the ninth month of the second year of Darius). Antagonism from the adversaries was ineffective, for the temple was completed on the third of Adar (March 10) 516 (Ezra 6:15), approximately seventy years after the first temple was destroyed in Jerusalem.[26]

The prophets Haggai and Zechariah compared the paneled houses of the recently returned residents of Jerusalem to the ruined state of the temple. They proclaimed it was past time to "arise and build," for the temple lay in ruins. *In that day* (Hag 2:6–7)—a reference to the Day of the LORD—Yahweh was going to shake the cosmos and overturn the military might of the nations, which is expanded in 2:21–22 (see especially LXX[A]) to thrones of kingdoms and the power of nations. Chariots, horses and riders, and swords of men were all to be overturned.

---

26. Williamson, "Ezra and Nehemiah," 421. See also Pennant, "Haggai," 857.

Looking Back for Jehoiachin

King Jeconiah, the preexilic signet, was hurled into Babylon, but that imagery gives way to Zerubbabel son of Shealtiel, the postexilic signet prefiguring the return of Yahweh to Jerusalem.

Haggai 2:20–23 by verses

2:20: Haggai 2:10 refers to the twenty-fourth day of the ninth month in the second year of Darius. Because it is present in both the MT and LXX, there is no textual warrant for dismissing the twenty-fourth day of the month as dittography. "This day was identified in 2:18 as the day on which the 'foundation' of the Lord's temple was laid."[27] Likewise, 2:20 (שנית, "a second time") is the same date—December 18, 520, at the end of the exilic period.[28]

2:21: Haggai was commanded to speak to Zerubbabel, the governor of Judah. Zerubbabel is identified by his Persian title "governor," but not by the patronymic "son of Shealtiel" (cf. 1:1, 12, 14; 2:2, 23). Haggai was to reveal what Yahweh was about to do, i.e., "shake the heavens and the earth" (from 2:6). Von Rad draws attention to exodus divine-warfare motifs in this and the following verse.[29]

2:22: Yahweh twice announces the overturning (הפך) of the thrones and the might of the kingdoms and the chariots and drivers. All of the horses and their riders were going to perish (lit. ירד "go down") by the weapons of their own army. Each man falling by the sword of his brother suggests "divinely inspired panics of the early Israelite period (Judg 7:22; cf. Ezek 38:21; Zech 14:13)."[30] Wolff eliminates the second iteration of ממלכות "of the kingdoms" due to metrical considerations. He inserts LXX^A in brackets.[31]

2:23: The oracle-link formula "on that day" (only used in Haggai) refers to the future. This verse is unusual in that it has three occurrences of the (צבאות twice) נאם יהוה "declaration of Yahweh (of hosts)," adding emphasis with each iteration.[32] Yahweh himself would appoint or

---

27. Verhoef, *The Books of Haggai and Malachi*, 141.

28. Wolff, *Haggai: A Commentary*, 15. See also Stuhlmueller, *Haggai and Zechariah*, 37.

29. Von Rad, "Der heilige Krieg im alten Israel," 65ff.

30. Wolff, *Haggai: A Commentary*, 103.

31. Ibid., 98.

32. See Wolff, *Haggai: A Commentary*, 100, for an excursus on (צבאות) נאם יהוה in the book of Haggai. "The thrice-used formula for a divine saying shows how in this

Jehoiachin in Other Prophetic and Narrative Literature

designate (lit. שׂים "set") Zerubbabel as the signet at his own sovereign initiative. He was specified as "son of Shealtiel" (full plene spelling) and called "my servant"—a common title appended to David and others (2 Sam 7:5–8; 1 Kgs 11:32–34; Ezek 34:23ff.; 37:24; Ps 78:70; 89:3; 132:10) and "the servant of the LORD," a royal designation in Isaiah 40–55. He was divinely placed as a signet or seal, for (כִּי) Yahweh had chosen him. A comparable OT text is Jeremiah 22:24; there, Coniah, "even if you were the signet on my right hand," was hurled into exile. With Zerubbabel, the God of Israel puts his seal to the promise of his presence, his blessing, and his peace (1:8b; 2:9b, 19b).

Wolff correctly notes that עַבְדִּי, "my servant" still belongs to the vocative of the person addressed as apposition, not to the assurance אֶקָּחֲךָ ("I will take you").[33] For "to take someone as servant," the construction would have to be לָקַח with accusative and לְ, as in 2 Kings 4:1b and Job 41:4b. He may overreach with his insistence that the similar concentration of messianic terms in Psalm 89:20 would mean Zerubbabel would be the new David. Verhoef is closer to the mark, saying he is "projected on the screen as a representative of the coming Messiah, perhaps as being the Messiah."[34]

How Haggai 2:20–23 informs our understanding of Jeconiah

The curse upon Coniah in Jeremiah 22:24–30 was that he would be the cast-out signet. Yahweh repudiated all that had come to be expected for the sons of David ruling on the throne in Jerusalem. It is entirely likely that Zerubbabel had known his grandfather Jeconiah in Babylonian captivity—perhaps he was also familiar with the curse obviating any of Jeconiah's offspring from occupying the throne of David. But in Haggai 2:23, Zerubbabel is taken (לְקַח), designated in the likeness of royalty ("my servant," עַבְדִּי), and chosen (בחר) as the signet (כְּחוֹתָם) of Yahweh. This prophecy would have reassured Zerubbabel of divine favor if opposition to the temple rebuilding occured. Ezra 1–4 prefigures the difficulties of the initial rebuilding effort in 536. Sixteen years later, during Zerubbabel's and Jeshua's leadership, the encouragement of Haggai

---

oracle every word has the greatest possible weight." His translation of נְאֻם יהוה is interesting: ". . . is the saying . . . is Yahweh's saying . . . —the saying of Yahweh of hosts."

33. Wolff, *Haggai: A Commentary*, 98.
34. Verhoef, *The Books of Haggai and Malachi*, 131.

91

and Zechariah would have invigorated the work. Opposition had not decreased after the temple was rebuilt and before the wall-building efforts of Nehemiah commenced eighty years later in 445–433.

Zerubbabel son of Shealtiel would be more than a governor (פחה) but less than a king. He would be heir to the throne of his forebear and predecessor David.[35] This is not to say that David's distant son Zerubbabel was to inherit the title king (מלך). However, there is a very nice movement of the implied signet of Yahweh from David, as the earthly regent, by primogeniture; to Jeconiah as the rejected and hurled-out signet imprisoned in Babylon; to the reversal of the oracle in the return of Zerubbabel set like a signet. Indeed, Zerubbabel is addressed not as an individual, but as the holder of the Davidic office.[36]

The reverberations of these rich attributes continue in Psalm 89:3–4, which will be explored in more depth in the next chapter. Zerubbabel son of Shealtiel is in both the genealogies of Jesus (Matt 1:1–16; Luke 3:23–38), although ascribed a son of Solomon in Matthew and a son of Nathan in Luke.

It appears that Yahweh's election of Zerubbabel as signet restored favor to the Davidic line, but did not gainsay the curse of Jeremiah 22:30 that no offspring of Jeconiah would succeed in ruling on the throne of David.

The apocryphal book Sirach reprises the imagery of Zerubbabel as signet (49:11–12) and combines it with the notation of the right hand from Jeremiah 22:24–27.

> How shall we magnify Zerubbabel? He was like a signet on the right hand, and so was Jeshua the son of Jozadak; in their days they built the house and raised a temple holy to the LORD, prepared for everlasting glory.

This prophecy of Haggai 2:20–23 should be seen alongside the prophecy of Zechariah 6:11–12. Together, Zerubbabel son of Shealtiel and Jeshua son of Jehozadak receive the messianic titles of signet, crown, and name (the Branch). The implications continue beyond the earthly lifetimes of both governor and priest.

The following pericope, Esther 2:5–6, will investigate a descendent (Mordecai) of a Benjaminite who was taken into exile in Babylon with Jeconiah.

---

35. Ibid., 146.
36. Achtemeier, "Nahum–Malachi," 105.

Jehoiachin in Other Prophetic and Narrative Literature

ESTHER 2:5–7: MORDECAI IN SUSA, EXILED WITH JECONIAH

Introduction

In this pericope,[37] we investigate the link between Jeconiah and the main characters of the book of Esther. Mordecai (or his great-grandfather) was linked to the exile of 597. Like the judges raised up to deliver Israel from oppression, the book of Esther portrays Mordecai and Esther as deliverers.

Scholarly opinion is split over whether Mordecai was exiled with Jeconiah (which would make him more than 100 years old) or whether Kish was exiled with Jehoiachin (which would be an unusual grammatical use of the relative pronoun אשר). Also of interest in this passage is the genealogy of Mordecai—were these his actual father, grandfather, and great-grandfather, or distant relations used for literary effect (Mordecai, descendant of Saul, opposed by Haman, descendant of Agag)? Although there are significant variations in the Greek and Hebrew manuscripts of the book of Esther, they are less significant in this pericope.[38]

Reconstructed text of Esther 2:5–7

5 אִישׁ יְהוּדִי הָיָה בְּשׁוּשַׁן הַבִּירָה ᵃ וּשְׁמוֹ מָרְדֳּכַי בֶּן יָאִיר בֶּן שִׁמְעִי
בֶּן קִישׁ אִישׁ יְמִינִי 6 ᵃ אֲשֶׁר הָגְלָה מִירוּשָׁלַיִם עִם הַגֹּלָה אֲשֶׁר ᵃ הָגְלְתָה
עִם יְכָנְיָה מֶלֶךְ יְהוּדָה ᵃ אֲשֶׁר הֶגְלָה נְבוּכַדְנֶאצַּר מֶלֶךְ בָּבֶל 7 וַיְהִי
אֹמֵן אֶת ᵃ הֲדַסָּה הִיא אֶסְתֵּר ᵇ בַּת דֹּדוֹ כִּי אֵין לָהּ אָב וָאֵם וְהַנַּעֲרָה
יְפַת תֹּאַר וְטוֹבַת מַרְאֶה וּבְמוֹת אָבִיהָ וְאִמָּהּ לְקָחָהּ מָרְדֳּכַי לוֹ לְבַת

Text notes

5a: The LXX adds τῇ πόλει, "the city."

6a-a: The LXX does not reflect the phrase "who were exiled with Jeconiah king of Judah."

7a: The LXX does not reflect "Hadassah."

---

37. Esther 2:5–7 is a parenthetic explanation of why Mordecai and Esther were in Susa. The transitional passage fits between the decree to find virgins for Ahasuerus (2:4) and Esther's move into the harem (2:8).

38. See Additions to Esther 11:2–4 in chapter 5.

7b: The LXX adds the name of her father Aminadab (Αμιναδαβ), probably from 9:29.

Translation of Esther 2:5-7

5There was a Jew in the citadel of Susa whose name was Mordecai, son of Jair, son of Shimei, son of Kish of the tribe of Benjamin. 6He had been carried away in the exile from Jerusalem among the captives taken with Jeconiah king of Judah by Nebuchadnezzar king of Babylon. 7Now Mordecai had brought up Hadassah, *known as* Esther, the daughter of his uncle, for she had neither father nor mother. The maiden was beautiful *with* lovely *features*. When her father and mother died, Mordecai adopted her as his own daughter.

Background of the Esther 2:5-7 account

Darius the Great (Hystaspis) 522-486 (Hag 1:1; Zech 1:1) was the father and predecessor of the Persian king Ahasuerus (Xerxes, 486-465) mentioned in the book of Esther. According to Esther 2:17, Esther ruled as his queen during a time of overt and simmering hostility to the Jews from within the Persian kingdom, which had displaced the earlier Babylonian kingdom.

The claims of many scholars that the book of Esther is fictional, or at least an improbable record of historical persons, need not concern us here.[39] Literarily, the book of Esther claims a linkage of events transpiring in the fifth century to the early sixth-century exile of Jeconiah.

Esther 2:5-7 by verses

2:5: "Jew" was the name given to the people of Judah after the Babylonian Exile of 586 and afterward was applied to Israelites more generally, including people of the tribe of Benjamin. Although the Hebrew says only that Mordecai was "in" Susa, the meaning is probably that he lived there.[40]

---

39. JG Baldwin, "Esther" in *NBC*, p. 445—"Historians have verified the (book of Esther) author's accurate knowledge of Persian royal palaces and customs, and independent evidence has come to light that a certain Marduka (Mordecai) was in authority in Susa."

40. Omanson, *A Handbook on the Book of Esther*, 59.

The name *Mordecai* (which does not occur in Israel before the exile) occurs with another captive who returned with Zerubbabel (Ezra 2:2; Neh 7:2). It is probably based upon Marduk, the state god of Babylon, and may be a Hebrew version of the common name *Mardukaya*.[41] It occurs in several forms in the treasure tablets found at Persepolis, It appears as *Mrdk* in a fifth-century Aramaic document and in an undated text, coming probably from either the last years of Darius I or the early years of Xerxes I, where mention is made of a man named Marduka who served as an accountant on an inspection tour from Susa.[42] Cassel speculates that Mordecai the Jew got his name from the son of Nebuchadrezzar, Evil-merodach, who released Jeconiah from prison in Babylon.[43] He further opines that, if the patronymic has a historical basis, Mordecai was not the one taken into exile with Jeconiah (due to the Babylonian etymology of his name), but his predecessor Kish. It is certainly an unhebraic, if not objectionable, name for a Jewish official. Because Esther has both a Hebrew and Persian name, possibly Mordecai's Hebrew name was not preserved.

Any negative connotation associated with Mordecai and Esther for failing to return to Jerusalem after the Decree of Cyrus is overcome by their roles as deliverers of the Jews. One might wonder whether Mordecai was longing for Jerusalem as his predecessor captive-in-chief Jeconiah. Cyrus's decree was voluntary, and Moore speculates that not all provinces of Persia were notified of the restoration.[44]

The majority of commentators see the names of Mordecai's patronymic as distant, well-known ancestors rather than of his actual grandfather and great-grandfather. Thus Shimei represents the one who cursed David in 2 Samuel 16:5, and Kish refers to the father of Saul (1 Sam 9:1–2). Moore argues tentatively for the historicity of Mordecai, stating that, had Mordecai been a totally fictitious character, the author would have made him a direct descendant of Saul, thus setting up a perfect parallel with Haman, who was a descendant of Agag.[45] This could be an example of telescoping the past for the sake of literary effect. Note the Greek forms of

---

41. *IBD* II, 1024.
42. Baldwin, "Esther," 65.
43. Cassel, *An Explanatory Commentary on Esther*, 50.
44. Moore, *Esther*, 19–20.
45. Moore, *Esther*, 19–20.

Looking Back for Jehoiachin

the names in the ancestral chain ὁ τοῦ Ιαρου τοῦ Σεμειου τοῦ Κισαιου, which would not suggest distinguished forebears.

2:6: It is not clear as to which name the "who" refers; grammatically, Mordecai is indicated, but this would make both him and Esther too old by 480. There are other examples of a telescoping of generations, in keeping with the awareness of family solidarity (cf. Gen 46:27).[46] Omanson concludes, "on both grammatical and exegetical grounds, it is most likely that the antecedent of the pronoun must be Mordecai and not Kish."[47]

Cassel's contrary opinion is, however, worthy of note: "Mordecai was not one of those who was exiled. . . . [T]he enumeration of the four generations [reflects a] period of about 115–120 years."[48]

In Hebrew, the words "had been carried away" and "the captives" have the same root. A rather literal translation of this verse reads, "who had been exiled from Jerusalem in the exile that had been exiled with Jeconiah." The repetitive use of (גלה) adds poignancy to the account. The linking of the book of Esther to the exile of 586 (in the LXX), and more specifically to Jeconiah (the MT), underscores this resonance.

2:7: "Hadassah" is possibly related to "myrtle," following the Targums. II Targum says, "as the myrtle spreads fragrance in the world, so did she spread good works; And for this cause she was called in the Hebrew language Hadassah because the righteous are likened to myrtle."[49]

Esther is a name of uncertain origin. If it is of Babylonian origin, it is a variant of the name Ishtar, the Babylonian goddess of love. But, if it is of Persian origin, then it comes from the word for "star."[50]

The LXX and *Megilla* 13a both have "he took her to himself for a wife." The problem here clearly lies with the Greek, not with the Hebrew, for the latter makes perfectly good sense. Since Esther was taken to the king's harem (2:8), she was obviously regarded by all as a virgin.[51]

"Beautiful and lovely," Esther is similar to Rachel (Gen 29:17). Esther is described with two expressions, the first indicating that she was physically attractive (literally "lovely of form"), the second referring more to her general appearance (literally "good of vision"). Only the latter was

---

46. Baldwin, "Esther," 65.
47. Omanson, *A Handbook of Esther*, 61.
48. Cassel, *An Explanatory Commentary on Esther*, 52.
49. Moore, *Esther*, 20.
50. Omanson, *A Handbook of Esther*, 60.
51. Moore, *Esther*, 21.

Jehoiachin in Other Prophetic and Narrative Literature

used to describe Queen Vashti (1:11) and the young women who were to be gathered for the king (2:3).[52]

The major difficulty in translating this verse comes with the Greek preposition and noun that are translated "to womanhood." The noun may mean either "woman" or "wife." The preposition may indicate a temporal relationship; that is "until [she had become] a woman," or "until she was grown" (TEV). Or, the preposition may indicate purpose; that is, "intending [to make her his] wife." The more natural reading of the Greek, however, favors the interpretation found in the REB: "intending to make her his wife."[53]

How Esther 2:5–7 informs our understanding of Jeconiah

The book of Esther is a postexilic composition. The genealogy of Mordecai establishes that he had a royal pedigree and was in Susa as an opponent to Haman, a descendant of Agag. He probably lived in the citadel of Susa. His relationship with Esther, regardless of his original intention, must have been viewed as guardian and ward, for Esther was taken into the harem without suspicion that she had been betrothed.

The significance of the names Jair, Shimei, and Kish implies that these were distant ancestors of Mordecai, not his father, grandfather, and great-grandfather. In the realm of probability, Mordecai would have been well over 100 years old if he were meant as the antecedent of the relative pronoun אשר. Although this is grammatically and exegetically the most appropriate conclusion, it is not the only explanation. Perhaps telescoping of the generations was in view, or a notation that Mordecai's family had been exiled with Jeconiah, and thus of royal significance.

The memory of exile was very fresh to the author of Esther. The resounding note of impending peril to be inflicted upon the Jews at the hand of Haman (keeper of the signet of Xerxes) surely is a century-later reverberation from the exile of the kingdom of Jerusalem and Judah at the hand of Nebuchadrezzar.

So what is the significance of the recalling of Jeconiah for Mordecai's family? Perhaps it is to sound again the unpleasant but dominant note of the "good figs" exile of 597 instead of the "bad figs" exile of 586. Four generations after the exile—approximately 120 years later—Jeconiah was

52. Ibid., 63.
53. Omanson, *A Handbook of Esther*, 64.

dead, Zerubbabel was in Jerusalem, and Mordecai and Esther were performing as deliverers for the Jewish remnant still in Persia.

CHAPTER 3 CONCLUSION

This chapter suggests that Jehoiachin/Jeconiah's captivity was far more significant than the fifteen collected verses of Ezekiel, 1 Chronicles, Haggai, and Esther might otherwise indicate. The chapter title "Jehoiachin in Other Prophetic and Narrative Literature" implies that the pericopes do not fit neatly into a category. Ezekiel uses the name Jehoiachin, whereas Chronicles and Esther reflect the name Jeconiah. The book of Haggai does not refer directly to this Judean king; however, the resonance of Zerubbabel taken (from Babylon), chosen to be a servant, and made like a signet is surely an echo of the cast-out signet Coniah in Jeremiah 22:24–30.

The grouping of pericopes suggests the idea of afterthought. The fifth year of Jehoiachin's captivity provides the dating baseline for the book of Ezekiel. All further dates up to the twenty-seventh year (Ezek 29:17) are related to the captivity of Jehoiachin. This is the latest date of Ezekiel. The release of Jehoiachin in the thirty-seventh year of his captivity (2 Kgs 25:27; Jer 52:31) is not reflected in Ezekiel. It is significant that Ezekiel 1:2 dates the captivity precisely to the exile of Jehoiachin and not simply to the less-specific fifth year, tenth year, eleventh year, etc. Although potentially a gloss, this verse underscores the dating of the exile from the young king's departure into Babylon.

Ezekiel also refers to Jehoiachin as "king"—a significant title contrasted to the "prince" remaining in Jerusalem. We will examine the implications of Ezekiel 17 and 19 in the next chapter. It is sufficient to observe now that Ezekiel attaches more significance to the גולה community than to those remaining in Israel who were destined for exile.

We were unable to explain fully the differences between the Chronicler's reporting of Jeconiah's successor to the throne or his progeny with that of 2 Kings and Jeremiah. The Chronicler's reporting is a discordant voice in the chorus of historical records. We translated אסר as "the captive" rather than as the name of a firstborn son of Jeconiah. This was based on the historical circumstances of his thirty-seven year captivity and the weight of the combined reports of 2 Kings and Jeremiah. We furthermore believe the Zedekiah of 1 Chronicles 3:17 to

Jehoiachin in Other Prophetic and Narrative Literature

be either the *successor* rather than the *son* of Jeconiah, or a different person from the king who succeeded him. We noted the difference in spelling between the two similar names, i.e., צִדְקִיָּה and צִדְקִיָּהוּ. We concluded that the parentage of Zerubbabel could be either Pedaiah (by Levirate custom) or Shealtiel (as reported in Ezra, Nehemiah, Haggai, and Zechariah), but that Jeconiah was his grandfather, thus maintaining the Davidic linkage while in exile.

The marked movement from Coniah as the cast-out signet to Zerubbabel returning as the Lord's signet reverses at least portions of the curse of Jeremiah 22:24–30. The concentration of apocalyptic terms in Haggai 2:20–23, combined with the thrice-repeated oath formula in verse 23, indicates that this was especially important as a capstone prophecy in the five months following Cyrus's decree for the restoration of the exiles to Judah. King Jeconiah had been the captive-in-chief without a kingdom at the outset of the exile, and his grandson Zerubbabel was the leader of the restoration.

Finally, we concluded that Mordecai's predecessors were exiled with Jeconiah. This afterthought links the Diaspora to the "good figs" captivity of Jeconiah instead of the "bad figs" of Zedekiah and the final destruction of Jerusalem.

Chapter 4

Reflections of Jehoiachin in the Poetry of Israel

INTRODUCTION

IN THE PRECEDING THREE chapters, we investigated the biblical passages that mention Jehoiachin/Jeconiah by name. The methodology was useful for building up the composite portraits of this king from the narrative, Jeremianic and other passages where he was named.

In the poetry under consideration in this chapter, we adopt a revised approach. Rather than a proposed reconstructed Hebrew text, we quote from the *Tanakh*[1] for each passage. Text-critical issues are only introduced in specific situations. Verse-by-verse exegesis is replaced by summary comments, frequently on large swaths of poetic texts. We attempt to answer whether the passages inform our understanding of Jehoiachin. This change in procedure is necessary for several reasons. Firstly, none of these passages mentions Jehoiachin by name, although the allusions to his captivity and exile may be implicit. Secondly, the allusions are set within extensive sections of the text, e.g., Psalm 89 and the book of Lamentations, making reconstruction and verse-by-verse exegesis unwieldy. Thirdly, evocative cultural and theological implications of the exile resonated far beyond the early sixth century BCE. Consequently, we will not

---

1. Jewish Publication Society, *Tanakh*.

Reflections of Jehoiachin in the Poetry of Israel

look at every aspect of these poems (as we did with the historical and prophetical passages), but just those aspects that shed light on Jehoiachin.

This chapter investigates the following pericopes: Ezekiel 17 (allegory of the top bough of the cedar taken to a land of traders), Ezekiel 19 (lament of a lioness left without a scepter to rule), Lamentations 3 and 4 ("I am the man who has known affliction"), Isaiah 52:13—53:12 ("Behold my servant"), Psalm 61 ("Hear my cry, O God"), and Psalm 89 (lament over David's debased throne).[2] Allusions to the exiled Jehoiachin are embedded within Ezekiel 17 and 19. The suggestions of modern scholars that the plight of Jehoiachin is recounted in the following pericopes is examined and less certainly established.

INTRODUCTION TO EZEKIEL 17

The mixed poetry-prose of Ezekiel 17 follows the unusually graphic condemnation of Jerusalem (the whore) in Ezekiel 16. There is the touchpoint in 16:7 ("I let you grow up like the plants of the field . . .") for the use of natural imagery in 17:5-6 ("a seed of the land" that grows into a low vine). Yahweh entered into covenant with Jerusalem in 16:7, only for her to trust in her beauty and lavish her whoring on passersby (16:15, 25). Yahweh's rebuke of Jerusalem, who "spurned the pact and violated the covenant" (בזית אלה להפר ברית, 16:59) anticipates the rebuke of the unnamed "prince" for identical violations of 17:15 (הפר ברית), 17:16 (בזה אלה להפר) and 17:18 (הפר את בריתו בזה את אלתו), and 17:19 (אלתי אשר בזה ובריתי אשר הפיר). Indeed the fable of Ezekiel 17 seems to be an extension of the rebuke of the whore in Ezekiel 16 in the language of fable, allegory, and riddle. Just as Jerusalem violated the covenant made with Yahweh (16:8, 15-34), so had the "prince" in Jerusalem violated the suzerainty covenant made with the king of Babylon to which Yahweh was party (17:5-8, 13-15). The tone of 17:16 is judgmental and predicts that the "prince" would die in Babylon for the trespass he committed against the LORD (17:20).

---

2. We will investigate various scholarly opinions alleging that Jehoiachin's exile is in view in these pericopes.

Looking Back for Jehoiachin

Ezekiel 17

The use of images from the animal and plant kingdoms (17:3–10) to decry the untoward activities of the "prince" זרע המלוכה, is interpreted in 17:13–21. Ezekiel 17:11–12 is the revelatory formula and the initial moral pointer of the fable—proof that this is not a simple observation from the kingdoms of animals and plants. "Do you not know what these things mean?" This rhetorical question (17:12) focuses the readers' attention. "These things" would include not only the specific symbols of the fable, but also, and more urgently, the interpretations of the activity. Ezekiel's fable had more than passing interest for the disconsolate and disillusioned exiles wondering if there was meaning in their situation in Babylon of the early sixth century and that of the remnant in Jerusalem.

The imagery of Ezekiel 17:1–21 is then revisited by the prophecy of a future ruler, "a slip from the lofty top of the cedar" (17:22) who becomes a noble cedar in the mountain height of Israel.

Ezekiel 17:1–10

In 17:1–2, the revelatory formula ("The word of the LORD came to me saying . . .") announces the requirement for Ezekiel to propound a riddle and relate an allegory. "It is thus a fable . . . traditionally used as a political cartoon in order to either challenge leadership or affirm it (Judg 9:8–15; 2 Kgs 14:9)."[3] Kimchi explained that a *riddle* (חידה) is an obscure saying from which something else is to be understood, while a *fable* (משל) is a likening of one matter to another—so this fable, in which the great eagles transplant cedar boughs and seeds, is at the same time a riddle, since none but the discerning can understand it.[4]

17:3–4: The messenger formula ("thus says the LORD God") opens the description of the variegated eagle who came to the Lebanon range, took the top of the cedar, and carried it to a land of traders and merchants (cf. 16:29; 17:12). Allen observes a "come-take-bring" theme, recurring at several points throughout the fable, e.g., 17:12, 19–20, 22–23. The extensive description of the eagle contrasts markedly with the terse description

---

3. Solomon, "Fable," 114–25. Solomon makes the etymological link between משל ("to employ a fable") and משל ("to rule over") as the basis for a prophet's "political oracle" (151, n. 16). See also Greenberg, "Ezekiel 17 and the Policy of Psammetichus II," 304–09; and Allen, *Ezekiel 1–19*, 254.

4. Cf. Greenberg, "Ezekiel 17 and the Policy of Psammeticus II," 309.

of "the top of the cedar . . . topmost bough." The stature and magnificence of the eagle of the fable dwarfs even the very top of the Lebanon cedar—famous for its size and value. As the eagle is the king of the birds, so the cedar is the king of trees.[5] In biblical literature, Lebanon's cedars symbolized (royal) majesty (Judg 9:15; 1 Kgs 5:13; 2 Kgs 14:9; Isa 10:33; Song 5:15).

17:5–6: We notice the difference in stature of the top of the cedar and the seed of the land: the first at the crown of the tree, the other at the base, potentially growing into a tree. Verse 17:6 reports that the seed grew into a spreading vine of low stature rather than into a cedar tree. This growth was unremarkable in the fabulous account, but was probably intended to strike the hearers as significant. Regardless of the disappointing growth (from the viewpoint of the vine), the great eagle intended the low vine would grow up for him.

17:7–8: The entry of "another great eagle" sets up the conflict of the fable. Though the "prince" had been planted "like a willow beside abundant waters" (17:5), "in rich soil beside abundant water" (17:8), the low vine bent its roots in the direction of the second eagle that he might "water it more than the bed where it was planted" (17:7) The low vine intended to become a "noble" vine.

17:9–10: The messenger formula (with the following questions) ties the interpretation of these verses to the fable. The first great eagle would not expend great effort in uprooting the low ambitious vine. The vine would "wither" (יבש) "on the bed where it grew."

Ezekiel 17:11–21

17:11–15: The revelatory formula established the link to the foregoing fable. Ezekiel was commanded to narrate the meaning of the fable's events to "the rebellious breed," associating the vine's rebellion and covenant violation with the audience in Babylon. The great, variegated eagle stood for the king of Babylon (cf. 2 Kgs 24; Jer 22; 2 Chr 36). He came to Jerusalem, "carried away its king and its officers and brought them back to Babylon," a probable reference to Jehoiachin and the nobles exiled in 597. "One of the seed royal" was placed under a vassal covenant to the king of Babylon. The purpose of the covenant was explained in 17:14: "so that [Judah] might be a humble kingdom and not exalt itself, but keep his

---

5. Wevers, *Ezekiel*, 134.

Looking Back for Jehoiachin

covenant and so endure." The conflict between the two eagles (17:7–10) was explained in 17:15. The "prince" rebelled. He sent envoys to the other eagle (Egypt) asking for relief. Pharaoh's help would only offer a temporary reprieve in the siege of Jerusalem (cf. Jer 37:5, 11 [prophecy] and 37:6–10 [interpretation]).

Allen translates 17:13b, "he included in the treaty the leading people in the country."[6] We favor the more traditional *Tanakh* view, that this was a reference to the nobles carried away in 598, as a simpler and more straightforward rendering.

The rhetorical questions all expect negative answers, indicating that the violations of the covenant sworn by the "prince" at the direction of the great eagle would be punished. According to the fable, it was not possible to violate the suzerainty treaty of Babylon with impunity. Would the rebellion succeed? Would he escape? These questions were painfully answered in 2 Kings 25:5–7, 2 Chronicles 36:17–20, Jeremiah 52:7–11, and the poignant laments of the book of Lamentations.

We discover further in the interpretation of 17:19–21 that the covenant violation was also of Yahweh's (אלתי) oath and covenant (בריתי). The king of Babylon who made him king (הממליך, cf. Jer 37:1) caused the "prince" to swear allegiance by God (2 Chr 36:13).

Ezekiel 17:22–24

This pericope presents a messianic promise under the guise of interpreting the fable. God was going to select "a slip from the lofty top of the cedar." He was going to take "a tender twig from the tip of its crown" for his planting in Israel. This twig of the cedar would grow into the noble tree. "This messianic cedar, a new king from the Davidic line, God's faithful 'servant' (34:24; 37:24–25) would grow into the full potential of the divine promise."[7]

How Ezekiel 17 informs our understanding of Jehoiachin

The great eagle that came to Lebanon (17:3) was King Nebuchadrezzar of Babylon (land of traders and city of merchants, 17:4). "The top of the cedar" (17:3) and "topmost bough" (17:4) were the chief men and

---

6. Allen, *Ezekiel 1–19*, 259.
7. Ibid., 260.

Reflections of Jehoiachin in the Poetry of Israel

Jehoiachin exiled in 597 to Babylon (cf. 17:12–13). A "seed royal of the land" (17:5, 13) that became a "spreading vine of low stature" (17:6) was Zedekiah. It was clear that the first eagle wanted the low vine to grow up under his oversight. "Another great eagle" (17:7) was the Egyptian pharaoh. This established the tension in the plant and animal kingdoms, which Ezekiel used to engage his Babylonian audience. The fable focused on Nebuchadrezzar's installation of Zedekiah under oath, to be his vassal, in place of the deposed King Jehoiachin (2 Chr 36:10). Zedekiah rebelled and was severely punished. Although the focus of the fable is that rebellion against the covenant of Babylon was a violation of Yahweh's covenant, the inactivity of the "topmost bough" was more positive than the rebellion of the "seed royal." Duguid observes on 17:12, "If exile was the fate of Jeconiah when he fought against Nebuchadrezzar, though he merited the more exalted title מלך, what are the prospects for Zedekiah, who is never explicitly termed מלך by Ezekiel, and who owes his very throne to Nebuchadrezzar (17:16)?"[8]

The pericope specifies that Yahweh himself "will take ... a slip from the lofty top of a cedar ... a tender twig from the tip of its crown" (17:22), which will "grow into a noble cedar" (17:23). The oaths of Yahweh, "As I live, declares the Lord GOD" (17:16, 19) and "I the LORD have spoken" (17:21 24), further solemnify the prediction. Ezekiel 17:22–24 is a messianic prophecy awaiting fulfilment in the years after Jehoiachin's and Zedekiah's reigns (cf. Jer 23:5–6). Ezekiel's fable extends the rule of David's house beyond Jehoiachin and Zedekiah's times in a Messianic ideal.

INTRODUCTION TO EZEKIEL 19

At the beginning and ending of Ezekiel 19, the poetry of this fable is identified as a lament, a *qinah* for the princes (נשיאי) of Israel. It reuses the language of Jacob's blessing of Judah in Genesis 49:9–11.[9] The lioness motif links 19:1–9 and 10–14, although there is a significant shift in imagery from the lion cubs to the vine of blood. "One of her cubs" (19:3) "brought ... to the land of Egypt" (19:4) is surely Jehoahaz/Shallum, the only one of the final kings to be deposed and exiled to Egypt.

---

8. Duguid, *Ezekiel and the Leaders of Israel*, 25.

9. See Begg, "The Identity of the Princes in Ezekiel 19," 358–69. Begg provides an excellent survey of the history of interpretation and concludes that Ezekiel used Gen 49:9–11 and Jer 22:10—23:8 as exemplars upon which he modeled his fable.

Looking Back for Jehoiachin

"Another of her cubs" (19:5) "brought... to the king of Babylon" (19:9) could be either Jehoiakim, Jehoiachin, or Zedekiah. "Your mother was like a vine in a vineyard" (19:10) may be an allusion to the vine of 17:8. The "strongest stem(s)" that became a "ruler's scepter(s)" in 19:11 is most likely Jehoiachin or Zedekiah. But there remains "no strong stem, no scepter for ruling" (19:14). The questions we must attempt to answer are the following: (1) What activity of the princes is Ezekiel lamenting? (2) What do the fabulous elements represent? (3) What does this fable tell us concerning Jehoiachin?

Ezekiel 19:2–4

The mother lioness of the lament bore many cubs, but she raised one to be dominant. When he had grown into a great beast, he hunted prey and devoured men. When he was at the point of his final challenge with the other great beasts, he was "caught in their snare and dragged off to Egypt" (19:4). At this point, the lament moved beyond the pride of lions into the human sphere of snares, pits, and hooks. Nations heeded the call to trap the cub. This prince of the lions was removed from his exalted position and taken away from the mother lioness and the other cubs.

The dirge about a prince in the guise of a lion cub taken to Egypt would have reminded Ezekiel's audience of Jehoahaz, deposed by Pharaoh and exiled to Egypt. The "nations" (Assyria, Babylon, and Egypt) were at war in Carchemish, and Josiah and then Jehoahaz were caught in their snare. Whether any of the audience recognized an allusion to Jeremiah 22:10–12 ("do not weep for the dead... weep rather for him who... has gone forth... he shall die in the place to which he was exiled") is uncertain, but Begg correctly recognizes Jeremiah's template in Ezekiel's fable.[10]

Ezekiel 19:5–9

The mother lioness lamented her lost cub, but took another cub and set him up as a great beast. He was more ferocious than the first cub: "He stalked among the lions" (19:6a), "devoured men" (19:6b), "ravished their widows, laid waste their cities" (19:7a), until "the land and all in it were appalled at the sound of his roaring" (19:7b). His power was eclipsed

10. Ibid., 368.

when the "nations from the countries round about arrayed themselves against him" (19:8). This lion was also caught in a snare with hooks and a cage.

If the audience understood the first prince to be Jehoahaz, the most likely candidate for the second cub would be Jehoiakim, remembered as a king intent "only on ill-gotten gains, on shedding the blood of the innocent... committing fraud and violence" (Jer 22:17). Jehoiakim merited the castigations of the fable regarding the second cub. He stalked among the nations, formed covenants first with Egypt, and then with Babylon. His "roaring" was muffled by the incursions of the surrounding nations (2 Kgs 24:2), and he was finally caught in the siege of Jerusalem when he broke the suzerainty covenant with Nebuchadrezzar.

If Begg is correct in his identification of the four princes in Ezekiel 19 as an overlay on the template of Jeremiah 22:10—23:8, we would expect to see the third cub at this point in the fable. Jehoiachin was elevated to the throne by primogeniture (mother lioness?) at some point before or during the siege of Jerusalem. He was caught in the snares, hooks, and cages of Chaldean reprisals initiated by his father, the covenant breaker.

Perhaps Ezekiel 19:8–9 portrays the second lion Jehoiakim in accord with 2 Chronicles 36:6–7. This is a possible solution to the plight of Jehoiakim being "carried... to the king of Babylon and confined in a fortress" (Ezek 19:9), although it more reasonably fits with the accounts regarding Jehoiachin/Coniah (2 Kgs 24:11–15; 2 Chr 36:10; Jer 22:24–30), especially confinement and the silencing of his roar on the hills of Israel. The violence of the second cub does not typify the short reigns of Jehoahaz or Jehoiachin, or the capricious rule of Zedekiah. Thus, we propose Jehoiakim as the most likely referent of the second cub and Ezekiel 19:8–9 as referring to the third prince, Jehoiachin.

Ezekiel 19:10–14

There is a shift in the lament at 19:10, from lions to vines, "under the influence of Gen 49:9–11"[11] which we believe to be correct. The Genesis passage reads:

> Judah is a lion's whelp; / On prey, my son, have you grown. / He crouches, lies down like a lion, / Like the king of beasts—who dare rouse him? / The scepter shall not depart from Judah, /

---

11. Ibid., 368.

> Nor the ruler's staff from between his feet; / So that tribute shall come to him / And the homage of peoples be his. / He tethers his ass to a vine, / His ass's foal to a choice vine; / He washes his garment in wine, / His robe in blood of grapes.

The combination of lion and vine imagery with reference to Judah also occurs here at Ezekiel 19:10. Ezekiel may have used this shift in metaphors to signal the arrival of the next cub. It is also possible that he was referring back to Ezekiel 17, his earlier vine analog (Jehoiachin and Zedekiah). The metaphor of the vine "planted beside streams, with luxuriant boughs and branches thanks to abundant waters" (19:10) sounds like 17:5–6, 8, previously identified as Zedekiah, the prince who rebelled and was caught in nets and snares (17:20).

The mother lioness, now portrayed as a vine, has "a mighty rod" (19:11–12), "fit for a ruler's scepter" (19:11a) and "conspicuous for its height" (19:11b). This stature and height may be reflections of the "top of the cedar" (17:3) and "topmost bough" (17:4). The "east wind withered her branches" and "her mighty rod was consumed by fire" (19:12) suggest the arrival of the Babylonians (from the east) who exiled Jehoiachin in 597.

The disjunctive adverb ועתה "now" signals a new prince, "planted in the desert, in ground that is arid and parched" (19:13), a possible allusion to the situation Zedekiah faced after he suffered the exile of 586. "Fire has issued from her twig-laden branch and has consumed her boughs" (19:14) could be a reference to Zedekiah's own complicity in the destruction of Jerusalem because of his foolish violation of the covenant of Yahweh and Nebuchadrezzar.

Although none of these identifications can be positively established because there are no decisive clues in the dirge beyond the evident one in 19:4 (Egypt), the suggestion of the next three kings of Judah follows the dirge closely.[12]

HOW EZEKIEL 19 INFORMS OUR UNDERSTANDING OF JEHOIACHIN

Ezekiel 19 is a lament about the disastrous activities of the final four kings of Judah immediately prior to the Babylonian captivity. It is helpful to see

---

12. For further discussion of the interpretive history of Ezek 19, the reader is referred to Begg.

Reflections of Jehoiachin in the Poetry of Israel

Jehoiachin in the context of each of these other kings. He can be compared in reign duration and early exile to Jehoahaz, the first of the mother lioness's cubs. Each became a "great beast," but was caught in snares and dragged off with hooks to a foreign land. Jehoiachin was additionally "put in a cage . . . and confined in a fortress" (19:9), alluding to his imprisonment. Neither voice was ever heard again on the hills of Israel. They died in the land of their exile.

Jehoiakim was much more savage than his son. He "stalked among the lions," both Egypt and Babylon, and was well acquainted with the incursions of the surrounding hostile nations. He devoured men and their widows, laid waste their cities, and all the land was appalled at his roaring. His son Jehoiachin did not rule long enough to prowl. He never confronted Egyptian might, but felt the full weight of Babylonian power crushing the rebellion set in motion by his father. Jehoiachin was taken from Jerusalem into exile with his mother, wives, children, advisors, and thousands of skilled craftsmen.

Jehoiachin did not reign long. Zedekiah, on the other hand, had eleven years to display his own (indecisive) commitment to Babylon, to Egypt, and to the LORD. The harangues of Ezekiel 16, 17, and 19 fell heaviest on him.

Although neither Jehoiachin nor Zedekiah was named in Ezekiel 17 and 19, the fable and allegory had implicit allusions to their reigns in Judah. The following pericopes do not mention any proper names, and the allusions must be carefully considered as to whether they shed light on Jehoiachin's life.

INTRODUCTION TO LAMENTATIONS 3 AND 4

Nearly all scholars agree that the setting of the book of Lamentations is the exile of Judah commencing in 587. We turn now to investigate the claims of Rudolph (that Lamentations 3 represents a dating to Jehoiachin's, not to Zedekiah's, time) and Porteous (that Lamentations 3 and 4 may represent the voice of King Jehoiachin in exile).

The LXX preface preceding Lamentations 1:1 states, "And it came to pass after Israel had been taken captive and Jerusalem had been laid waste, Jeremiah sat weeping and lamented this lament over Jerusalem, and said. . . ." Though a later addition, based on Jeremianic authorship of Lamentations, this ascription is early. Any scholar who posits that

Looking Back for Jehoiachin

Lamentations 3 and 4 are describing or giving voice to Jehoiachin's exile must grapple with this addition.

Having already established the canonical portraits of Jehoiachin's life in chapters 1 to 3, we considered the idea that the tragic reign of Jehoiachin could have been recorded by the author of the poems. The following allusions within Lamentations 3 and 4 potentially might refer to Jehoiachin in exile:

"I am the man who has known affliction" (3:1)

"... unrelieved darkness" (3:2)

"He has worn away my flesh and skin" (3:4)

"He has made me dwell in darkness" (3:6)

"He has walled me in and I cannot break out" (3:7)

"He has weighed me down with chains" (3:7)

"when I cry and plead, / He shuts out my prayer" (3:8)

"He has walled in my ways with hewn blocks" (3:9)

"He has left me numb" (3:11)

"I have become a laughingstock to all people" (3:14)

"I thought my strength and hope / Had perished before the LORD" (3:18)

"To recall my distress and my misery / Was wormwood and poison" (3:19)

"All the prisoners of the earth" (3:34)

They have ended my life in a pit" (3:53)

"The breath of our life, / The LORD's anointed (מְשִׁיחַ יהוה), / Was captured in their traps— / He in whose shade we had thought / To live among the nations." (4:20)

Background of Lamentations 3 and 4

There is a definite shift in voice between Lamentations 1–2 (feminine voice of Zion) and Lamentations 3 (masculine voice "I am the man" [אֲנִי הַגֶּבֶר]). Although these excerpts may suggest the plight of the young prisoner, we turned to Rudolph's and Porteous's specific assertions to see if they shed light on allusions to Jehoiachin.

Rudolph

Wilhelm Rudolph argued that Lamentations 1 dated from the first capture of Jerusalem by the Babylonians, that is, from shortly after 597, not from after 587. He based his conjecture on the lack of notice of the destruction of the city and temple in Lamentations 1, which speaks only of the capture of Jerusalem. Hillers dispensed with this argument from silence as insufficient to remove the dating from Lamentations 2 and 3.[13] Additionally, the references to severe famine ("All her inhabitants sigh / As they search for bread; / They have bartered their treasures for food, / To keep themselves alive" [1:11]; "My priests and my elders / Have perished in the city / As they searched for food / To keep themselves alive" [1:19]) do not fit the quick siege of Jerusalem and capitulation of Jehoiachin in 597 described by the Babylonian Chronicle.

Rudolph's suggestion that the "I" of 3:1 was Jeremiah was engaging. In this identification, he was not suggesting that Jeremiah wrote the poem, only that the anonymous author wanted to make the work appear as if it were penned by Jeremiah as an example of how faith triumphs in suffering. Rudolph rejected any collective interpretation.[14] Hillers again found this argument unconvincing, going on to conclude, "There is nothing in Lam 3 that makes it necessary to think that Jeremiah, or for that matter *any of the writer's contemporaries*, is the one who speaks."[15] Hillers's view is that the man of Lamentations 3 is neither a specific historical individual nor a collective, but instead is an "Everyman—a figure who represents what any man may feel when it seems that God is against him."

Provan agrees with this generic everyman or anyman. He states:

> The biblical texts have retained a lasting value for their readers precisely because of their ability to transcend the particular and embrace the general in human experience. Especially in the case of poetry, to be overly concerned with the historical roots of the literature is to risk missing the point. For whatever else poems exist for, they do not exist primarily to impart information.

---

13. Hillers, *Lamentations*, xviii–xix.

14. Albrektson, *Studies in the Text and Theology of the Book of Lamentations*, 126. "The overwhelming majority of commentators (Ewald, Keil, Budde, Löhr, Rudolph, Haller, Wiesmann, Meek, Weiser, Kraus, Balla) are agreed that this poem must be a personal lament and that a collective interpretation is impossible."

15. Hillers, *Lamentations*, 63, emphasis added.

Appreciation of them is hindered rather than helped by a historical mind-set.[16]

Porteous

Norman W. Porteous, in a festschrift for Rudolph,[17] suggested that the individual lament of Lamentations 3 could have been intended to describe the bitter experiences of Jehoiachin. He amended Rudolph's view (that Jeremiah was the man of Lamentations 3:1), proposing instead that the speaker of 3:1 fit the experience Jehoiachin had in prison. Furthermore, he thought the reference to "The kindness of the LORD" (3:22, cf. 3:32) suggested the חסד of Yahweh towards his covenant with David and his successors.

In Porteous's argument, he suggested that the part of the exiled Jehoiachin might be played by a priest. "If Jehoiachin is indeed kept in mind in Lam 3, the assertion (3:31–33) that the Lord would not reject forever but would yet have mercy would be fulfilled" by the King Evil-merodach's release of Jehoiachin from captivity.[18]

Provan discounts "possible historical events which might have been in the author's mind as he wrote."[19] He asserts that what is in the mind of the author is unknowable and irrelevant to our reading of the ancient texts.

We find Porteous's suggestion intriguing despite Provan's reservations. Although it is impossible to know what the author of Lamentations 3 was thinking, we do see a fit between some of the clauses and the experience of the king who experienced suffering. Reading the poem with Jehoiachin's situation in mind does not detract from the poignancy of the lament, especially if it is recalled that Jehoiachin did not initiate the retributive siege of Jerusalem—he was simply the recipient of Nebuchadrezzar's wrath.

Lamentations 4:20 has traditionally been seen to refer to Zedekiah's desperate flight from Jerusalem after the breaching of the wall by the Chaldean forces (Jer 52:6–9; 2 Kgs 25:3–6; cf. Jer 39:1–5). Porteous conjectured that the author of Lamentations took part in the flight; standing

---

16. Provan, *Lamentations*, 29.
17. Porteous, "Jerusalem-Zion: The Growth of a Symbol," 235–52.
18. Porteous, "Jerusalem-Zion: The Growth of a Symbol," 244–45.
19. Provan, *Lamentations*, 29.

fairly close to King Zedekiah, and was much grieved at his capture (4:20). To be sure, he deliberately used somewhat exaggerated language in speaking of the king in order to sharpen the contrast between their hopes in the king and the bitter actuality.

How Lamentations 3 and 4 inform our understanding of Jehoiachin

The poems of Lamentations 3 and 4 *could* fit the experience of King Jehoiachin. We agree that a collective interpretation of 3:1ff is most unlikely. Given that the speaker is male (הגבר) and not the same speaker of Lamentations 1–2, we believe Porteous may have correctly identified the *possible* referent. Of course, this is speculative, and we conclude that Lamentations 3 *may* have been recorded with him in mind. We disagree with the conjecture that Jehoiachin fits 4:20. He surrendered to Nebuchadrezzar rather than being "captured in their traps." Although the suggestion that Lamentations 3 reflects Jehoiachin's exile is only a possible solution, that may be the best option.

INTRODUCTION TO ISAIAH 52:13—53:12

Michael Goulder of Birmingham concludes that Jehoiachin is the Suffering Servant of Isaiah 52:13—53:12.[20] Jehoiachin was certainly an important figure in the tragic downfall of Jerusalem at the time of the Babylonian captivity. But to consider that he could be the fulfillment of this vastly allusive pericope seems to be stretching the text. We believe Goulder's argument outstrips his evidence. He deserves credit for contributing to the possibilities regarding the Suffering Servant.

Goulder

Goulder credits Sellin with the initial identification of Jehoiachin as the Suffering Servant, although he then denigrates Sellin's innovations: "a fertile imagination which suggested ever new ideas"[21] and improper

---

20. Goulder, "Behold My Servant Jehoiachin," 175–90, esp. 176.

21. Ibid., 175. Goulder says of E. Sellin, "In 1898 he thought the Servant was Zerubbabel; in 1901 Jehoiachin; in 1922 Moses; in 1930 Deutero-Isaiah, in 1933 the same with elaborations."

Looking Back for Jehoiachin

application of Jehoiachin to all four of Duhm's Servant Songs. Goulder sees 2 Kings 25:27–30 (the release of Jehoiachin from prison by Evil-merodach) as the impetus for Isaiah 52:13–15. He suggests that Deutero-Isaiah, living in Jerusalem, wrote a poem of five stanzas of three verses each to give a prophet's insight into the news of Jehoiachin's release.

Goulder suggests that Isaiah 52:13–15 is the account of Jehoiachin at the royal banquet in Babylon. Furthermore, Goulder opines that Isaiah 53 recounts successive stages of that young king's experience: 53:1–3, Jehoiachin's early life; 53:4–6, the significance of his sufferings; 53:7–9, his imprisonment; and 53:10–12, his reward.

Although he rejects Duhm's hypothesis that the four Servant Songs are separate units, he does agree that 52:13—53:12 should be taken as a unified pericope based on the inclusio of 52:13–15 (spoken by Yahweh) answered in 53:11b–12, both with the common theme of exaltation of the servant.

He amasses data on the probability that עבדי means practically, "my servant," and in this pericope, specifically, "my king." Having asserted that, he concludes that, therefore, King Jehoiachin must be in the mind of Deutero-Isaiah.

Goulder presents his evidence summarily, then announces that (obviously) Jehoiachin is the referent. We detect possible circularity. He states that Jehoiachin is the Suffering Servant, observes that Deutero-Isaiah could have intended this, then concludes that it must be thus. He does not adequately address the other significant opinions in a vast amount of literature on the passage. This age-old mystery will not die out by speculations supported only by circumstantial evidence.

As an example of circularity, it seems to us that Goulder suggests a linkage between 2 Kings 25:27–30 and Isaiah 52:13–15, then states, "the language recalling..." followed by "the picture is that of Jehoiachin" without showing the linkage. He describes the prison setting more graphically than we can know for certain. His speculations are plausible, but not compelling. We believe that he extrapolates from what the text says without due regard for caution, e.g., "For most of a lifetime below ground, without much light, if any, very likely in the damp, with we know not what diet or means of washing, racked with sickness: he must indeed have looked a scarecrow."[22] Further on, Goulder attributes the verb (יזה) "to sprinkle"—normally the role of the priest—to Jehoiachin, "here taking

---

22. Ibid., 178.

authority to cleanse, or to consecrate, the worship of Gentiles. Such a figure is no mere prophet: he is the presiding figure in the nations' worship, high-priest after the exile, king before."[23] One further example of this phenomenon is sufficient. Goulder argues that the Suffering Servant is indeed Jehoiachin, depicts his appearance after the thirty-seven years in prison, then explains Isaiah 53:1–3 as the evidence for Jehoiachin.[24]

In Isaiah 53:1–3, Goulder admits that Clines[25] has an interesting treatment of the "we" of chapter 53, but then dismisses it for his own interpretation, namely, that the "we" is the Jewish community. By dismissing Clines's point, he fails to address the other shifts in pronouns in the pericope, i.e., "you," "he," and "they." He states that Jeremiah contemptuously called Jehoiachin Shallum and Coniah. We believe Goulder is mistakenly confusing Jeremiah 22:10–11 (regarding Shallum son of Josiah) and Jeremiah 22:24–30 (Coniah son of Jehoiakim). His characterization of this name as contemptuous is unique. No other scholar has so typified it.

His explanation of 53:4–6 is unconvincing. "With his stripes we are healed" is attributed to the (*probable*) flogging inflicted by Nebuchadrezzar on Jehoiachin (our emphasis). He claims "it was an easy move from 'as a result of our sins' to 'in satisfaction of our sins'"[26] without further supporting data. This has the depressing effect of rendering the transcendence of this song to a fixed historical point without the sense of wonder inherent in the passage. Truly, as Goulder himself says, "new solutions to age-old riddles do not easily win acceptance."[27]

How Isaiah 52:13–53:12 inform our understanding of Jehoiachin

Goulder suggests the possibility that Jehoiachin is the intended referent of the pericope, but the exile and punishment of Jehoiachin do not seem to fulfill the requirement of atoning sacrifice specified in the pericope, e.g., "My servant" (עבדי) "shall prosper" (ישכיל); "be exalted and raised to great heights" (52:13); "like a tree trunk out of arid ground" (53:2); "despised, shunned by men; a man of suffering, familiar with disease" (53:3);

23. Ibid., 179.
24. Ibid., 180.
25. Clines, *I, He, We, and They*.
26. Goulder, "Behold My Servant Jehoiachin," 182.
27. Ibid., 175.

Looking Back for Jehoiachin

"Yet it was our sickness that he was bearing" (53:4); "but he was wounded because of our sins, crushed because of our iniquities" (53:5); "and the Lord visited upon him the guilt of us all" (53:6); "and his grave was set among the wicked and with the rich in his death" (53:9); "he might see offspring, and have long life; and that through him, the Lord's purpose might prosper" (53:10); "assuredly, I will give him the many as his portion, and he shall receive the multitude as his spoil" (53:12).

As interesting as Goulder's argument is, it is too speculative. We are left to inquire with the Ethiopian Eunuch of Acts 8:34 of whom the prophet is speaking. Surely he means someone in the lineage of the kings of Judah, but more reflective of atonement than the pitiable Jehoiachin.

INTRODUCTION TO PSALM 61

The author of this psalm appears to be crying out of his extremity (exile?) to God and is in fear of "the enemy" (61:2–4); he has received an answer to his prayers (61:5); he prays now in fervent yet restrained language for his king (61:6, 7).

Barnes

> [T]he king is to be identified with Jeconiah, the captive king of Judah in the hands of the Chaldeans. For him the Psalmist may pray that he may have long life, that he may abide before God, that loving kindness and truth may preserve him. . . . On the other hand he confesses that his former prayers have been heard. May not this confession point to the favour shown to Jeconiah by Evil-merodach the successor of Nebuchadrezzar (2 Kgs 25:27–30)?[28]

Barnes's opinion is in the minority of commentators among whom there is no clear consensus. Tate offers this summary of the opinions regarding setting and form of Psalm 61:

> Several interpreters assign the Psalm to the period of the pre-exilic monarchy, and even to David when he was forced to flee from Absalom to the other side of the Jordan (e.g., Delitzsch, Perowne, Kirkpatrick, and Kissane). Others, however, think of the period of the exile after 597 BC, when the prayer could have

---

28. Barnes, *The Psalms with Introduction and Notes*, 288–89.

been for Zedekiah in Jerusalem and for Jehoiachin, who as an exile himself received favorable treatment by the Babylonian king, Evil-merodach (Barnes). Those who hold to the exilic setting do not think of the king as the speaker but of an Israelite who prays for the king.[29]

Although Barnes's comments are interesting for discussion, they are speculative. He provides no evidence, merely suggesting that it is possible. He does not account for the superscription (לדוד) or the change between first and third person in the psalm.

How Psalm 61 informs our understanding of Jehoiachin

Lacking additional information, we are forced to pass over Barnes's suggestions and say that nothing can be conclusively stated about the setting of Psalm 61 *vis-à-vis* Jehoiachin/Jeconiah.

INTRODUCTION TO PSALM 89

This royal psalm has numerous verses that *may* depict the exile of Jehoiachin. Anticipating Goulder's argument that this may be the case, we review *Tanakh* extracts (selected verses refer to the Hebrew).

"Yet You (ואתה) have rejected, spurned, and become enraged at Your anointed (משיחך)" (89:39)

"You have repudiated the covenant with Your servant (עבדך); / You have dragged his dignity in the dust" (89:40)

"You have breached all his defenses, shattered his strongholds" (89:41)

"All who pass by plunder him; he has become the butt of his neighbors" (89:42)

"You have exalted the right hand of his adversaries, and made all his enemies rejoice" (89:43)

"You have turned back the blade of his sword, and have not sustained him in battle" (89:44)

"You have brought his splendor to an end and have hurled his throne to the ground" (89:45)

---

29. Tate, Marvin E. *Psalms* 51–100. The Word Biblical Commentary, Vol. 20, Edited by David E. Hubbard, et. al. (Dallas: Word Press, 1990), pp. 288–89.

Looking Back for Jehoiachin

"You have cut short the days of his youth; You have covered him with shame" (89:46)

"O remember how short my life is" (89:48)

"O LORD, where is Your steadfast love of old which You swore to David in Your faithfulness?" (89:50)

"Remember, LORD, the abuse flung at Your servants (עבדיך) that I have borne in my bosom from many peoples" (89:51)

"abuse at Your anointed (משיחך) at every step" (89:52)

Goulder

Goulder proposes that the referent for Psalm 89 is King Jeconiah of Judah.[30] He supports his premise in a number of ways. Firstly, he states that the original psalm core (89A) was 89:1–2, with 5–18 written in the Israelite area at Tabor. It was accepted into liturgical use in Jerusalem and amended to fit the needs of the Judahite priesthood. Secondly, Goulder interprets משכיל from the superscription as "a skillful psalm" incorporating כון (from Jeconiah) into the body of the psalm as an indication that it was finally adapted after the exile of Jeconiah and the nobility of Judah. Thirdly, Goulder points to some of the historical corpus to buttress his findings. We find his proposition engaging and illustrative of his great analytical skills, but, ultimately, speculative.

Goulder sees in Psalm 89:12, "Tabor and Hermon sing forth Your name," an indication that the northern priests at Tabor brought the psalm south after the fall of Israel to the Assyrians. "The northern tradents had to amend their sanctuary's texts ... seeing the real fulfillment of the divine promises in Jerusalem."[31] Presumably, this would include the emendation of cultic references to the Dan or Bethel altars and any other material at odds with the Jerusalem temple and liturgy.

Goulder maintains the lament of Psalm 89 (89:3–4, 19–51) was added to the core material after Nebuchadrezzar's siege and capture of Jerusalem in 598/597. Reworked portions of 2 Samuel 7 were incorporated as 89:3–4, the references to the Davidic dynasty were added as 89:19–37, and, finally, 89:38–51 was added to pose the question why Yahweh would apparently repudiate the eternal covenant to David and his seed. This revised psalm was appended onto the last portion of Book 3 of the Psalter,

---

30. Goulder, *The Psalms of the Sons of Korah*, 211–38.
31. Ibid., 216.

Reflections of Jehoiachin in the Poetry of Israel

thus explaining the last verse, "Blessed is the LORD forever; Amen and Amen."

Goulder posits that *Selah* (סלה) is a literary convention, a sort of pointer to a supporting text. He envisions a break in the liturgical reading of the psalm, a reading of the associated text, then return to the psalm. In Psalm 89, *Selah* occurs after 89:5, 38, 46, and 49. Goulder suggests that the associated texts would probably be 2 Samuel 7 and 2 Kings 24:8–17. His choice of supporting texts is reasonable. That the worshiping community would understand the background to the psalm is likely even if Goulder has overstated the likelihood that *Selah* is such a convention.

Goulder translates משכיל as "a skillful psalm" and believes, based on the occurrence of the root כון (89:2, 4, 21, and 37), that these are pointers to the exiled King Jeconiah.

How Psalm 89 informs our understanding of Jehoiachin

We recall that Goulder proposed Jehoiachin as the referent of the Suffering Servant, Isaiah 52:13—53:12. Whereas in that analysis we were unconvinced, we believe his analysis of Psalm 89 is possible. His rationale for משכיל, סלה, and the use of כון as a pointer to the exiled Jehoiachin is fascinating. We would have expected, based on our understanding of his proposition, that כון would have occurred in the lament of 89:38–51, since that section relates to Yahweh's apparent rejection of the Davidic king. Furthermore, we thought his analysis of the superscription was weighted toward משכיל and somewhat arbitrary regarding authorship. But his conjecture that a northern psalm (Tabor and Hermon) was reworked into a lament for the debased Davidic throne of Jehoiachin is possible. It would apply to the 597 exile or to any time afterward, including that of 586.

CHAPTER 4 CONCLUSION

The allegory of Ezekiel 16 and the fable of Ezekiel 17 reinforce the sanctity of covenant oaths, e.g., Yahweh–Jerusalem (16:8, 59) and Great Eagle–"prince" (17:13–14). God always abides by his covenants, and he demands the same of a vassal. The exile was the regrettable but necessary corrective for covenant violation by Judah and Jerusalem. Ezekiel's fable addressed the first question in the minds of his audience: "Why has the LORD done this to us?" They ("top of the cedar") were in captivity with Jehoiachin ("topmost bough") under the power of Nebuchadrezzar ("great eagle"). The fable also answered their second unspoken question: "What of those in Jerusalem?" The low vine looked to another eagle in order to be a noble vine. The audience would have recognized the answer to Ezekiel's rhetorical question, "Can he indeed break the covenant and escape?" The demanded response was, "No, nor can anyone else who violates the covenant." (We can only wonder what Jehoiachin thought about being "the topmost bough" in his prison cell.)

To demonstrate his faithfulness, Yahweh promised to take "a slip from the lofty top of a cedar," plant it in Israel, and watch it grow into a noble cedar. Ezekiel 17:22–24 extends the rule of David's house beyond Jehoiachin and Zedekiah in a Messianic ideal (cf. Jer 23:5–6). There was yet hope in God for the "good figs."

Ezekiel 19 is a lament that, although Israel produced "princes" from the abundant waters where the lioness dwelt (vine was planted), there was no strong branch fit for a ruler's scepter. Jehoiachin is a lamented prince only by allusion. Perhaps 19:9 "put in a cage . . . confined in a fortress" refers to his captivity. It is also possible that 19:11–12 is allusive to his accession to the throne ("a mighty rod fit for a ruler's scepter"), the siege of Jerusalem ("plucked up in a fury"), and exile (hurled to the ground").

None of the "princes" was named in Ezekiel 17 and 19, yet the fable and allegory had implicit allusions to the reigns of Jehoiachin and Zedekiah in Judah.

Porteous correctly identified that a *possible* referent to Lamentations 3 could be Jehoiachin's situation. His plaintive lament, "I am the man who has known affliction," could have been read (by a priest) as a part of a cultic ritual. Lamentations 4:20 is probably not a reference to Jehoiachin.

Goulder's argument that Jehoiachin is the referent of Isaiah 52:13–53:12 is too speculative. We can say nothing conclusive regarding Psalm 61 *vis-à-vis* Jehoiachin. Goulder's suggestion that Psalm 89 reflects Jeconiah/Jehoiachin is possible.

CHAPTER 5

Reflections of Jeconiah in Intertestamental and New Testament Literature

INTRODUCTION

ALL OF THE CITATIONS of this chapter are written considerably after the death of Jeconiah in Babylon; e.g., 1 Esdras 1 was written approximately 165 BCE, about the time of the final redaction of the apocryphal book of Baruch, approximately four hundred years after Jeconiah's death. His life as portrayed by the canonical accounts was established primarily in chapters 1 to 3 with additional insights from poetry in chapter 4. This chapter is an investigation of the occurrences of the name Jeconiah (and byforms) in the Apocrypha, Josephus, rabbinical literature, and the New Testament. It is to be expected that the reminiscences of Jeconiah's life would deviate from that of the canonical writings, which were much closer to his reign. There was a clear rehabilitation of Jeconiah after the close of the canonical accounts, occasioned by his captivity. This rehabilitation continues in the New Testament. Matthew's genealogy does not mention Jehoiakim or Zedekiah, Jeconiah's father and uncle; rather, the fourteen-generation motif highlights the progression from Abraham to David to Jeconiah and the exile. From the exile, there are fourteen generations to Jesus Christ. This mnemonic does more than ease memorization. It magnifies the significance of the covenants to Abraham and David and shows Jesus as the heir of the House of David. Although the great failure of the exile seems to be irreconcilable with the Davidic covenant, the construction of the genealogy implies that the redemption of the line of David was accomplished through Jeconiah, Zerubbabel, and Jesus Christ.

INTRODUCTION TO 1 ESDRAS

The pericope in 1 Esdras mentioning Jehoiachin/Jeconiah begins abruptly with a description of the Passover of Josiah in Jerusalem (about 621). First Esdras 1 mimics the canonical accounts (2 Kgs 23, 24; 2 Chr 35, 36) with some notable changes. The book was written after 165 and before Josephus wrote *Antiquities of the Jewish People* (93–94 CE).[1] So at the least the 1 Esdras tradition was written four hundred years after the events described in the canonical narratives.[2] The chapter provides a different outline of the names of the kings and what befell them during their reigns, as shown below.[3]

Figure 2: The Kings of Judah according to 1 Esdras 1

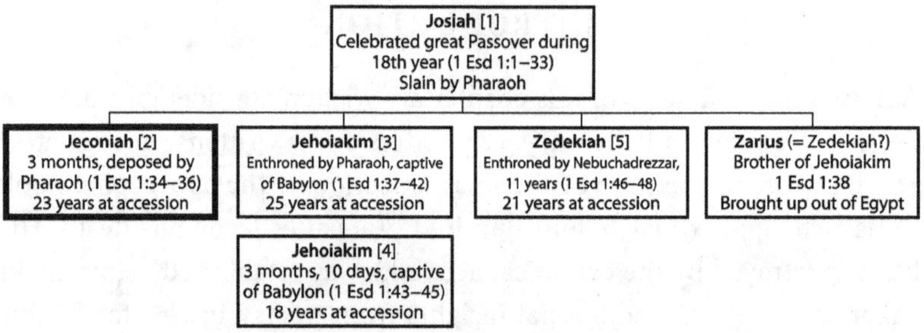

```
                        Josiah [1]
              Celebrated great Passover during
                   18th year (1 Esd 1:1–33)
                       Slain by Pharaoh

Jeconiah [2]        Jehoiakim [3]         Zedekiah [5]           Zarius (= Zedekiah?)
3 months, deposed by Enthroned by Pharaoh, captive Enthroned by Nebuchadrezzar, Brother of Jehoiakim
Pharaoh (1 Esd 1:34–36) of Babylon (1 Esd 1:37–42) 11 years (1 Esd 1:46–48)    1 Esd 1:38
23 years at accession  25 years at accession   21 years at accession    Brought up out of Egypt

                    Jehoiakim [4]
              3 months, 10 days, captive
              of Babylon (1 Esd 1:43–45)
                 18 years at accession
```

Josiah (1 Esdras 1:1–33)

The account begins abruptly during the Passover celebrated by King Josiah in his eighteenth year (1 Esd 1:22). There is no mention of his age upon accession, his mother's name, or the length of his reign. The 1

---

1. Metzger, *The Oxford Annotated Apocrypha*, 1.

2. The implication of these changes is that 1 Esd 1 is a confused account of the last five kings of Judah just prior to the exile to Babylon.

3. In addition to the five named kings, this account includes Zarius, the brother of Jehoiakim, rescued from Egypt (1 Esd 1:38). He is otherwise unknown.

Reflections of Jeconiah in Intertestamental and New Testament Literature

Esdras 1 account also differs from the canonical reports in two distinct ways: (1) the number of calves provided by the Levites (700 in 1 Esd 1:9, 500 in 2 Chr 35:9), and (2) in the warning that Josiah disobeyed in order to confront Neco in battle (Jeremiah in 1 Esd 1:28, Neco in 2 Chr 35:22). The 1 Esdras summary also extends Josiah's deeds beyond that of the canonical summary, i.e., "every one of the acts of Josiah, and his splendor, and his understanding of the law of the Lord, and the things that he had done before and these that are now told, are recorded in the book of the kings of Israel and Judah" (1 Esd 1:33).

The additions to the canonical portrait tend to amplify Josiah's righteousness as a king, but bring into question his wisdom in engaging the Egyptian Pharaoh in battle by disobeying the word of Jeremiah, rather than Pharaoh in 2 Chronicles 35:22.

Jeconiah/Conaniah (1 Esdras 1:9)

In addition to the deviations from the canonical account of Josiah, the author of 1 Esdras also changes the names of the first of three captains over a thousand Levites participating in the Passover (not shown in Fig. 2). Conaniah (Χωνενιας and כוננניהו, 2 Chr 35:9) is changed to Jeconiah (Ιεχονιας) in 1 Esdras 1:9. There is a *kethib/qere* issue over the *waw* in the name Conaniah in the Chronicles account. The *kethib* reflects the *po'lel* form כוננניהו ("Yahweh is strengthened") whereas the *qere* reflects the *qal* כנניהו ("Yahweh strengthened"). The name Conaniah also occurs with the *kethib/qere* in 1 Chronicles 15:27 (וכנניה) and 2 Chronicles 31:12-13 (כוננניהו). Lowery is correct that this could be "for theological reasons (Yahweh could hardly need to be strengthened or made righteous) or the change could be a dialectical difference in the pronunciation between two vowels or a historical difference."[4]

Either the author of 1 Esdras was using a different source, or, more likely, he simply substituted the byform Jeconiah for Conaniah. The reporting of this name Jeconiah in the same chapter with a king by the same name adds to the confusing portrait by the author of 1 Esdras 1.

---

4. Lowery, "Conaniah," 1:1124-25.

Jeconiah (1 Esdras 1:34-36)

1 Esdras 1:34 states that the king who succeeded Josiah was his son Jeconiah, i.e., "the men of the nation (οἱ ἐκ τοῦ ἔθνους) took Jeconiah (Ιεχονιαν) the son of Josiah . . . and made him king in succession to his father." This deviates from the canonical accounts, which report that "the people of the land (עַם הָאָרֶץ) took Jehoahaz (יְהוֹאָחָז) son of Josiah and made him king to succeed his father in Jerusalem" (2 Chr 36:1; 2 Kgs 23:30b; cf. Jer 22:11). It is possible that the author of 1 Esdras misunderstood or downplayed the significance of עַם הָאָרֶץ,[5] for the phrase "the people of the land" (עַם הָאָרֶץ) does not occur in 1 Esdras. As far as the canonical accounts report, there was no Jeconiah son of Josiah. First Chronicles 3:15 lists the sons of Josiah as "Johanan the firstborn, the second Jehoiakim, the third Zedekiah, and the fourth Shallum." The otherwise unknown Johanan son of Josiah might have been confused by the author of 1 Esdras and reported as Jeconiah, but this would be a corruption indeed, for, as far as it is knowable, Johanan never ruled in Judah. The canonical reports are consistent that Jehoahaz (Shallum) succeeded his father when he was 23 years old, reigned three months, and was deposed by Pharaoh.

In the portrait of Jeconiah in 1 Esdras 1:34-35, the author has confused the canonical Jehoahaz son of Josiah with an otherwise unknown Jeconiah son of Josiah. The reign, age upon accession, and particulars about his captivity in Egypt are parallel to the canonical account with the important change from עַם הָאָרֶץ to οἱ ἐκ τοῦ ἔθνους.

Jehoiakim (1 Esdras 1:37-42)

The 1 Esdras 1 account does not mention the name change from Eliakim to Jehoiakim (cf. 2 Kgs 23:34; 2 Chr 36:4). This third king to reign following Josiah was twenty-five years old upon accession, but there is no indication how long he ruled. There is also the otherwise unattested account in 1 Esdras 1:38 that "Jehoiakim put the nobles in prison, and seized his brother Zarius (Ζαριου) and brought him up out of Egypt."[6] Presumably these nobles would be those who opposed Pharaoh Neco, Jehoiakim's

---

5. Myers, *I and II Esdras*, 32.

6. Metzger, *The Oxford Annotated Apocrypha*, 3, opines that "the name *Zarius* is apparently an orthographic corruption (through confusion of the Hebrew letters ד and ר) of Zedekiah, who was a brother of Jehoiakim (2 Kgs 24:17)."

accession, or the fine imposed by Jehoiakim to pay off Neco. It does seem difficult that the vassal (King Jehoiakim) would "seize" his brother in the suzerain's (Neco) kingdom and bring him up "out of Egypt." First Esdras 1:39 adds that "he did evil in the sight of the Lord"—the negative summary that describes him and his two successors portrayed in 1 Esdras 1. First Esdras 1:40–41 reports the binding and transporting of Jehoiakim to Babylon along with some of the vessels of the temple (cf. 2 Chr 36:6–7; 2 Kgs 24:1). The elusive phrase of 2 Chronicles 36:8, "what was found against him," becomes "his uncleanness and impiety" in 1 Esdras 1:42.

The portrait of Jehoiakim in 1 Esdras 1 is similar to that of the canonical accounts (2 Kgs 23:34—24:6; 2 Chr 36:4–8) with the omissions of his name change, the length of his reign, and the circumstances of his death. Notable additions (the imprisonment of the nobles, the seizing of his brother Zarius in Egypt, and his transport in chains to Babylon) tend to amplify Jehoiakim's significance as a wicked king.

Jehoiakim (Ιωακιμ) his son (1 Esdras 1:43–45)

The Greek text of 1 Esdras 1:43 reports that the successor to Jehoiakim was Jehoiakim (Ιωακιμ) his son. This is a significant deviation from the canonical reports (2 Kgs 24:6; 2 Chr 36:8; Jer 22:24 [Coniah, byform of Jehoiachin], cf. 1 Chr 3:16–17), which all specify that Jehoiachin succeeded his father Jehoiakim. First Esdras 1:43–45 reports that this king was eighteen upon accession and ruled three months and ten days. Like Jehoiakim and Zedekiah, but unlike Jeconiah son of Josiah before him, this king did evil in the sight of the Lord. First Esdras 1:45 is confusing. It reports that "after a year (καὶ μετ' ἐνιαυτὸν) Nebuchadrezzar sent and removed him to Babylon, with the holy vessels of the Lord." This conflicts with the note that he completed a reign of three months and ten days. Perhaps it implies the turn of the year, as in 2 Chronicles 36:10 (לתשובת השנה and ἐπιστέφοντες τοῦ ἐνιαυτοῦ), or in Nebuchadrezzar's next regnal year. The canonical reports specify that Nebuchadrezzar came physically to Jerusalem to besiege the city and capture the king (2 Kgs 24:11; 2 Chr 36:10; Esth 2:6; Ezek 17:12).

The portrait of Jehoiakim son of Jehoiakim is of a wicked king who was deposed by the king of Babylon after a short reign. The three months and ten days is telescoped in the following verse, becoming "after a year." Whereas the canonical accounts and the Babylonian Chronicle report that Nebuchadrezzar came personally to depose Jehoiachin, 1 Esdras states that Nebuchadrezzar sent and removed him to Babylon.

Zedekiah (1 Esdras 1:46–48)

Like the previous accounts, 1 Esdras 1:46–48 does not reflect the name change of the king from Mattaniah to Zedekiah (2 Kgs 24:17). The account leaves unnamed Zedekiah's father, which obscures his relationship to Josiah, Jehoiakim, and Jehoiachin. First Esdras 1:48 highlights that, although Nebuchadrezzar made him swear an oath in the name of the Lord (cf. Ezek 17:13–15), "he stiffened his neck and hardened his heart and transgressed the laws of the Lord, the God of Israel." The chapter does not report what happened to Zedekiah. It is vague whether he was slain by the Chaldeans (1:52–53) or transported with the survivors (1:56) to Babylon. This obscures the personal responsibility incumbent upon this king for the downfall of the nation.

The author of 1 Esdras 1 does not explain Zedekiah's relationship to Josiah, Jehoiakim, or his predecessor, Jehoiakim son of Jehoiakim. He did what was evil and did not obey the prophecies of Jeremiah. He violated the oath that Nebuchadrezzar made him swear, but the account left his end uncertain. This incomplete portrait of the final king of Judah and Jerusalem leaves the reader unsettled and unsure of the fate of the kingdom.

How 1 Esdras 1:9ff informs our understanding of Jeconiah

It appears that 1 Esdras 1 is a dubious witness to the reigns of the final kings of Judah. There is evident confusion of the name of the Levite Conaniah, the name of the successor to Josiah, the role of the עַם הָאָרֶץ, and the name of the successor to Jehoiakim. It leaves Zedekiah's reign unresolved. This apocryphal book is not helpful in painting an accurate portrait of the Judean king Jehoiachin/Jeconiah/Coniah taken to Babylon by Nebuchadrezzar in 597. The text of 1 Esdras is replete with errors. The dubious historical account written by the author of 1 Esdras confuses the names of Conaniah (Jeconiah the Levite), Jehoahaz (Jeconiah), Jehoiakim, Jehoiachin (Jehoiakim son of Jehoiakim), and Zedekiah into a collection of byforms and a suspicious succession of kings that deviates from the canonical reports. The account does not have an internally consistent portrait of the kings it depicts. (It was perhaps composed in order to set up the tale of the three wise children and to portray Ezra as one of the key players in the formation of the Old Testament.)

Four hundred years after the events of the downfall of Jerusalem, this author provided a spurious recording of the history of the kingdom of Judah that obscured the importance of these last five kings in Jerusalem. The specific interest of this study regarding Jehoiachin is especially opaque in the reporting of 1 Esdras 1. The account tends to excise Jehoiachin from history.

Williamson raises the possibility that 1 Esdras is an early form of "rewritten Bible,"[7] citing the earlier characterization used explicitly by Vermes with regard to such texts as the *Genesis Apocryphon* from Qumran.[8]

INTRODUCTION TO JOSEPHUS'S WRITINGS REFLECTING JEHOIACHIN

Josephus was born in 37 CE, just a few years after Jesus' death and not much later than Paul's conversion to Christianity. He grew up in Jerusalem, studied with Pharisees, Sadducees, and Essenes, and worked for a time in Jesus' home region of Galilee. Josephus moved to Rome within a decade of Paul's execution there.[9] Josephus comments upon Jeconiah in four passages: *Antiquities of the Jews* (*AJ*) 10:96–102, 139, 229–230; and *Wars of the Jews* (*WJ*) 6:103, which we introduce and then quote.

In the first cited passage, Josephus recounts Nebuchadnezzar's[10] expedition in the eleventh year of Jehoiakim's reign. According to Josephus, Jehoiakim opened the gates so that Nebuchadnezzar could observe the situation in the city. Josephus alludes to covenants agreed by Nebuchadnezzar not to harm the citizens of Jerusalem—covenants that he broke.

---

7. Williamson "The Problem with 1 Esdras," 202.

8. Vermes, *Scripture and Tradition in Judaism*, 67–126. See also Nickelsburg, "The Bible Rewritten and Expanded," 157–84. Nickelsburg explains "rewritten Bible" as "literature that is very closely related to the biblical texts, expanding and paraphrasing them and implicitly commenting on them" (89). See discussion of Feldman regarding "rewritten Bible" later in this chapter.

9. Mason, *Josephus and the New Testament*, 1–3. See also Begg, *Josephus' Story of the Later Monarchy*, and Cohen, *Josephus in Galilee and Rome*.

10. Whereas *Nebuchadrezzar* is the spelling of this name, we retain Josephus's spelling for consistency.

Looking Back for Jehoiachin

The passage explains Jehoiakim's death at the command of Nebuchadnezzar (cf. Jer 22:18–19), posits an exile of three thousand (including the prophet Ezekiel), and states that Nebuchadnezzar installed Jehoiachin, although in other ways it agrees with the canonical reports.

> Now, a little time afterwards, the king of Babylon made an expedition against Jehoiakim, whom he received [into the city], and this out of fear of the foregoing predictions of this prophet [Jeremiah], as supposing he should suffer nothing that was terrible, because he neither shut the gates, nor fought against him; yet when he was come into the city, he did not observe the covenants he had made, but he slew such as were in the flower of their age, and such as were of the greatest dignity, together with their king Jehoiakim, whom he commanded to be thrown before the walls, without any burial; and made his son Jehoiachin king of the country, and of the city: he also took the principal persons in dignity for captives, three thousand in number, and led them away to Babylon; among which was the prophet Ezekiel, who was then but young. And this was the end of king Jehoiakim, when he had lived thirty-six years, and of them reigned eleven. But Jehoiachin succeeded him in the kingdom, whose mother's name was Nehushta; she was a citizen of Jerusalem. He reigned three months and ten days. (*AJ* 10:96–98)

The continuation of the passage relates that Nebuchadnezzar regretted his decision to install Jehoiachin and returned to Jerusalem to remove Jehoiachin and install Zedekiah in his stead. Again, Josephus alludes to covenants agreed by Nebuchadrezzar, but again broken in the siege of Jerusalem. Josephus described Jehoiachin as kind (χρηστός) and just (δίκαιος), the same pair of adjectives that he used of Samuel (*AJ* 6:194), Hezekiah (*AJ* 9:260), Jehoiada (*AJ* 9:166), and Nehemiah (*AJ* 11:183), each of whom was a pivotal figure in Judean history. He attributed Jehoiachin's motive for his surrender to a desire "not . . . to see the city endangered on his account." All of these accolades exceed what the canon reports concerning Jehoiachin, who did evil in the eyes of the Lord (2 Kgs 24:9; 2 Chr 36:9).

> But a terror seized on the king of Babylon, who had given the kingdom to Jehoiachin, and that immediately; he was afraid that he should bear him a grudge, because of his killing his father, and thereupon should make the country revolt from him; wherefore he sent an army, and besieged Jehoiachin in Jerusalem; but because he was of a kind and just disposition, he did not desire to

> see the city endangered on his account, but he took his mother and kindred, and delivered them to the commanders sent by the king of Babylon, and accepted of their oaths, that neither should they suffer any harm, nor the city; which agreement they did not observe for a single year, for the king of Babylon did not keep it, but gave orders to his generals to take all that were in the city captives, both the youth and the handicraftsmen, and bring them bound to him; their number was ten thousand eight hundred and thirty-two; as also Jehoiachin, and his mother and friends. And when these were brought to him, he kept them in custody, and appointed Jehoiachin's uncle, Zedekiah, to be king; and made him take an oath, that he would certainly keep the kingdom for him, and make no innovation, nor have any league of friendship with the Egyptians. (*AJ* 10:99–102)

Josephus relates how Nebuchadnezzar confronted Zedekiah for breaking the covenant and being ungrateful. Josephus reproaches Zedekiah, who received his reign after Nebuchadnezzar deposed Jehoiachin. After killing Zedekiah's sons, Nebuchadnezzar gouged out Zedekiah's eyes and took him to Babylon, where he presumably died.

> When he was come, Nebuchadnezzar began to call him a wicked wretch, and a covenant-breaker, and one that had forgotten his former words, when he promised to keep the country for him. He also reproached him for his ingratitude, that when he had received the kingdom from him, who had taken it from Jehoiachin, and given it to him, he had made use of the power he gave him against him that gave it; "but," said he, "God is great, who hated that conduct of thine, and hath brought thee under us." And when he had used these words to Zedekiah, he commanded his sons and his friends to be slain, while Zedekiah and the rest of the captains looked on; after which he put out the eyes of Zedekiah, and bound him, and carried him to Babylon. (*AJ* 10:138–139)

The Josephus narrative continues with the destruction of Jerusalem and events of the next several years, which we bypass. In *AJ* 10:229–30, Josephus comments upon the release of Jeconiah from prison. Josephus noted that Evil-merodach "esteemed [Jeconiah] among his most intimate friends" and "gave him many presents." The motive for this largesse was his own father Nebuchadnezzar's unfaithfulness to the covenant with Jeconiah at the installation and siege of Jerusalem earlier. Again, this account makes much of the fact that Jeconiah "voluntarily" surrendered in order to save Jerusalem.

> But now, after the death of Nebuchadnezzar, Evil-merodach his son succeeded in the kingdom, who immediately set Jeconiah at liberty, and esteemed him among his most intimate friends. He also gave him many presents, and made him honorable above the rest of the kings that were in Babylon; for his father had not kept his faith with Jeconiah, when he voluntarily delivered up himself to him, with his wives and children, and his whole kindred, for the sake of his country, that it might not be taken by siege, and utterly destroyed. . . . (AJ 10:229–30)

Josephus does not mention Jehoiachin/Jeconiah again in *AJ*, but has recourse to invoke his alleged selflessness in *Wars of the Jews*. In 70 CE, Vespasian approached the city of Gischala and commanded Josephus (at this time a Roman collaborator) to compel the city's capitulation. Josephus initially attempted to decry the character of John of Gischala, who resisted the Romans and stopped offering sacrifices for the emperor.

> . . . Josephus stood in such a place where he might be heard, not by John only, but by many more, and then declared to them what Caesar had given him in charge, and this in the Hebrew language. So he earnestly prayed them to spare their own city, and to prevent that fire which was just ready to seize upon the temple, and to offer their usual sacrifices to God therein. At these words of his a great sadness and silence were observed among the people. But the tyrant himself [John of Gischala] cast many reproaches upon Josephus, with imprecations besides; and at last added this withal, that he did never fear the taking of the city, because it was God's own city. In answer to which Josephus said thus with a loud voice: "To be sure thou hast kept this city wonderfully pure for God's sake; the temple also continues entirely unpolluted! Nor hast thou been guilty of any impiety against him for whose assistance thou hopest! He still receives his accustomed sacrifices! Vile wretch that thou art! If any one should deprive thee of thy daily food, thou wouldst esteem him to be an enemy to thee; but thou hopest to have that God for thy supporter in this war whom thou hast deprived of his everlasting worship; and thou imputest those sins to the Romans, who to this very time take care to have our laws observed, and almost compel these sacrifices to be still offered to God, which have by thy means been intermitted! Who is there that can avoid groans and lamentations at the amazing change that is made in

> this city? Since very foreigners and enemies do now correct that impiety which thou hast occasioned; while thou, who art a Jew, and wast educated in our laws, art become a greater enemy to them than the others." (*WJ* 6:93–102)

When Josephus realized this stratagem was ineffective in dislodging the Judean resisters, he invoked the example of Jeconiah's surrender of Jerusalem. It is difficult to avoid the conclusion that Josephus had mixed motives in his use of this "evidence." He probably would not have pointed to his own surrender of Jotapata to the Romans under shameful circumstances; i.e., Josephus counseled the entire garrison to commit suicide, but when there was only one remaining defender, Josephus convinced his comrade to surrender the garrison and avoid Roman retaliation. Josephus's encomium that Jeconiah was celebrated among the Jews, in their memorials, etc., is not in the canon.

> But still, John, it is never dishonorable to repent, and amend what hath been done amiss, even at the last extremity. Thou hast an instance before thee in Jeconiah, the king of the Jews, if thou hast a mind to save the city, who, when the king of Babylon made war against him, did of his own accord go out of this city before it was taken, and did undergo a voluntary captivity with his family, that the sanctuary might not be delivered up to the enemy, and that he might not see the house of God set on fire; on which account he is celebrated among all the Jews, in their sacred memorials, and his memory is become immortal, and will be conveyed fresh down to our posterity through all ages. This, John, is an excellent example in such a time of danger.... (*WJ* 6:103–106)

Feldman provides the best summary of Josephus's motives in summoning Jehoiachin as exemplar:

> Josephus saw a striking parallel between the events leading to the destruction of both the First and Second Temples, and because he himself acted in a fashion similar to that of Jehoiachin in surrendering to the enemy, he felt a greater necessity to defend Jehoiachin's decision.... As a sole precedent, he cites the instance of Jehoiachin, whose action he refers to as a noble example, in that he voluntarily endured captivity together with his family rather than see the Temple go up in flames. He then, in a veritable peroration and clearly disregarding the biblical

statements that he did evil, remarks that because of this action Jehoiachin is celebrated in sacred story by all Jews and will be remembered forever. It is significant, too, that aside from David and Solomon, Jehoiachin is the only king mentioned by name in the *Jewish War*.[11]

How the writings of Josephus inform our understanding of Jeconiah

Josephus has been bitterly condemned for his (cowardly) surrender to the Romans of the garrison at Jotapata. He was probably aware of the rabbinic traditions that Jehoiachin was motivated to surrender Jerusalem to the Babylonians in order to forestall the burning of the city and razing of the temple. Feldman notes, "This action ... is then blamed not on Jehoiachin but on Nebuchadnezzar, who, we are told, failed to keep his pledge to Jehoiachin"[12] (*AJ* 10:101). Feldman may be too generous to the historian when he states that Josephus was aware of a rabbinic tradition that "Evil-merodach ... rehabilitated and indeed honored Jehoiachin, and that sorrow and suffering changed the latter ... into a saint."[13] While it is true that the rabbinic texts redeem Jehoiachin's activities (see discussion later in this chapter), it is also evident that Josephus tried to mitigate his own conduct by citing his own account of Jehoiachin's activity and neglecting to mention his own perfidy at Jotapata. That Jehoiachin surrendered Jerusalem is clear from the canon and the Babylonian Chronicle. What is less clear is that his motivation was as pure as Josephus portrayed it.

Josephus's writings redeemed Jeconiah's accession, surrender, confinement, and release from captivity. According to Josephus, Nebuchadnezzar initially installed Jehoiachin on the throne of his father Jehoiakim, but later removed him because he feared Jehoiachin might lead a revolt due to the actions taken against his father. This would tend to forestall criticism of Jehoiachin regarding his conduct prior to the siege of Jerusalem in 598. That he was installed and then removed from power by Nebuchadnezzar is nowhere else noted in the literature. This appears to attribute too convenient an investiture to the young king. It also alludes

---

11. Feldman, *Studies in Josephus' Rewritten Bible*, 443–44.
12. Ibid., 444.
13. Ibid., 445.

Reflections of Jeconiah in Intertestamental and New Testament Literature

to Nebuchadnezzar as a covenant breaker with both Jehoiakim and Jehoiachin, which would be corruptions of the canonical accounts, the Babylonian Chronicle, and his status as suzerain over Judah.

Based on Josephus's self-interest, it is apparent that he redeemed Jeconiah's activities in both his *Wars of the Jews* and to a lesser extent the *Antiquities of the Jews*. Although the biblical accounts had their own unique perspectives, Josephus's "rewritten bible," at least in the case of Jeconiah, fits his circumstances too conveniently. (Although our characterization of Josephus may seem a bit harsh, we are grateful that his writings are still extant. Mason's maxim: "Josephus' works often suffer the same fate as the King James Version of the Bible: a perennial bestseller, much loved, occasionally quoted, hardly ever read."[14])

INTRODUCTION TO ADDITIONS TO ESTHER 11:2-4

The Greek additions to the Hebrew text of Esther were probably introduced by Lysimachus, an Alexandrian Jew who lived at Jerusalem and who translated the canonical book of Esther about 114 CE.[15] The additions made the story more vivid, but principally supplied a religious element lacking in the canonical book of Esther. The additions occasionally contradict the canonical book and have little or no historical value. Metzger observed, "both the external and internal evidence indisputably indicate that they were not originally a part of the Esther story but were added later."[16]

Text of Additions to Esther 11:2-4

2In the second year of the reign of Artaxerxes the Great, on the first day of Nisan, Mordecai the son of Jair, son of Shimei, son of Kish, of the tribe of Benjamin, had a dream. 3He was a Jew, dwelling in the city of Susa, a great man, serving in the court of the king. 4He was one of the captives whom Nebuchadnezzar king of Babylon had brought from Jerusalem with Jeconiah king of Judea.

---

14. Mason, 3.
15. Metzger, *The Oxford Annotated Apocrypha*, 96.
16. Moore, *Daniel, Esther and Jeremiah*, 153.

Looking Back for Jehoiachin

How Additions to Esther 11:2–4 informs our understanding of Jeconiah

The Greek additions to Esther are not helpful or necessary for our accounting of Jeconiah. The additions stated that Mordecai came to Babylon with the exiles with Jeconiah (in 597), making him well over one hundred years old. The canonical (Hebrew) account left unsettled whether Mordecai or Kish was exiled with Jeconiah. Esther's great beauty would be unlikely had she come to Babylon with Mordecai, as she would have been very old herself (but compare Sarai's age when she accompanied Abram to Egypt, Gen 12:10–20). As Dancy observes, "Obviously the historical gap was not taken into account by the narrator who, centuries later, was not concerned about, or informed in, chronological data of that type."[17]

INTRODUCTION TO RABBINICAL LITERATURE

The literature we cite is not exhaustive; i.e., there are passages that relate to Jeconiah's circumstances that we will not explore. However, because of the vast amount of material, we have selected representative portions of the Mishnah (*circa* first and second centuries CE) as well as the Palestinian (fifth century CE) and Babylonian Talmuds (sixth century CE).

Midrash by the end of the last century BCE had come to stand for the oral interpretation of the Torah. Haggadah (as opposed to Halakhah commentary on the normative practice of the law) included narratives, historical composition, poetry, speculation, genealogical records, fanciful interpretation, and moral exhortation from all parts of the Bible. Midrash haggadah often indulged in apologetics, rehabilitating the questionable behavior of the patriarchs and Israel's heroes. Piety of conduct and piety of thought were exemplified.[18]

Rabbinic citations

Midrash Rabbah, Leviticus 19:6: This Midrash on the command in Torah for menstrual purity provided a point of departure for the rabbis to illustrate the point. It is an extended haggadah ranging far beyond the initial

---

17. Dancy, *The Shorter Books of the Apocrypha*, 140.
18. Goldin, "Midrash and Aggadah," 9:509–15.

Reflections of Jeconiah in Intertestamental and New Testament Literature

Halakhah, but commenting upon Jeconiah's strict observance of Torah while in the Babylonian prison.

> "And if a woman have an issue of her blood many days . . . All the days of the issue of her uncleanness she shall be as in the days of her impurity: she is unclean." Who observed the precept relating to menstruation? Jeconiah, the son of Jehoiakim. . . .

A long interlude in this midrash addresses the activities of Jehoiakim that do not contribute to our understanding of Jehoiachin. The rabbis' account is similar to that narrated by Josephus; i.e., Nebuchadrezzar installed Jehoiachin on the throne, then changed his mind and removed him to captivity. We will return to the Midrash Rabbah of Leviticus 19:6 after this haggadah about Jehoiachin's return of the temple keys.

> When Nebuchadnezzar put Jehoiakim to death, he appointed Jeconiah king in his place, and went down to Babylon. All the Babylonians came out to praise him, and said to him: "What have you accomplished?" Said he to them: "Jehoiakim rebelled against me and I put him to death, and set up his son Jeconiah as king in his place." Said they to him: "A proverb says: Do not rear a gentle cub of a vicious dog, much less a vicious cub of a vicious dog." He hearkened to them at once and went up to Daphne Antiochena. The Great Sanhedrin went down to meet him, and said to him: "Has then the time arrived for the House [i.e., Temple] to be destroyed?" He said to them: "No, but hand over to me him whom I have set up as king, and I shall depart." They went and said to Jeconiah: "Nebuchadnezzar demands you." What did he [Jeconiah] do?—He collected all the keys of the Temple and ascended the roof [of the Temple], and said: "Lord of the Universe! Seeing that we have hitherto not proved worthy stewards, faithful custodians for Thee, from now and henceforth, behold Thy keys are Thine." Two *Amoraim* [differ as to what followed]. One said: A kind of a fiery hand descended and took them from him; the other said: As he threw them upward they did not come down any more.

Certainly, there is no canonical account of this return of the temple keys to Yahweh. The nature of this midrash is that it comments upon the Torah and helps the reader to understand the rabbis' interpretation of the account. The Midrash Rabbah of Leviticus 19:6 continues with the account of Jeconiah and his wife in his captivity.

Looking Back for Jehoiachin

When Nebuchadnezzar came to have marital intercourse with (his wife), she said to him: "You are king. Is not Jeconiah, too, a king? You desire your sexual satisfaction. Does not Jeconiah, too, desire his sexual satisfaction?" Nebuchadnezzar thereupon ordered that Jeconiah be given his wife. And how did they lower her [into the dungeon] to him? Rabbi Shabbethai said: They lowered her down to him over the bars, whilst the rabbis said: They opened the ceiling and let her down to him. When he was about to have marital intercourse with her, she said to him: "I have seen a discharge the color of a red lily," and he then withdrew from her, and she went away and counted [the seven days of separation] and observed the ritual of purification and of immersion. The Holy One, blessed be He, then said: "In Jerusalem you did not observe the precept relating to issues, but now you are fulfilling it," as it is said, As for thee also, because of the blood of thy covenant I send forth thy prisoners out of the pit (Zech 9:11) [which means], You have remembered the blood at Sinai, and for this do "I send forth thy prisoners." Rabbi Shabbethai said: He [Jeconiah] did not move thence before the Holy One, blessed be He, pardoned him all his sins.

Midrash Rabbah, Song of Songs 7:20: In this midrash, Jeremiah 24:1ff is summoned to comment upon Song of Songs 7:20. Rabbi Levi says Jeconiah and Zedekiah both gave forth a fragrance (both are redeemed by suffering in the rabbinic texts).

"The mandrakes give forth fragrance": . . . Rabbi Levi said: It is written, The Lord showed me, and behold two baskets of figs . . . one basket had very good figs—this refers to the captivity of Jeconiah; the other basket had very bad figs (Jer 24:1f): this refers to the captivity of Zedekiah. Shall we say that the captivity of Jeconiah repented and the captivity of Zedekiah did not repent? Not so, since it says, "the mandrakes give forth fragrance": both the baskets, of the good and of the bad, gave forth fragrance.

Midrash Rabbah, Song of Songs 8:5: Jeremiah 22:24–30, Haggai 2:20–23, and 1 Chronicles 3:17 are all used in this midrash. Note the clear redemption of Jeconiah in the days of his (grand)son Zerubbabel.

Rabbi Meir said: "Set me as a seal upon thy heart, as a seal upon thine arm:" like Jehoiachin. For Rabbi Meir said: The Holy One, blessed be He, swore an oath that He would pluck the kingdom of the house of David from his hand, as it says, As I live, saith the Lord, though Coniah the son of Jehoiakim king of Judah were the signet upon My right hand, yet would I pluck thee thence (Jer 22:24). Rabbi Hanina ben Isaac said: [It means], from there I would pluck the kingdom of the house of David. Another explanation: . . . "I will repair thee," with repentence; in the place from which I plucked thee, there will be thy reparation. Rabbi Ze'ira said: I heard Rabbi Isaac sitting and giving this exposition, and I do not know how he makes it out. Rabbi Aha Arika said to him: Perhaps you may find this lesson in the text, "Write ye this man childless, a man that shall not prosper in his days": [as if to say], in his own days he shall not prosper, but he will prosper in the days of his son, as it is written, In that day, saith the LORD of hosts, will I take thee, O Zerubbabel My servant, the son of Shealtiel, saith the Lord, and will make thee as a signet (Hag 2:23). Rabbi Aha ben Rabbi Abun ben Benjamin said in the name of Rabbi Aha the son of Rabbi Pappi: Great is the power of repentance, which can nullify a decree and nullify an oath. Whence do we know that it nullifies a decree? Because it says, "Write ye this man childless" and yet it says, "In that day, saith the Lord of hosts, will I take thee, O Zerubbabel My servant, etc." Whence do we know that it nullifies an oath? Because it says, "As I live, saith the LORD, though Coniah the son of Jehoiakim were the signet on My right hand, etc.,' and it says elsewhere, And the sons of Jeconiah—the same is Assir-Shealtiel his son (1 Chr 3:17). Rabbi Tanhum ben Rabbi Jeremiah said: He was called Assir because he was fettered in the prison; he was called Shealtiel because from him the kingdom of the house of David was replanted. Another explanation: Assir, because God bound Himself with an oath; Shealtiel, because He applied to the celestial council, and they released Him from His vow.

Midrash Rabbah: Lamentations Prologue 23: This is the poignant account of the exiles of 587 inquiring about the welfare of the 586 exiles.

"And the caperberry shall fail" (Eccl 12:5): this refers to ancestral merit. "Because man goeth to his long home": from Babylon they came and there shall they return. "And the mourners go about the streets": this refers to the exile of Jeconiah. You find that when Nebuchadnezzar went down to Babylon after capturing Jerusalem and the exiles of Zedekiah with him, the exiles of Jeconiah came out to meet him, wearing black underneath but white outside, and hailed him as "conqueror of barbarians!" The exiles of Jeconiah asked those of Zedekiah, "What happened to my father? What happened to my brother? What happened to my children?" They replied, "Such as are for death to death, and such as are for the sword to the sword" (Jer 15:2). They thus praised Nebuchadnezzar with one breath and mourned with the other, to fulfill that which was said, 'Your turbans shall be upon your heads, and your shoes upon your feet; ye shall not make lamentation nor weep' (Ezek 24:23).

Soncino Zohar, Shemoth, Section 2, Page 106a: Jeconiah is shown as an example of repentance; Jeremiah 22:24-30 and 1 Chronicles 3:17 support the haggadah.

> Most assuredly the Holy One accepts every sinner who turns to Him. Such a one is set upon the way of life, and, notwithstanding his former stain, everything is put right and restored to its former position. Even when the Holy One has decreed most solemnly against a person, He forgives entirely where there is a perfect repentance. Thus we find it written concerning Jehoiachin: "As I live, says the Lord, if thou Coniah the son of Jehoiakim were the signet upon my right hand, yet would I pluck thee hence . . . write ye this man childless . . ." (Jer 22:24-30); and yet, when he repented and turned again unto the Lord, we read: "And the sons of Jeconiah, Assir, etc." (1 Chr 3:17), showing that after all he was not childless: which proves that repentance annuls all decrees and judgments, and breaks many an iron chain, and there is nothing that can stand against it.

Talmud, Ma'asroth Sanhedrin 37b-38a: Jeremiah 22:24-30 was again used to support this haggadah that exile as well as repentence are honorable. Note the speculation that Nehemiah was a pseudonym for Zerubbabel.

> Rabbi Johanan said: Exile atones for everything, for it is written, Thus saith the Lord, write ye this man childless, a man that shall not prosper in his days, for no man of his seed shall prosper sitting upon the throne of David and ruling any more in Judah. Whereas after he [the king] was exiled, it is written, And the sons of Jeconiah, — the same is Assir — Shealtiel his son etc. [He was called] Assir, because his mother conceived him in prison. Shealtiel, because God did not plant him in the way that others are planted. We know by tradition that a woman cannot conceive in a standing position. Yet she did conceive standing. Another interpretation: Shealtiel, because God obtained [of the Heavenly court] absolution from His oath. Zerubbabel [was so called] because he was sown in Babylon. But [his real name was] Nehemiah the son of Hachaliah.

Reflections of Jeconiah in Intertestamental and New Testament Literature

Mishna, Ma'asroth Sheqalim Chapter 6: Similarly, *Ma'asroth Middoth* Chapter 2, regarding one of the temple gates:

> "And wherefore was its name called the gate of Jeconiah?" Because through it Jeconiah went forth into his captivity.

How the rabbinical literature informs our understanding of Jeconiah

The rabbis, writing in the Mishnah and Talmuds, had the ability to look back upon the canonical writings of the Hebrew Bible at a distance and with the clarifying purge of the Babylonian captivity. Although Jeconiah's accession, surrender, and exile occurred in 598/597, the rabbis had the benefit of unimpeded views of 2 Kings, 1 and 2 Chronicles, Isaiah, Jeremiah, Ezekiel, Haggai, Esther, Lamentations, and the Psalter. Whether they had or used apocryphal writings is uncertain, although 1 Esdras 1 was followed in Josephus, and the rabbinic traditions cohere with Josephus in many places. Because of this viewpoint, they were able to interpret a wide range of Scriptures of interest to their communities. The Davidic line was of special interest because of the covenant in 2 Samuel 7. When Zedekiah's sons were killed in Hamath in 586, the only Davidic survivors were those born to Jeconiah. Reflections on the historical events gave an opportunity for their theological reflections. Many of these were wildly speculative, e.g., Midrash Rabbah Leviticus 19:6, Jeconiah collecting the keys of the temple and returning them to God. This midrash follows the account of Nebuchadrezzar installing Jeconiah as king, then returning later to depose him just as Josephus outlined the events in *AJ* 10:99–102. That this deviates from the canonical text was not the principal concern. It is interesting that King Jeconiah was chosen to return the keys rather than one of the Levitical priests, as one one might have expected. Could this be a "good figs" reflection from Jeremiah 24:1?

The midrash states that Nebuchadrezzar put Jehoiakim to death and installed Jeconiah in his stead. This would have necessitated Nebuchadrezzar's follow-on decision. That the Babylonians referred to Jeconiah as a "vicious cub of a vicious dog" may reflect the tone of the fable of Ezekiel 19—the mother lioness trained her cubs to "tear the prey and devour men." For this reason, Nebuchadrezzar came down to besiege

Looking Back for Jehoiachin

Jerusalem a second time. The great Sanhedrin explained to Jeconiah that Nebuchadrezzar "demands you." This provoked Jeconiah to surrender the keys to the temple.

Louis Feldman, citing Margaliyot, remarks that "the Bible says not a word that is positive about Jeconiah, whereas the rabbinic tradition has only complimentary statements and not a single negative remark about him."[19] It seems that the rabbinic tradition, presumably based upon 2 Kings 25:27–30 and Jeremiah 52:31–33, rehabilitated and honored Jehoiachin and declared that sorrow and suffering had changed him into a saint. Indeed, so great is the tradition's regard for Jehoiachin that one of the gates of the temple, when it was rebuilt, was named for Jeconiah.[20] A rabbinic tradition holds that Jeconiah brought the ark from the Jerusalem temple and built a synagogue in the Babylonian city of Nehardea, and that the Shekinah dwelt there from time to time.[21]

INTRODUCTION TO BARUCH 1:3–9

The apocryphal book Baruch purports to be written by Jeremiah's amanuensis and secretary, but "there is no valid reason to regard any of Baruch as being composed by Baruch son of Neriah."[22] The text of the book is confusing, disjointed, and problematic. Baruch 1:1 states that the book was written in Babylon, yet Baruch son of Neraiah was taken to Egypt from Judah with Jeremiah after the assassination of Gedaliah (Jer 43:6–7). Baruch 1:2 incorrectly dates the destruction of Jerusalem to the fifth year. Furthermore, Baruch 1:3 states that Baruch read the words of the book in the hearing of Jeconiah, yet 1:5–14 recount events after this supposed reading of the book. Presumably, whatever was read aloud by Baruch (not the text of 1:5–14) resulted in mourning and contributing money to be sent to the high priest in Jerusalem. Further undermining the veracity of the book is the indication in 1:2 that this all transpired after Jerusalem had been burned, yet the book was to be provided to priests performing ritual sacrifice at the (currently razed) temple (1:10, 12). The

---

19. Feldman in *Studies*, 445–46. Margaliyot, Eliezer. *Positive [Depictions] in the Bible and Negaitve [Depictions] in the Talmud and in the Midrashim*. London: Ararat, 1949.

20. Feldman, *Studies*, 445.

21. *Seder Olam* 25, Tosefta *Sheqalim* 2.18, cited by Feldman, *Studies*, 445–46.

22. Moore, *Daniel, Esther, and Jeremiah: The Addtions*, 255.

Reflections of Jeconiah in Intertestamental and New Testament Literature

"silver vessels which Zedekiah . . . had made" could not have been taken into exile with Jeconiah. In reality, Zedekiah's vessels had been made in Jerusalem after Jeconiah's exile in order to replace the vessels taken to Babylon. The vessels of the temple were in Babylon and Nebuchadrezzar would not have surrendered them to Baruch to transport. The evident confusion of events, sequences, and details underpins the expectation that this book will not be a helpful resource in shedding light on Jeconiah. Baruch 1:1–14 mentions Jeconiah twice, neither time very helpfully.

But, recognizing that the scribe Baruch son of Neraiah[23] did not write the apocryphal book that bears his name, there is still utility in asking who wrote it and what was the purpose in linking it to Jeconiah and the exile. As to the actual author, we know little (cf. Lysimachus, the author of Additions to Esther). But we can surmise why this author, writing between 150 and 60, might have used this setting.[24] Once the decision to write under the pseudonym Baruch son of Neraiah was made, a setting contemporaneous to his existence had to be selected. Perhaps the public readings portrayed by Jeremiah 36 suggested the need for an expansion upon the canonical account, e.g., "It was then that Baruch—in the chamber of Gemariah son of Shaphan the scribe, in the upper court, near the new gateway of the House of the LORD—read the words of Jeremiah from the scroll to all the people in the House of the LORD," (Jer 36:10). This suggests the activity of the opening section of the apocryphal account. Perhaps the author could not resist fleshing out the idea of a letter read before the exiles in Babylon concerning a descendent of Shallum and the House of the LORD (Jer 29:1–3). A setting in the midst of the Babylonian exiles would have elicited far greater interest due to the cumulative weight of adherence to Jeremiah's prophecies and those of Ezekiel. Very little weight was attached to literature from an Egyptian provenance after the return of the exiles under Cyrus.

The Text of Baruch 1:1–14[25]

1 These are the words of the book which Baruch the son of Neraiah, son of Mahseiah, son of Zedekiah, son of Hasadiah, son of Hilkiah, wrote in Babylon, 2 in the fifth year, on the

---

23. See Avigad, *Jewish Quarter Excavations*.
24. Metzger, *The Oxford Annotated Apocrypha*, 198.
25. From the NRSV.

Looking Back for Jehoiachin

seventh day of the month, at the time when the Chaldeans took Jerusalem and burned it with fire. 3And Baruch read the words of this book in the hearing of Jeconiah the son of Jehoiakim, king of Judah, and in the hearing of all the people who came to hear the book, 4and in the hearing of the mighty men and the princes, and in the hearing of the elders, and in the hearing of all the people, small and great, all who dwelt in Babylon by the river Sud.

5Then they wept, and fasted, and prayed before the Lord; 6and they collected money, each giving what he could; 7and they sent it to Jerusalem to Jehoiakim the high priest, the son of Hilkiah, son of Shallum, and to the priests, and to all the people who were present with him in Jerusalem. 8At the same time, on the tenth day of Sivan, Baruch took the vessels of the house of the LORD, which had been carried away from the temple, to return them to the land of Judah—the silver vessels which Zedekiah the son of Josiah, king of Judah, had made, 9after Nebuchadnezzar king of Babylon had carried away from Jerusalem Jeconiah and the princes and the prisoners and the mighty men and the people of the land, and brought them to Babylon.

10And they said: "Herewith we send you money; so buy with the money burnt offerings and sin offerings and incense, and prepare a cereal offering, and offer them upon the altar of the LORD our God; 11and pray for the life of Nebuchadnezzar king of Babylon, and for the life of Belshazzar his son, that their days on earth may be like the days of heaven. 12And the LORD will give us strength, and he will give light to our eyes, and we shall live under the protection of Nebuchadnezzar king of Babylon, and under the protection of Belshazzar his son, and we shall serve them many days and find favor in their sight. 13And pray for us to the LORD our God, for we have sinned against the LORD our God, and to this day the anger of the LORD and his wrath have not turned away from us. 14And you shall read this book which we are sending you, to make your confession in the house of the LORD on the days of the feasts and at appointed seasons.

How Baruch 1:1–14 informs our understanding of Jeconiah

The notation that Baruch is a work of fiction by an author writing more than four hundred years after the death of Jeconiah does not oblige us to dismiss the work. We venture into the uneasy arena of speculation when asking why the author would have chosen to link the work to Jeconiah.

That the book is not linked to the destruction of Jerusalem in 586, but rather to that of the exile eleven years earlier, seems to suggest that Jeconiah was the legitimate king of Judah even during Zedekiah's reign. Beyond this uncertain explanation, we can only appreciate that the author felt Jeconiah's situation warranted sufficient interest to include his name twice.

Introduction to Matthew 1:1-17

According to Hagner, the literary genre of Matthew 1:1-17 is midrashic haggadah, "consisting of an historical core with theological elaboration."[26] We do not mean to suggest that Matthew ignored the historical antecedents of this name list, but rather that he used existing genealogies (1 Chr 1:34; 2:1-13; 3:1-19; Ruth 4:18-22) and shaped them to show their theological significance. There were names omitted from the Davidic kings (Ahaziah, Jehoash, Amaziah) and emphasis on four women (though they had no legal status in Jewish genealogies), all incorporated into three groups of fourteen generations in order to show God's faithfulness in fulfilling the covenants with Abraham and David despite the chastening of the captivity. The chiastic design of the genealogy is evident from the inclusio of 1:1: Χριστου . . . Δαυίδ . . . Αβρααμ, and 1:17, Αβρααμ . . . Δαυίδ . . . Χριστοῦ.

"The story of Jesus doesn't begin with Jesus."[27] Matthew set forth Jesus' pedigree at the outset of his account of the gospel.[28] Although this genealogy begins with Abraham, it extends through the line of David to Jeconiah, culminating in Jesus Christ. Matthew's intent is to set Jesus in his "world historical context."[29] We could never mistake Matthew 1:1-17 as the story of Jeconiah. He is only a linking player in the drama beginning with Abraham and culminating in Jesus Christ. In this pericope, there are four names (Abraham, David, Jeconiah, and Jesus) as the terminal points of three sections of salvation history. The period from Abraham to David (1:2-6a) establishes a template for the succeeding generations; i.e., "Abraham was the father of Isaac, Isaac the father

---

26. Hagner, *Matthew 1-13*, 27. Although the terms "midrash haggadah" are very imprecise, we employ them for now.

27. E. H, Peterson, *The Message Remix*, 1764.

28. Mounce, *Matthew*, 7.

29. Ibid., 1764.

Looking Back for Jehoiachin

of Jacob, Jacob the father of Judah and his brothers" is the motif we see repeated in succeeding sections. Section two encompasses the period from David to Jeconiah and the Babylonian exile (1:6b–11). "And David became the father of Solomon . . ." begins the section that ends with, "and Josiah the father of Jeconiah and his brothers, at the time of the exile to Babylon." The closing of this section is parallel to the opening of section one. Section three contains the period from (Jeconiah) the exile to Jesus: "And after the exile to Babylon, Jeconiah became the father of Shealtiel . . ." and closes with "Jacob was the father of Joseph, the husband of Mary, of whom God brought forth Jesus who is called 'Christ.'" This last list of forebears is not otherwise attested. The genealogy in Luke differs from the Matthean genealogy at Zerubbabel son of Shealtiel (Luke 3:27), skipping the kings of Judah (Jeconiah to Solomon), and tracing the lineage from Nathan son of David. From 3:32–34, the generations David to Abraham agree with Matthew 1:2–6.

Text of Matthew 1:11–17

11 Josiah became the father of Jeconiah[a] and his brothers,[b] at the time of the deportation to Babylon.

12 After the deportation to Babylon:[a] Jeconiah became the father of Shealtiel,[b] and Shealtiel the father of Zerubbabel. 13 Zerubbabel was the father of Abihud, Abihud the father of Eliakim, and Eliakim the father of Azor. 14 Azor was the father of Zadok, Zadok the father of Achim, and Achim the father of Eliud. 15 Eliud was the father of Eleazar, Eleazar the father of Matthan, and Matthan the father of Jacob. 16 Jacob was the father of Joseph the husband of Mary, by whom Jesus was born,[a] who is called the Messiah.

17 So all the generations from Abraham to David are fourteen generations; from David to the deportation to Babylon, fourteen generations; and from the deportation to Babylon to the Messiah, fourteen generations.

Text notes

11a: Several late uncials (M U Θ S) and other witnesses (ƒ1 33 661 syh) add "τὸν Ἰωακίμ . . . Ἰωακίμ δὲ ἐγέννησεν," rendering 1:11, "Josiah became the father of Jehoiakim, and Jehoiakim became the father of

Jeconiah and his brothers." This accomplishes a harmonization with 1 Chronicles 3, 2 Kings 24, and Jeremiah 22, but changes the second section of the genealogy to fifteen names instead of the fourteen that Matthew accounted for in 1:17. The English spelling of Jec(h)oniah with and without the medial "h" is a function of the rendition of the Hebrew כ or the Greek χ.

11b: καὶ τοὺς ἀδελφοὺς αὐτοῦ, "and his brothers," seems to be a stylistic device used to bring the account of Jeconiah into parallel with "Judah and his brothers" (1:2), a reference to the twelve tribes of Israel.

12a: Rather than repeating Jeconiah's name, the significant event of the Babylonian exile becomes the reference point. This fits the disruptive pattern of 1:6 where "the king" intervenes between the first section and the second section. In this second section, the "exile to Babylon" performs as the disjunctive departure into the third section.

12b: Shealtiel is the spelling of the Greek Σαλαθιήλ, the NT rendering of שאלתיאל, in 1 Chronicles 3:17. English versions use alternate spellings, e.g., NASB, JPS, NIV, and RSV use Shealtiel; NRSV and KJV use Salathiel.

16a: "Of whom was born" reflects ἐξ ἧς ἐγεννήθη, an aorist passive change to the repetition of unbroken aorist active ἐγέννησεν, from γεννάω. This follows the disjunctive pattern ("the king" in 1:6, "the exile to Babylon" in 1:11–12) and brings the third section to a close. Furthermore, it shifts the genealogy from that of Joseph to Mary and ultimately to Jesus, "who was called Christ."

How Matthew 1:11–16 informs our understanding of Jeconiah

Matthew's genealogy provides the ultimate rehabilitation of the legacy of Jeconiah. In his lifetime, he did not prosper on the throne of David, underlined in the genealogy with the moniker "Babylonian exile."

A key textual issue is found at 1:11, "Josiah became the father of Jeconiah." Josiah was the father of Jehoiakim who was the father of Jeconiah according to the genealogies in 2 Kings and 1 Chronicles. But Matthew was not required to include every name in the genealogy. It is possible that Jehoiakim ended the second group of fourteen names and was lost in copying due to haplography. If this were true, Jeconiah began the third group of names—but this would not follow the template of repeating names in sections one and two. Without additional evidence, we retained 1:11 and left the number of names in the third section at thirteen.

The reference to "Jeconiah and his brothers" (1:11) suggests the earlier occurrence of "Judah and his brothers" (1:2) rather than the three brothers of Jehoiakim (Johanan, Zedekiah, and Shallum) named in 1 Chronicles 3:15 (contra Hagner), two of whom ruled, but none of whom was counted in Matthew's name list. If this reflects a midrash haggadah as we propose, then the deletion of kings Jehoahaz, Jehoiakim, and Zedekiah places a premium on the last member of the fourteen-generation list. Certainly, in his three-month reign, there was nothing to set Jeconiah apart, other than the desire (proclaimed by Josephus) to avoid the destruction of Jerusalem. Otherwise, in his service in Jerusalem, Jeconiah was undistinguished, but in his exile he gained a prominent place in the salvation history of Israel and Judah. His "son" Jesus Christ provided the ultimate rehabilitation of his legacy.

CHAPTER 5 CONCLUSION

This chapter has been an investigation of the later writings about Jeconiah. The reflections of his life and legacy were written four hundred or more years after his death in Babylon, well after the conclusion of Chronicles. There is minor tension between the accounts of Jeconiah's life in 2 Kings and 2 Chronicles—e.g., age at accession (eighteen or eight), reign duration (ninety or one hundred days), and relation to his successor (nephew or brother)—over the couple hundred years between the recordings of those books. So it should not be surprising that the many centuries-on reflections should introduce even more tension. There is a weighty disparity between the canonical view that Jeconiah "did evil in the eyes of the LORD" (2 Kgs 24:9; 2 Chr 36:9) and that he was "kind and just" (*AJ* 10:100), "celebrated among all the Jews, in their sacred memorials, and his memory is become immortal" (*WJ* 6:103). The rabbis said that God was so impressed with Jeconiah's observance of Halakhah that "He pardoned him all his sins"—a considerable revision for the man called "a vicious cub of a vicious dog" (Midrash Rabbah, Lev 19:6).

The 1 Esdras 1 account is a dubious recording of the final years of Judah, e.g., after Josiah's celebration of Passover and untimely death, he was succeeded by Jeconiah son of Josiah. This error and the following account are obvious departures from the canonical age, reign, appointment,

Reflections of Jeconiah in Intertestamental and New Testament Literature

and removal of Jehoahaz. Additional errors in the 1 Esdras 1 portraits of Jeconiah render Esdras suspect for accurate accounts of this king. The book may have been written as an apology for the three children (1 Esd 3:1—5:6), or to "emphasize the contributions of Josiah, Zerubbabel, and Ezra to the reform of Israelite worship,"[30] but it offers nothing of substance in our quest to understand Jeconiah's life and legacy.

The doubtful contribution of Additions to Esther 11 was that Mordecai, exiled with Jeconiah in 597, was at least one hundred twenty-two years old at the time of the events of the canonical book of Esther. Mordecai was not one of the exiles from the third year of Jehoiakim (Dan 1:1–3) or the "bad figs" of 586. His distinguished genealogy and the circumstances for his arrival in Susa made him a suitable champion for the Jews in the Persian kingdom.

Baruch reputedly read his treatise in the ears of Jeconiah in Babylon. Although this patently conflicts with the biblical location of Baruch son of Neraiah in Egypt (Jer 43:6–7), it was perhaps suggested by the public reading of Jeremiah's scroll (36:10). It could be that the apocryphal author wrote to pique the interest of the descendants of the Babylonian exile.

The genealogy in Matthew 1 is the most significant amendment to the legacy of Jeconiah in the Bible. He is the linking name between Abraham, David, and Jesus Christ. His name would always be associated with the exile, even though there were four kings in the decaying spiral that led to the Babylonian captivity. When considered with the genealogy in Luke 3, the gospel lineage of Jesus begins in Abraham, coheres in David, diverges at Jeconiah, and recommences at Zerubbabel.

The process of rehabilitating Jeconiah by these later authors seems to relate to their different motives. Josephus's agenda appeared to be self-interest. By summoning Jeconiah's voluntary surrender of Jerusalem, Josephus was able to commend a similar action to John of Gischala. By so doing, he could also set aside his own surrender of Jotapata. The Rabbis were involved in reading rabbinic Judaism back into the biblical account. The practice of Halakhah and haggadah were means of interpreting for their Jewish constituents the implications of life after the exile. Matthew employed this midrash haggadah to shape the previously existing name lists into a genealogy that shows Jesus as the inheritor and fulfillment of the covenants of Abraham (Gen 12:1–3; 15:4–6, 18–21; 17:1–21) and David (2 Sam 7). Despite the exile intimated by Jeremiah's curse of Jeconiah

---

30. Metzger, *The Oxford Annotated Apocrypha*, 1.

Looking Back for Jehoiachin

(Jer 22:24–30), Yahweh elected to set Zerubbabel as the signet (Hag 2:23), a position that Jesus rightfully occupied.

CHAPTER 6

Conclusion

THIS BOOK ATTEMPTS TO assemble the biblical, postbiblical, and inscriptional portraits of Jehoiachin son of Jehoiakim, the last living king of Judah. His life provoked an extraordinary amount of literature. We argue for an optimistic portrayal of Jehoiachin's tragic life and redeemed legacy: tragic in that he was cast-off due to curses on the kings from Hezekiah to Zedekiah, yet redeemed by Yahweh, the covenant-keeping God who chose to return his signet to Jerusalem, temporarily in Zerubbabel and eternally in the Son of God.

In *Looking Back for Jehoiachin*, it may be useful to consider the pericopes as portraits in a gallery of Israel's history. In this conclusion, we will revisit Jehoiachin's part in that history by viewing the portraits in the introduction and the successive chapters.

In the introduction, the metaphorical foyer of our portrait gallery, we considered the method involved in looking back for this king. We examined his various names (Jehoiachin, Coniah, Jeconiah, and *Yaukin*), a chart of the Davidic dynasty (see page xiv), and a sketch of the setting in which he was a participant. We looked briefly at some inscriptions that attest the historical details of the portraits. An overview of the gallery by chapters (call them halls) led us out of the introduction and into the portrait halls.

In the first hall, we saw only four Jehoiachin portraits. We did not focus on portraits of kings, pharaohs, and scenes of the sixth-century Levant. We did glance at the portraits of the kings immediately preceding

Conclusion

and following the 597 BC exile. In the *Surrender* paintings on one side of the hall, we noted that the artist of the 2 Kings 24 portrait has painted an eighteen-year-old prince surrounded by Chaldean chaos, surrendering with his family and 10,000 citizens. The artist of 2 Chronicles 36, with a later view of the surrender scene, painted it slightly differently, but only by nuance: exile/tribute of the last four kings, brother (אחיו) instead of uncle (אחי אביו), and a misplaced עשרה regarding Jehoiachin's age/reign. This (flaw?) persisted in portraits seen later in the gallery (1 Esd 1; *AJ* 10.98).

Still in the first hall, but on the opposite wall, labeled *King's Coda*, are the happier portraits of the recently released old king at a banquet, 2 Kings 25 and Jeremiah 52. Reclothed for a royal audience, he sat at his exalted seat above the other captive kings. Jeremiah 52 was probably a revision of 2 Kings 25 with the appending of Jehoiachin's obituary. When these two portraits are viewed beside the perspective of the 2 Chronicles 36 restoration of Cyrus, we sense that Yahweh was performing a new work out of the tragedy of the exile. Understanding what we saw in the foyer and first hall helps as we move forward.

In the second hall, there were eight (Jeremiah) portraits of this king who had three names. We were drawn to the first two that did not mention him by name, but his situation is outlined in the sketches: Jeremiah 36 "None to Sit on David's Throne" and Jeremiah 13 "All Judah Going into Exile."

The artist of 2 Kings 22–23 painted a positive likeness of Josiah, the king of restored covenants. "None to Sit on David's Throne" is a rousing condemnation of Jehoiakim, king of broken covenants. Yahweh was going to punish (פקד) Jehoiakim, his son (זרעו), Judah, and Jerusalem.

"All Judah Going into Exile" is pathetic and instructive, probably spoken to Jeconiah and Nehushta. The young king's surrender to Nebuchadrezzar may have had its inspiration here.

We moved on in the Jeremiah hall to the *Afterthoughts*, paintings on both the (preferred LXX) thin canvas and the MT enriched fabric by artists (Jeremiah 27:22 extends the provision of Yahweh's watch-care to the temple vessels).

The dominant painting in the Jeremiah hall is the violent "Signet Hurling," Jeremiah 22. Coniah had once been, but was no longer to be, Yahweh's signet. He was plucked off, handed off to those whom he feared, and cast off (טול) into a foreign land to die. He was declared "childless" (ערירי), for none of his offspring (זרע) would reign on the throne of

Conclusion

David (a brush stroke from "None to Sit on David's Throne," Jeremiah 36). When we came to the gallery, we were sure that the exile was God's punishment, but perhaps Yahweh had a provision planned. We saw the unexpected "Good Figs" portrait (Jeremiah 24) and two side-by-side paintings depicting the ultimate fate of the temple vessels. (God is more interested in obedience than sacrifice). The first showed a letter to the exiles: "Build and Multiply," (Jeremiah 29). The second (Jeremiah 37) was a portrait of Coniah's ne'er-do-well uncle Zedekiah—a pitiable *prince*, not in the line of succession, appointed by Nebuchadnezzar, and encumbered with a disobedient bureaucracy—leader of the pejorative "bad figs" exile.

Strolling into the third hall, we briefly observed four miscellaneous portraits. The first (Ezekiel 1) shows that the dating of Ezekiel is based on the exile of Jehoiachin, *not* Zedekiah. The second (1 Chronicles 3) is a genealogy portrait with brushstrokes from the Chronicler's sketchbook: the descendants of King David, including Jeconiah (the captive), Zerubbabel, and (seven?) generations into the time of Herod's temple. The Haggai 2 portrait looks like a major repainting of the term (החותם) of Jeremiah. Unusually precisely dated, it depicts Yahweh taking his servant Zerubbabel and setting him like a signet (כחותם) because he was chosen. Lastly, there is a small likeness of Mordecai (Esther 2), whose distinguished forebears were exiled with Jeconiah.

The fourth hall on the left is full of poetic murals. There are no names because these works illustrate concepts more profound than Jehoiachin or any individual's life story. An allegory of cedars and vines (Ezekiel 17) is next to a painting of lions and vines (Ezekiel 19). These are full of mysterious and meaningful allusions, but there are strong indications that Jehoiachin is in both paintings. Nearby is a poignant painting, "The Man who Has Known Affliction," which may show our exiled king in Lamentations 3. The Psalm 61 portrait could be of any Davidic king. The Psalm 89 portrait starts by rejoicing in Yahweh's promise of an eternal throne for David, but is blemished by the profound tragedy of David's debased throne (marks from Jer 13?). We may see Jehoiachin's complicity in that portrait; he was portrayed in the curses in 2 Kings and 2 Chronicles (ויעש הרע בעיני יהוה). The dominant image in this hall is that of the Suffering Servant (Isaiah 53). One observer is positive that it is a portrait of Jeconiah.

(Although we feel Professor Goulder may be very close to the mark with Psalm 89, we are dubious about his speculation that Jeconiah is

Conclusion

the Suffering Servant. Staying with the gallery metaphor, we recall that, when an American buyer duped the unsuspecting owner of Peter Paul Rubens's painting *Daniel in the Lion's Den* for £1000 and fled the country, the British public was mortified. In a similar way, we are chagrined that the exquisite literary masterpiece of Isaiah 52:13—53:12 is *solved* by substituting Jeconiah's name against that of the Suffering Servant. As interesting as Goulder's speculations are, if we are to consider this tragic king the fulfillment of the portrait, perhaps we have sold the Suffering Servant too cheaply.)

The portraits in the last hall of the gallery are reflections upon Jeconiah's legacy four hundred years after his epitaph in Babylon, well after the completion of the Chronicler's portraits. The colors in this hall reflect a much brighter shade than those of the Hebrew Bible. There is a weighty disparity between the canonical portraits that Jeconiah "did evil in the eyes of the LORD" (2 Kings 24 and 2 Chronicles 36) and that he was "kind," "just," and "celebrated among all the Jews," (Josephus).

Off in a dreary corner of this intertestamental hall hang three apocryphal paintings of kings and priests (1 Esdras 1), a caricature of Mordecai as an old man (Additions to Esther), and a strange letter to the exiles (Baruch 1). These confused likenesses are dwarfed by three large sectional paintings. The Josephus paintings show our king with powerful strokes saving Jerusalem; Jeconiah appears more heroic than in any of the other halls. Rabbis from an artist's school also painted Jeconiah better than life, but they had the benefit of careful study in all the previous halls and a hermeneutical flair for telling their congregations how to live under Torah. The last mural is a NT genealogy (Matthew 1) showing three unmistakably imposing kings and our own diminutive Jeconiah. Covenant favor was promised to Abraham in Genesis 12 and David in 2 Samuel 7 and Psalm 89. (We know God always keeps covenant even if we don't understand. The Gallery of Ancient Israel is full of portraits of his faithfulness and mercy.) Yet, Jeconiah stands in the trough of the exile. We suggest he did not understand his part in the gallery. But God is faithful and will not cast-out his signet forever. Jeconiah died in Babylon shortly after he was providentially invited to the table of the king. His grandson Zerubbabel, the temporary signet (כחותם), was the leader of the restoration decreed by Cyrus in 2 Chronicles 36. But the profound and permanent redemption of Jeconiah's legacy was in God's covenant faithfulness in providing Jesus Christ.

Conclusion

Matthew 1 is not the legacy of Jeconiah in the Bible. Matthew 1 is the trajectory of God's faithfulness to Abraham and David, even through exile, redeemed by Christ. Jeconiah is forever associated with the exile (suggesting אסר?), linking Abraham, David, and Jesus Christ. When considered even tangentially with the Luke 3 genealogy, the lineage of Jesus originates in Abraham, concentrates at David, is cast-off at Jeconiah, and recommences at Zerubbabel. Despite the exile intimated by Jeremiah 22:24–30, Yahweh set Zerubbabel as the signet (Haggai 2:23), a position that Jesus would rightfully fulfill.

This was a limited study. Because of our specific interests, we did not consider Joseph's elevation as Pharaoh's regent, Mephibosheth's elevation to David's table, Mordecai's election as Ahasuerus's signet keeper, or Daniel's elevation as Nebuchadrezzar's vizier as historic antecedents to Jehoiachin's elevation to the Babylonian table. We bypassed the ending of the Solomonic line and did not investigate the Luke 3 genealogy that excludes the kings, favoring instead the line of Nathan son of David. We did not consider Gedaliah in the portraits of the final kings or a royal pedigree of Nehemiah (suggested in *AJ* and Talmud *Ma'asroth Sanhedrin* 37b–38a, 183). The study did not delve into the exile of Jehoiakim's third year described in Daniel 1:1–3. We did not work on Nehushta daughter of Elnathan and artifacts that link her to Jerusalem. We did not work on the successors to Zerubbabel in 1 Chronicles 3:19b–24 or investigate the reference to Zerubbabel in Sirach 49. We steered clear of the Sheshbazzar/Shenazzar controversy.

We were anticipating a discussion of the implications of the Dead Sea Scrolls (4QJer^c, 1QIsa^b, 4QPs^e, 4Q174, and 5QLam^{a-b}), but the required text-critical work (primarily in poetry) took us beyond the scope of this defined project. Regrettably, we had to fence them from this study because the details exceed our parameters. We only provided a surface treatment of rabbinical literature and Josephus writings, relying on expert assistance from the faculty at New College.

Perhaps future studies could focus on these areas. We believe Stephen G. Dempster's Biblical Theology reflecting Jehoiachin's release as a key to the structure of the *Tanakh* will be a profitable pursuit.

Bibliography

Achtemeier, Elizabeth R. *Nahum-Malachi*. Interpretation: A Bible Commentary for Teaching and Preaching. Atlanta: John Knox Press, 1986.
Ackroyd, P. R. "The Temple Vessels—A Continuity Theme." In *Studies in the Religion of Ancient Israel*, Vetus Testamentum Supplement 23, 46-60. Leiden: Brill, 1972.
———. "Chronicles-Ezra-Nehemiah: Concept of Unity." Zeitschrift für die alttestamentliche Wissenschaft Supplement 100 (1988): 189-201.
———. "Historians and Prophets." *Svensk Exegetisk Årsbok* 33 (1968): 18-54.
Adler, William. "Exodus 6:23 and the High Priest from the Tribe of Judah." *Journal of Theological Studies* 48 (1997): 24-47.
Aharoni, Y. *The Land of the Bible*. Translated by A. F. Rainey. Philadelphia: Westminster, 1979.
———. "Arad: Its Inscriptions and Temple." *Biblical Archaeologist* 31 (1968): 2-33.
Albertz, Rainer. "Wer waren die Deuteronomisten? Das historische Rätsel einer literarischen Hypothese." *Evangelische Theologie* 57 (1997): 319-38.
Albrektson, B. *Studies in the Text and Theology of the Book of Lamentations*. Lund: Gleerup, 1963.
———. *History and the Gods: An Essay on the Idea of Historical Events as Divine Manifestations in the Ancient Near East and Israel*. Lund: Coniectanea Biblica, 1967.
Albright, W. F. "King Jehoiachin in Exile." *Biblical Archaeology Review* 1 (1956): 106-12.
———. "The Seal of Eliakim and the latest Pre-exilic History of Judah." *Journal of Biblical Literature* 51 (1932): 77-106.
———. *Archaeology and the Religion of Israel*, 4th ed. Baltimore: Johns Hopkins, 1946.
Allen, L. C. "Kerygmatic Units in 1 and 2 Chronicles." *Journal for Biblical Literature* 41 (1988): 21-36.
———. *Ezekiel 1-19*. Word Biblical Commentary 28. Dallas: Word, 1994.
Andreasen, A. "The Role of the Gebira." *Catholic Biblical Quarterly* 45 (1983): 192.
Applegate, John. "The Fate of Zedekiah: Redactional Debate in the Book of Jeremiah. Part I and II." *Vetus Testamentum* 48 (1998): 137-60.
Auerbach, E. "Wann eroberte Nebukadnezzar Jerusalem?" *Vetus Testamentum* 11 (1961): 128-36.
Auld, A. G. *Kings Without Privilege*. Edinburgh: T&T Clark, 1994.
Avigad, N. "Baruch the Scribe and Jerahmeel the King's Son." *Biblical Archaeologist* 42 (1979): 114-18.

Bibliography

———. *Jewish Quarter Excavations in the Old City of Jerusalem: Conducted by N. Avigad, 1969-82*. Jerusalem: Israel Exploration Society, 2000.
———. *Bullae and Seals from a Post-exilic Judean Archive*. Qedem IV: Jerusalem, 1976.
Bach, R. *Königsbücher*. Tübingen: Mohr, 1929.
Bade, W. F. "The Seal of Jaazaniah." *Seitschrift* 51 (1933): 150-56.
Baldwin, J. G. "Esther." In *New Bible Commentary, 21st Century Edition*, edited by G. J. Wenham, J. A. Motyer, D. A. Carson, and R. T. France, 442-52. Downers Grove: InterVarsity, 1994.
Baltzer, Klaus. "Das Ende des Staates Juda und die Messias-Frage." In *Studien zu Alttestamentlichen Überlieferung*, edited by R. Rendtorff and K. Koch, 3-43. Neukirchen: Neukirchener, 1961.
Barnes, W. E. *The Second Book of Kings*. Cambridge Bible for Schools and Colleges. Cambridge: University Press, 1908.
———. *The Psalms with Introduction and Notes*. Westminster Commentaries. Edited by W. Lock and D. C. Simpson. London: Methuen & Co., 1931.
Barstad, H. "The Strange Fear of the Bible: Some Reflections on the 'Bibliophobia' in Recent Ancient Israelite Histography." In *Leading Captivity Captive*, Journal for the Study of the Old Testament: Supplement Series 278 edited by L. Grabbe, 120-27. Sheffield: JSOT Press, 1988.
Bayer E. *Das Dritte Buch Esdras und sein Verhältnis den Büchern Esra-Nehemi*. Freiburg: Jederische, 1911.
Becking, B. "Jehojachin's Amnesty, Salvation for Israel?" in *From David to Gedaliah: The Book of Kings as Story and History*, 174-90. Göttingen: Vandenhoeck & Ruprecht, 2007.

Becking, B., and Meindert Dijkstra, eds. *On Reading Prophetic Texts: Gender Specific and Related Studies in Memory of Fokkelien van Dijk-Hemmes*. Biblical Interpretation Series 18. Leiden: Brill, 1996.
Becking, B., and Majo C. A. Korpel, eds. *The Crisis of Israelite Religion: Transformation of Religious Tradition in Exilic and Post-Exilic Times*. Soesterberg Symposium. Leiden: Brill, 1999.
Begg, C. T. "The End of King Jehoiakim: The Afterlife of a Problem." *Journal of Semitics* 8 (1996): 12-20.
———. "The Identity of the Princes in Ezekiel 19: Some Reflections." *Ephemerides Theologicae Lovanienses* 65 (1989): 358-69.
———. "The Reading in Ezekiel 19:7a: A Proposal." *Ephemerides Theologicae Lovanienses* 65 (1989): 370-80.
———. "The Significance of Jehoiachin's Release: A New Proposal." *Journal for the Study of the Old Testament* 36 (1986): 49-56.
———. *Josephus' Story of the Later Monarchy*. Louvain: Louvain University Press, 2000.
Ben-Barak, Z. "The Status and Right of the Gebira." *Journal of Biblical Literature* 110 (1991): 23-34.
Benzinger, I. *Die Bücher der Chronik*. Leipzig: Mohr, 1901.
———. *Die Bücher der Könige*. Kurzer Hand-Commentar zum Alten Testament 9. Tübingen: Mohr, 1899.
Berridge, J. M. "Jehoiachin." In *Anchor Bible Dictionary*, edited by D. N. Freedman, 3:661-63. New York: Doubleday, 1992.
Bertheau, E. *Commentary on the Book of Chronicles*. Edinburgh: T&T Clark, 1857.

———. *Die Bücher der Chronik*. Kurzgefasstes exegethisches Handbuch zum Alten Testament 15. Leipzig: Hirzel, 1854.
Beyerlin, W. *Near East Religious Texts Relating to the Old Testament*. Translated by J. Bowden. Philadelphia: Westminster, 1978.
Bickerman, E. "The Edict of Cyrus in Ezra I." *Journal of Biblical Literature* 65 (1946): 249-75.
Blank, S. H. *Of a Truth the Lord Hath Sent Me: An Inquiry into the Source of the Prophet's Authority*. The Goldson Lecture for 1955. Cincinnati: Hebrew Union College, 1955.
Block, Daniel. *The Book of Ezekiel*. New International Commentary on the Old Testament. Grand Rapids: Eerdmans, 1997.
Born, A. van den. *Kronieken*. Rome: Roermond, 1954.
Botterweck, G. J. "Zur Eigenart der chronistischen Davidgeschichte." *Theologische Quartalschrift* 136 (1956): 402-35.
Braun R. L. *First Chronicles*. Word Biblical Commentary. Waco: Word, 1986.
———. *The Significance of 1 Chronicles 22, 28, and 29 for the Structure and Theology of the Work of the Chronicler*. St. Louis: Concordia Seminary, 1971.
———. "A Reconsideration of the Chronicler's Attitude toward the North." *Journal of Biblical Literature* 96 (1977): 59-62.
———. "Solomon, the Chosen Temple Builder: The Significance of 1 Chronicles 22, 28, and 29 for the Theology of Chronicles." *Journal for Biblical Literature* 95 (1976): 581-90.
———. "Solomonic Apologetic in Chronicles." *Journal of Biblical Literature* 92 (1973): 503-16.
———. "The Message of Chronicles: Rally 'Round the Temple." *Concordia Theological Monthly* 42 (1971): 502-14.
Brettler, Mark. "2 Kings 24:13-14 as History." *Catholic Biblical Quarterly* 53 (1991): 541-52.
Bright, John. *Jeremiah*. Anchor Bible 22. Garden City, NY: Doubleday, 1965.
———. *A History of Israel*. Philadelphia: Westminster, 1972.
Bronner, L. *The Stories of Elijah and Elisha*. Leiden: Brill, 1968.
Brown, F., S. R. Driver, and C. A. Briggs. *The New Brown-Driver-Briggs-Gesenius Hebrew and English Lexicon*. Peabody, MA: Hendrickson, 1979.
Brueggemann, W. *Isaiah 40-66*. Westminster Bible Companion. Louisville: Westminster John Knox, 1998.
———. *The Land*. Philadelphia: Fortress, 1977.
———. *To Pluck up, To Tear Down: A Commentary on the Book of Jeremiah 1-25*. International Theological Commentary. Grand Rapids: Eerdmanns, 1988.
———. *To Build, To Plant: A Commentary on Jeremiah 26-52*. International Theological Commentary. Grand Rapids: Eerdmans, 1988.
Bruet, G. "La prise de Jérusalem sous Sedecias." *Revue de l'histoire des religions* 167 (1965): 156-76.
Brunet, A. "La théologie du Chroniste: theocratie et messianisme." *Sacra Pagina* 1 (1959): 384-97.
———. "La théologie du Chroniste." *Revue Biblique* 61 (1954): 349-86.
———. "Le Chroniste et ses sources." *Revue Biblique* 60 (1953): 481-508.
Buckers, H. *Die Bücher der Chronik*. Frieburg: Herder, 1952.
Burney, C. F. *Notes on the Hebrew Text of the Book of Kings*. Oxford: Clarendon, 1903.

Bibliography

Cancik, H. "Das jüdische Fest: Ein Versuch zu Form und Religion des chronistischen Geschichtswerkes." *Theologische Quartalschrift* 150 (1970): 335–48.

Carr, C. L. *The Claims of the Chronicler for the Origin of the Israelite Priesthood*. Boston: Boston University Press, 1973.

Carroll, Robert P. *The Book of Jeremiah*, OTL. Philadelphia: Westminster, 1986.

———. *When Prophecy Failed: Cognitive Dissonance in the Prophetic Traditions of the Old Testament*. Norwich (UK): SCM Press, 2011.

Carter, C. S. *The Emergence of Yehud in the Persian Period*. Sheffield: Sheffield University Press, 1999.

Cassel, P. *An Explanatory Commentary on Esther*. Translated by A. Bernstein. Edinburgh: T&T Clark,1888.

Cazelles, H. *Les livres des Chroniques, la Sainte Bible*. Paris: Éditions du Cerf, 1954.

———. "Le roi Yoyakin et le Serviteur du Seigneur." In *Proceedings of the Fifth World Congress of Jewish Studies*, 121–125. Jerusalem: World Union of Jewish Studies, 1969.

Clements, R. E. *Jeremiah, Interpretation: A Bible Commentary for Teaching and Preaching*. Atlanta: John Knox Press, 1988.

———. *Prophecy and Covenant*. Studies in Biblical Theology, First series 43. Eugene, OR: Wipf & Stock, 2005.

———. "A Royal Privilege: Dining in the Presence of the Great King (2 Kings 25:27–30)." In *Reflection and Refraction: Studies in Biblical Historiography in Honour of A. Graeme Auld*, edited by Robert Rezetko, Timothy H. Lim, and W. Brian Aucker, 49–66. Leiden: Brill, 2007.

Clines, D. J. A. *I, He, We, and They: A Literary Approach to Isaiah 53*. Sheffield: JSOT Press, 1976.

Cogan, M. "Assyrian Royal Inscriptions." In *Empirical Models for Biblical Criticism*, edited by J. Tigay, 197–209. Philadelphia: University of Pennsylvania, 1985.

———. "Tendentious Chronology in the Book of Chronicles." *Zion* 45 (1980): 165–72.

———. *Imperialism and Religion: Assyria, Judah, and Israel in the Eighth and Seventh Centuries B.C.* Society of Biblical Literature Monograph Series 19. Missoula: Scholars Press, 1974.

Coggins, R. J. *The First and Second Books of the Chronicles*, Cambridge: University Press, 1976.

Cohen, S. J. D. *Josephus in Galilee and Rome: His Vita and Development as a Historian*. Leiden: Brill, 1979.

Craigie, P. C. *Deuteronomy*. New International Commentary of the Old Testament. Grand Rapids: Eerdmans, 1976.

Craigie, P. C., Page H. Kelley, and Joel F. Drinkard, Jr. *Jeremiah 1–25*. Word Biblical Commentary 26. Dallas: Word, 1998.

Croatto, J. S., and J. A. Soggin. "Die Bedeutung on 'sdmwt' im Alten Testament." *Zeitschrift für die alttestamentliche Wissenschaft* 74 (1962): 44–50.

Cross, F. M. "A Reconstruction of the Judean Restoration." *Journal of Biblical Literature* 94 (1975): 4–18.

———. "The Contribution of the Qumran Discoveries to the Study of the Biblical Text." *Israel Exploration Journal* 16 (1955): 81–95.

———. *Canaanite Myth and Hebrew Epic*. Cambridge: Harvard University Press, 1973.

Curtis, E. L., and A. A. Madsen. *A Critical and Exegetical Commentary on the Books of Chronicles*. International Critical Commenary. Edinburgh: T&T Clark, 1910.

Bibliography

Dahood, Mitchell J. "Two textual notes on Jeremia." *Catholic Biblical Quarterly* 23 (1961): 462–64.
Dancy, J. C. *The Shorter Books of the Apocrypha: Tobit, Judith, Rest of Esther, Baruch, Letter of Jeremiah, Additions to Daniel, and Prayer of Manasseh*. Cambridge: Cambridge University Press, 1972.
David, M. "The Manumission of Slaves under Zedekiah." *Oudtestamentische Studiën* 5 (1948): 63–79.
Davidson, Robert. *Jeremiah II with Lamentations*. Edinburgh: Saint Andrew Press, 1985.
Davis, J. D. "Names in the Hebrew Bible." In *International Standard Bible Encyclopedia*, edited by J. Orr, 2:1101. Cedar Rapids, IA: Parsons Technology, Quick Verse, version 6.02, 1995.
Déaut, R. L. and J. Robert. *Targum des Chroniques*. Analecta Biblica. Rome: Biblical Institute Press, 1971.
Deboys, D. G. "History and Theology in the Chronicler's Portrayal of Abijah." *Biblica* 71 (1990): 48–62.
Deltombe, L. F. "Josias, heros do l'independence judeene." *Bible et terre sainte* 63 (1945): 2–5.
Dempster, S. G. "Geography and Genealogy, Dominion and Dynasty: A Theology of the Hebrew Bible." In *Biblical Theology: Retrospect and Prospect*, edited by S. Hafeman, 66–82. Wheaton, IL: InterVarsity, 2002.
Dever, W. G., and S. M. Paul. *Biblical Archaeology*. Jerusalem: Keter, 1973.
DeVries, S. J. "Moses and David as Cult Founders in Chronicles." *Journal of Biblical Literature* 107 (1988): 619–39.
Dillard, R. B. "Reward and Punishment in Chronicles: The Theology of Immediate Retribution." *Westminster Theological Journal* 46 (1984): 164–72.
———. "The Chronicler's Jehoshaphat." *Trinity Journal* 7 (1986): 17–22.
———. "The Literary Structure of the Chronicler's Solomon Narrative." *Journal for the Study of the Old Testament* 30 (1984): 85–93.
———. "The Reign of Asa (2 Chr 14–16): An Example of the Chronicler's Theological Method." *Journal of the Evangelical Theological Society* 23 (1980): 207–18.
———. *2 Chronicles*. Word Biblical Commentary 15. Waco: Word, 1987.
———. "David's Census: Perspectives on 2 Samuel 24 and 1 Chronicles 21." In *Through Christ's Word: A Festschrift for Philip E. Hughes*, edited by Philip Edgcumbe Hughes, W. Robert Godfrey, and Jesse L. Boyd, 94–107. Phillipsburg, NJ: Presbyterian and Reformed, 1985.
———. "The Chronicler's Solomon." *Westminster Theological Journal* 43 (1980): 289–300.
Driver, S. R. *A Critical and Exegetical Commentary of Deuteronomy*. International Critical Commentary. Edinburgh: T&T Clark, 1903.
Duguid, I. M. *Ezekiel and the Leaders of Israel*. Leiden: Brill, 1994.
Dumbrell, W. "The Purpose of the Books of Chronicles." *Journal of the Evangelical Theological Society* 27 (1984): 257–66.
Eakin, F. E. "Yahwism and Baalism before the Exile." *Journal of Biblical Literature* 84 (1965): 407–14.
Eichrodt, Walther. *Ezekiel: A Commentary*. London: SCM, 1970.
Eisenstadt, S. N. *The Political Systems of Empires*. New York: MacMillan, 1963.
Eissfeldt, O. *The Old Testament: An Introduction*. Oxford: Blackwells, 1965.

Bibliography

Ellis, P. F. "1-2 Kings." *Journal of Biblical Literature* (1968): 44-78.

———. *1-2 Kings*. Jerome Biblical Commentary. Edited by R. E. Brown. Englewood Cliffs, NJ: Prentice Hall, 1968.

Elmslie, W. A. *The Books of Chronicles*. Cambridge Bible for Schools and Colleges. London: Cambridge University Press, 1916.

Engler, H. "The Attitude of the Chronicler Toward the Davidic Monarchy." Dissertation, Concordia Seminary, 1972.

Ephal, I. "Assyrian Dominion in Palestine." In *World History of the Jewish People, vol. 4, The Age of the Monarchy*, edited by A. Malamat, 276-89. Jerusalem: Masada, 1979.

Eshkenazi, T. "The Chronicler and the Composition of 1 Esdras." *Catholic Biblical Quarterly* 48 (1986): 39-61.

Feldman, L. H. *Studies in Josephus' Rewritten Bible*. Leiden: Brill, 1998.

———. "Josephus' Portrait of Jehoiachin." *Proceedings of the American Philosophical Society* 139 (1995): 11-31.

Finegan, Jack. "The Chronology of Ezekiel." *Journal for Biblical Literature* 69 (1950): 61-66.

Fischer, Georg, S. J. "Jeremia 52—Ein Schlussel zum Jeremiabuch." *Biblica*, 79 (1998): 333-59.

Fishbane, M. *Biblical Interpretation in Ancient Israel*. Oxford: Clarendon, 1985.

Fohrer, G. "Das Geschicht des Menschen nach dem Tode im Alten Testament." *Kerygma and Dogma* 14 (1968): 249-62.

———. *Die symbolischen Handlungen der Propheten*. Zurich: Zwingli, 1968.

Foulkes, F. "Theology of Jehoiachin." In *New International Dictionary of Old Testament Theology and Exegesis*, edited by W. A. VanGemeren, 744-45. Grand Rapids: Zondervan Reference Software, version 2.8, 1998.

Fowler, M. D. "The Israelite Bama: A Question of Interpretation." *Zeitschrift für die alttestamentliche Wissenschaft* 94 (1982): 203-13.

Freedman, D. N. "The Chronicler's Purpose." *Catholic Biblical Quarterly* 23 (1961): 436-42.

Freedy, K. S., and D. B. Redford. "The Dates in Ezekiel in Relation to Biblical, Babylonian, and Egyptian Sources." *Journal of the American Oriental Society* 90 (1970): 462-85.

Frick, F. S. *The City in Ancient Israel*. Missoula: Scholars, 1977.

Fricke, K. D. *Das Zweite Buch von den Königen*. Die Botschaft des Alten Testaments. Stuttgart: Calwer, 1972.

Galling, K. *Die Bücher der Chronik, Esra, Nehemiah*. Das Alte Testament Deutsch 12. Göttingen: Vandenhoeck und Ruprecht, 1954.

Genung, J. F. "Jehoiachin." In *International Standard Bible Encyclopedia*, edited by J. Orr, 2:975-76. Cedar Rapids, IA: Parsons Technology, Quick Verse, version 6.02, 1995.

Gerhards, Meik. "Die Beiden Erzählungen aus 2 Kön 20 und 2 Kön 20, 18 als Ankündigung der Begnadigung Jojachins (2 Kön 25, 27-30)." *Biblische Notizen* 98 (1999): 5-12.

———. "Die Begnadigung Jojachins: überlegungen su 2 Kön 25, 27-30 (mit einem Anhang su den Nennungen Jojachins auf Zuteilungslisten aus Babylon)." *Biblische Notizen* 94 (1998): 27-30.

Gerleman, G. *Studies in the Septuagint II*. Lunds Universitets Årsskrift, N.F. Lund: Gleerup, 1946.

Bibliography

Gese, H. "Geschichtliches Denken im alten Orient und im alten Testament." *Zeitschrift für katholische Theologie* 55 (1958): 127-45.
Geva, H. "The Western Boundary of Jerusalem at the End of the Monarchy." *Israel Exploration Journal* 29 (1979): 84-91.
Gibson, J. C. L. *Textbook of Syrian Semitic Inscriptions: Hebrew and Moabite Inscriptions*, vol. 1. Oxford: Clarendon, 1981.
Gichon, M., and C. Herzog. *Battles of the Bible*. London: Weidenfeld and Nicholson, 1978.
Gill, M. "Israel in the Book of Chronicles." *Beit Mikra* 13 (1968): 105-15.
Ginsberg, H. "Judah and the Transjordan States from 734-582 B.C." In *Alexander Marx Jubilee Volume*, edited by A. S. Halkin, 481-501. New York: Jewish Publication Society, 1950.
Ginsberg, L. *Legends of the Jews*, vol. 7. Translated by H. Szold. Philadelphia: Jewish Publication Society, 1913.
Goettsberger, J. *Die Bücher der Chronik oder Paralipomenon, die heilige Schrift des Alten Testaments*. Bonn: Hanstein, 1939.
Goldin, J. "Midrash and Aggadah." In *Encyclopedia of Religion*, edited by M. Eliade, 9:509-15. New York: MacMillan, 1987.
Goldingay, J. "The Chronicler as Theologian." *Biblical Theology Bulletin* 5 (1975): 99-126.
Görg, M. "Sur Dekoration der Tempelsäulen." *Biblische Notizen* 13 (1980): 17-21.
Goulder, M. D. "Behold My Servant Jehoiachin." *Vetus Testamentum* 52 (Jan 2002): 175-90.
———. *The Psalms of the Sons of Korah*. JSOT Supplement Series 20. Sheffield: JSOT Press, 1982.
Granowski, Jan Jaynes. "Jehoiachin at the King's Table: A Reading of the Ending of the Second Book of Kings." In *Reading Between the Texts*, edited by Danna Nolan Fewell, 173-90. Louisville: Westminster John Knox, 1992.
Gray, J. *1 and 2 Kings: A Commentary*. Old Testament Library, 2nd ed. Philadelphia: Westminster, 1970.
Grayson, A. K. *Texts from Cuneiform Sources: Assyrian and Babylonian Chronicles*, vol. 5. Locust Valley, NY: J. J. Augustine, 1975.
Green, A. "The Fate of Jehoiakim." *Andrews University Seminary Studies* 20 (1982): 103-09.
Greenberg. M. "Ezekiel 17 and the Policy of Psammeticus II." *Journal for Biblical Literature* 76 (1957): 304-09.
Gurewicz, S. B. "The Problem with Lamentations 3 (Jehoiachin's authorship defended)." *Australian Biblical Review* 8 (1960): 19-23.
Gurtner, Daniel M. "The 'Twenty-Fifth Year of Jeconiah' and the Date of 2 Baruch." *Journal for the Study of the Pseudepigrapha* 18.1 (2008): 23-32.
Hagner, D. A. *Matthew 1-13*. Word Biblical Commentary 33a. Dallas: Word, 1998.
Hamilton, V. P. "ירד." In *New International Dictionary of the Old Testament Theology and Exegesis*, edited by Willem A. VanGemeren, 3:534-35. Grand Rapids: Zondervan,1988.
Hanks, T. D. "The Chronicler: Theologian of Grace." *Evangelical Quarterly* 53 (1975): 16-28.
Haran, M. *Temples and Temple Service in Ancient Israel*. Oxford: Clarendon, 1977.

Bibliography

Hayes, J. H., and J. Max Miller. *Israelite and Judean History*. Philadelphia: Westminster, 1977.
Hellholm, D. *Apocalyticism in the Mediterranean World and the Near East*. Tübingen: Mohr, 1983.
Herbert, A. S. *1 and 2 Chronicles*. New York: Thomas Nelson, 1962.
Hermisson H. J. "Jeremias Wort über Jojachin." In *Werden und Wirken des Alten Testaments, Festschrift für C. Westermann*, edited by R. Albertz et al., 253–56 Göttingen:Vandenhoeck and Ruprecht, 1980.
Hillers, D. R. *Lamentations*. Anchor Bible. Garden City, NY: Doubleday, 1972.
Hobbs, T. R. *Second Kings*. Word Biblical Commentary 13. Waco: Word, 1985.
———. "Composition and Structure of the Book of Jeremiah." *Catholic Biblical Quarterly* 34 (1972): 257–75.
Holladay, W. *Jeremiah 1*. Hermeneia. Edited by P. D. Hanson. Philadelphia: Fortress, 1986.
———. *Jeremiah 2*. Hermeneia. Edited by P. D. Hanson. Minneapolis: Fortess, 1989.
Honeyman, A. M. "The Evidence for Regnal Names among the Hebrews." *Journal for Biblical Literature* 67 (1948): 16.
Horn, S. H. "The Babylonian Chronicle and the Ancient Calendar of the Kingdom of Judah." *Andrews University Seminary Studies* 2 (1967): 12–27.
Hughes, J. *Secrets of the Times: Myth and History in Biblical Chronology*. Journal for the Study of the Old Testament Supplement Series 66. Sheffield: Sheffield Press, 1990.
Hunter, J. *Faces of a Lamenting City: The Development and Coherence of the Book of Lamentations*. Frankfurt: Peter Lang, 1996.
Hyatt, J. P. "New Light on Nebuchadnezzar and Judean History." *Journal of Biblical Literature* 75 (1956): 277–84.
Im, T. S. *Das Davidbild im der Chronikbüchern: David als Idealbild des theokratischen Messianismus für den Chronisten*. Frankfurt: Lang, 1985.
Isbell, Charles D. "2 Kings 22:3—23:24 and Jeremiah 36: A Stylistic Comparison." *Journal for the Study of the Old Testament* 8 (1978), 33–45.
Janzen, J. G. *Studies in the Text of Jeremiah*. Harvard Semitic Manuscripts 6. Ann Arbor: AMI Press, 1991.
Japhet, S. "Conquest and Settlement in Chronicles." *Journal for the Study of the Old Testament* 98 (1979): 205–18.
———. "Sheshbazzar and Zerubbabel." *Zeitschrift für die alttestamentliche Wissenschaft* 94 (1982): 66–98.
———. "The Historical Reliability of Chronicles." *Journal for the Study of the Old Testament* 33 (1985): 83–107.
———. "The Supposed Common Authorship of Chronicles and Era-Nehemiah Investigated Anew." *Vetus Testamentum* 18 (1968): 330–71.
———. *1 and 2 Chronicles*, Old Testament Library. Louisville: Westminster John Knox, 1993.
———. *The Ideology of the Book of Chronicles and Its Place in Biblical Thought*. Jerusalem: Bialik, 1977.
Jewish Publication Society. *Tanakh: A New Translation of the Holy Scriptures According to the Traditional Hebrew Text*. Philadelphia: Jewish Publication Society, 1985.
Jobling, D. "The Quest of the Historical Jeremiah: Hermeneutical Implications of Recent Literature." In *A Prophet to the Nations*, edited by L. G. Perdue and B. W. Kovacs, 285–97. Winona Lakes, IN: Eisenbrauns, 1984.

Bibliography

———. "The Quest of the Historical Jeremiah: Hermeneutical Implications of Recent Literature." *Union Seminary Quarterly Review* 34 (1978): 3-12.
Jones, Douglas R. *Jeremiah*. New Century Bible Commentary. Edited by Ronald E. Clements and Matthew Black. Grand Rapids: Eerdmans, 1992.
Jones, G. H. *1 and 2 Kings*. New Century Bible Commentary. Grand Rapids: Eerdmans, 1992.
Kaiser, O. *Isaiah 13-39*. Old Testament Library. Philadelphia: Westminster, 1974.
Kalimi, I., and J. D. Purvis. "King Jehoiachin and the Vessels of the Lord's House in Biblical Literature." *Catholic Biblical Quarterly* 56 (1994): 449-57.
Katzenstein, H. J. *A History of Tyre*. Jerusalem: Goldbergs, 1973.
Kegler, J., and M. Augustin. *Synopsis zum chronistischen Geschichtswerk*. Frankfurt: Lang, 1984.
Keown, Gerald L., Pamela J. Scalise, and Thomas G. Smothers. *Jeremiah 26-52*. Word Biblical Commentary 27. Dallas: Word, 1995.
Kessler, John A. C. "The Shaking of the Nations: An Eschatological View." *Journal of the Evangelical Theological Society* 30 (1987): 159-66.
Kitchen, K. A. *The Third Intermediate Period in Egypt*. Warmister: Aris and Phillips, 1973.
Kittel, R. *Die Bücher der Könige*. Handkommentar zum Alten Testament 5. Göttingen: Vandenhoeck und Ruprecht, 1900.
———. *Die Bücher der Chronik*. Handkommentar zum Alten Testament 6. Göttingen: Vandenhoeck & Ruprecht, 1902.
Klein, Ralph W. "New Evidence for an Old Recension of Reigns." *Harvard Theological Review* 60 (1967): 93-105.
Knight, D. A. *Rediscover the Traditions of Israel*. Missoula, MT: Scholars, 1975.
Koch, K. *The Growth of the Biblical Tradition: The Form-critical Method*. Translated by M. Cupitt. London: A. C. Black, 1969.
Kraus, H. J. "Die Geschichte des Passah-Massot Festes im Alten Testament." *Evangelische Theologie* 18 (1958): 47-67.
Kropat, A. *Die Syntax des Autors der Chronik vergleichen mit der seiner Quellen*. Beihefte zur Zeitschrift für die alttestamentliche Wissenschaft 16. Giessen: Alfred Töpelmann, 1909.
Kutsch, E. "Das Jahr der Katastophe, 587 von Chronical." *Biblica* 55 (1974): 520-45.
Lance, H. D. "The Royal Stamps and the Kingdom of Judah." *Harvard Theological Review* 64 (1971): 315-32.
Langton, S. *Commmentary of the Book of Chronicles*. Edited by A. Saltman. Ramat-gan: Bar-Ilan University Press, 1978.
Larsson, G. "When Did the Babylonian Captivity Begin?" *Journal of Theological Studies* 18 (1967): 117-23.
Lemaire, A. *Inscriptions hebraiques: Les ostraca*. Paris: Editions du Cerf, 1977.
Lemke, W. E. "The Synoptic Problem in the Chronicler's History." *Harvard Theological Review* 58 (1965): 349-63.
Levenson, Jon D. "The last four verses in Kings (2 Kgs 25:27-30)." *Journal for Biblical Literature* 103 (Sep 1984): 353-61.
Lilley, J. "Jehoiachin." In *Zondervan Pictorial Encyclopedia of the Bible*, edited by Merrill C. Tenney, 3:416-18. Grand Rapids: Zondervan, 1975.
Lim, Timothy, H. *The Dead Sea Scrolls and their Historical Context*. Edinburgh: T&T Clark, 2000.

Bibliography

Lind, M. *Yahweh Is a Warrior: The Theology of Warfare in Ancient Israel.* Scottsdale: Herald, 1980.
Lindars, B. "Commentaries on Samuel and Kings." *Theology* 47 (1964): 11–15.
Lindbom, J. R. "Jerahmeel." In *The Anchor Bible Dictionary*, edited by David Noel Freedman, 3:683–84. New York: Harper, 1951.
Lindsell, H. *Battle for the Bible.* Grand Rapids: Zondervan, 1976.
Lipinski, E. "The Egyptian-Babylonian Wars of the Winter of 601–600 B.C." *Annali dell 'instituto orientale di Napoli* 22 (1972): 235–41.
Long, Burke. *Hazor: The Rediscovery of the Great Citadel of the Bible.* New York: Random House, 1975.
———. *The Forms of OT Literature*, vol. 10. Edited by R. P. Knierim and G. M. Tucker. Grand Rapids: Eerdmans, 1991.
———. *The Problem of the Etiological Narrative in the Old Testament.* Beihefte zur Zeitschrift für die altestamentliche Wissenschaft. Berlin: Walter de Gruyter, 1968.
Longacre, R. *Anatomy of Speech Notions.* Lisse: Peter de Ridder, 1976.
Lowery, K. E "Conaniah." In *The Anchor Bible Dictionary*, edited by David Noel Freedman, 1:1124–25. Garden City, NY: Doubleday, 1992.
Lundbom, J. R. "Jerahmeel." In *The Anchor Bible Dictionary*, edited by David Noel Freedman, 3:683–84. Garden City, NY: Doubleday, 1992.
Lust, Johan. "The Identification of Zerubbabel with Sheshbassar." *Ephmerides Theologicae Lovanienses* 63, no. 1 (1987): 90–95.
Malamat, A. "The Twilight of Judah in the Egyptian-Babylonian Maelstrom." *Supplements to Vetus Testamentum* 28 (1975): 23–145.
———. "Doctrines of Causality in Hittite and Biblical Historiography." *Vetus Testamemtum* 5 (1955): 1–22.
———. "The Last Kings of Judah and the Fall of Jerusalem." *Israel Exploration Journal* 18 (1968): 137–56.
———. "Jeremiah and the Last Two kings of Judah." *Palestine Exploration Quarterly* 83 (Jan–Apr 1951): 81–87.
Marcus, R. *Josephus, with an English Translation.* Antiquities Books IX–XI, Loeb Classical Library. Cambridge, MA: Harvard University Press, 1937.
Margaliyot, Eliezer. *Positive [Depictions] in the Bible and Negaitve [Depictions] in the Talmud and in the Midrashim.* London: Ararat, 1949.
Martin-Achard, R. *From Death to Life: A Study of the Development of the Doctrine of the Resurrection in the Old Testament.* Translated by J. P. Smith. Edinburgh: Oliver & Boyd, 1960.
Mason, R. "Some Echoes of the Preaching in the Second Temple? Tradition Elements in Zechariah." *Zeitschrift für die alttestamentliche Wissenschaft* 96 (1984): 221–35.
———. *Preaching the Tradition: Homily and Hermeneutics after the Exile.* Cambridge: Cambridge University Press, 1990.
Mason, S. *Josephus and the New Testament.* Peabody, MA: Hendrickson, 1992.
Mathias, D. *Die Geschichte der Chronikforschung in 19. Jarhundert under besonderer Berucksichtigung der exegetishen Behandlung der Prophetennachrischten des chronistischen Geschichtswerkes*, vol. 3. Leipzig: Karl-Marx Univerität, 1977.
Mauchline, J. *1 and 2 Kings.* Peake's Commentary on the Bible. Edited by H. H. Rowley and M. Black. London: Thomas Nelson, 1962.
May H. G. "Jehoiachin." In *Interpreters Dictionary of the Bible*, edited by G. A. Buttrick, 2:811–13. New York: Abingdon, 1962.

Bibliography

———. "Three Hebrew Seals and the Status of Exiled Jehoiachin." *American Journal of Semitic Languages and Literatures* 61 (1939): 146–148.
McAlpine, Thomas H. "Jehoiachin." In *Eerdman's Bible Dictionary*, edited by Allen C. Myers, 558. Grand Rapids: Eerdmans, 1987.
McConville, J. G. *Grace in the End: A Study in Deuteronomic Theology*. Grand Rapids: Zondervan 1993.
———. "Jeremiah." In *New Bible Commentary: 21st CenturyEdition*, edited by G. J. Wenham, J. A. Motyer, D. A. Carson, and R. T. France, 671–708. Downers Grove, IL: InterVarsity, 1994.
———. *Deuteronomy*. Apollos Old Testament Commentary. Leicester: Apollos, 2002.
———. *Judgment and Promise: An Interpretation of the Book of Jeremiah*. Leicester: Apollos, 1993.
———. *Reconsidering Israel and Judah: Recent Studies on the Deuteronomistic History*. Edited by G. Knoppers. Winona Lake, IN: Eisenbrauns, 2000.
———. *1 and 2 Chronicles*. Daily Study Bible. Philadelphia: Westminster, 1984.
McKane, W. A. *A Critical and Exegetical Commentary on Jeremiah*, vol. 1. Edinburgh: T&T Clark, 1986.
McKenzie, S. *King David: A Biography*. New York: Oxford University Press, 2000.
———. *The Trouble With Kings: The Composition of the Books of Kings in the Deuteronomistic History*. Leiden: Brill, 1991.
———. *The Chronicler's Use of the Deuteronomistic History*. Harvard Semitic Monographs. Atlanta: Scholars, 1985.
Meek, T. J. "Translation Problems in the OT." *Jewish Quarterly Review* 50 (1959): 45–54.
Mendenhall, E. *The 10th Generation*. Baltimore: Johns Hopkins Press, 1973.
Merser, M. K. "Daniel 1:1 and Jehoiakim's Three Years of Servitude." *Andrews University Seminary Studies* 27 (1989): 179–92.
Mettinger, T. N. D. *King and Messiah*. Lund: Gleerup, 1977.
Metzger, B. M., editor. *Oxford Annotated Apocrypha*. New York: Oxford University Press, 1973.
Michaeli, F. *Les livres des Chroniques, d'Esdras, et de Néhémie*. Commentaire de l'Ancien Testament. Neuchâtel: Delachaux et Niestlé, 1967.
Micheel, R. *Die Seher und Prophetenüberlieferungen in der Chronik*. Beträge sur Assyriologie und semitischen Sprachwissenschaft. Frankfurt: Lang, 1983.
Miller, P. D. *The Divine Warrior in Early Israel*. Harvard Semitic Monographs 5. Cambridge, MA: Harvard University Press, 1973.
Mitchell, H. G. "Isaiah on the Fate of His People and the Capital." *Journal of Biblical Literature* 37 (1918): 149–62.
Montgomery, J. A., and H. S. Gehman. *The Books of Kings*. International Critical Commentary. Edinburgh: T&T Clark, 1951.
Moore, C. A. *Daniel, Esther, and Jeremiah: The Additions: A New Translation with Introduction and Commentary*. Garden City, NY: Doubleday, 1977.
Mosis, R. *Untersuchungen zur Theologie des chronistischen Geschichtswerkes*. Freiburger Theilogische Studien. Frieburg: Herder, 1973.
Mottu, Henri. "Jeremiah versus Hananiah: Ideology and Truth in Old Testament Prophecy." In *The Bible and Liberation*, edited by Norm K. Gottwald, 235–51. Maryknoll, NY: Orbis, 1983.
Mounce, R. H. *Matthew*. New International Biblical Commentary. Edited by W. W. Gasque. Peabody, MA: Hendrickson, 1991.

Bibliography

Mowinckel, S. "Israelite Historiography." *Annual of the Swedish Theological Institute* 2 (1963): 7–12.

———. "Erwägungen zum chronistischen Geschichtswerk." *Theologische Literaturzeitung* 85 (1960): 1–8.

Murray, D. F. "Of All the Years the Hopes—or Fears? Jehoiachin in Babylon 2Ki 25:27–30." *Journal of Biblical Literature* 120 (Summer 2001): 245–65.

Myers, C. L. "The Elusive Temple." *Biblical Archaeologist* 45 (1981): 33–41.

Myers, J. M. *1 and 2 Chronicles*. Anchor Bible. Garden City, NY: Doubleday, 1965.

———. "The Kerygma of the Chronicler: History and Theology in the Service of Religion." *Interpretation* 20 (1966): 259–73.

———. *1 and 2 Esdras*. Anchor Bible. Garden City, NY: Doubleday, 1974.

Nelson, George. *First and Second Kings*. Atlanta: John Knox, 1987.

Newsome, J. D. "Toward New Understanding of the Chronicler and His Purposes." *Journal of Biblical Literature* 94 (1975): 201–17.

Nicklesburg, George W. E. "The Bible Rewritten and Expanded." In *Jewish Writings of the Second Temple Period: Apocrypha, Pseudepigrapha, Qumran Sectarian Writings, Philo, Josephus*, edited by M. E. Stone, 157–84. Philadelphia: Fortress, 1984.

———. *Jewish Literature Between the Bible and Mishnah*. Philadelphia: Fortress, 1981.

North, R "The Chronicler: 1–2." In *Jerome Bible Commentary*, edited by R. E. Brown, 639–55. Englewood Cliffs, NJ: Prentice Hall, 1968.

———. "Does Archaeology Prove Chronicles Sources?" In *Old Testament Studies in Honor of Jacob M. Myers*, edited by H. N. Bream et. al., 375–401. Philadelphia: Temple University Press, 1974.

———. "The Theology of the Chronicler." *Journal of Biblical Literature* 82 (1963): 369–81.

Noth, M. "Die Einnahme von Jerusalem in Jahre 597 von Chronik." *Zeitschrift des deutschen Palästine-Vereins* 74 (1958): 133–57.

———. "Jerusalem und die israelitische Tradition." *Oudtestamentische Studiën* 8 (1950): 28–46.

———. *The Deuteronomistic History*. Sheffield: JSOT Press, 1981.

Oded, B. "When Did the Kingdom of Judah Become Subjected to Babylonian Rule?" *Tarbiz* 25 (1965): 103–07.

———. "The Historical Background of the War between Rezin and Pekah against Ahaz." *Tarbiz* 38 (1969): 205–44.

Omanson, R. L. *A Handbook of Esther: The Hebrew and Greek Texts*. New York: United Bible Societies, 1997.

Parker, Richard, and Waldo H. Dubberstein. *Babylonian Chronology: 626 B.C.–A.D. 75*. Eugene, OR: Wipf & Stock, 2007.

Payne, J. B. "1 and 2 Chronicles." In *Wycliffe Bible Commentary*, edited by C. Pfeiffer and E. Harrison, 367–422. Chicago: Moody, 1962.

———. "The Validity of Numbers in Chronicles." *Bibliotheca Sacra* 136 (1979): 109–28, 206–20.

Pennant, D. F. "Haggai." In *New Bible Commentary, 21st Century Edition*, edited by G. J. Wenham, J. A. Motyer, D. A. Carson, and R. T. France, 857–62. Downers Grove: InterVarsity, 1994.

Person, Raymond F. "2 Kings 24:18–25, 30, and Jeremiah 52: A Text-Critical Study in the Redaction History of the Deuteronomistic History." *Zeitschrift für die Alttestamentliche Wissenschaft* 105, no. 2 (1993): 174–205.

Bibliography

Petersen, D. L. *Late Israelite Prophecy.* Society of Biblical Literature 23. Missoula, MT: Scholars, 1977.

———. "Zerubbabel and Jerusalem Temple Reconstruction." *Catholic Biblical Quarterly* 36 (July 1974): 366–72.

Peterson, E. H. *The Message Remix: The Bible in Contemporary Language.* Colorado Springs: NavPress, 2003.

Pohlmann, O. "Erwägungen um Schlußkapitel des deuteronomistischen Geschichtswerkes: Oder, Warum wird der Prophet Jeremia in 2 Kön. 22–25 nicht erwähnt?" In *Textgemäß, Aufsätze und Beiträge sur Hermeneutik des Alten Testaments, Festschrift E. Würthwein,* edited by A. H. J. Gunneweg and O. Kaiser, 94–109. Göttingen: Vandenhoeck & Ruprecht, 1979.

Polzin, R. *Late Biblical Hebrew: Toward an Historical Typology of Biblical Hebrew Prose.* Harvard Semitic Monographs 12. Missoula, MT: Scholars, 1971.

Porteous, N. W. "Jerusalem-Zion: The Growth of a Symbol." In *Verbannung und Heimkehr, Beiträge zur Geschichte und Theologie Israels im 6. und 5. Jahrhundert v. Christus, Festschrift für Wilhelm Rudolph,* edited by Arnulf Kuschke, 235–52. Tübingen: JCB Mohr, 1961.

Provan, I. W. *1 and 2 Kings.* New International Biblical Commentary 7. Peabody, MA: Hendrickson, 1995.

———. *Hezekiah and the Books of Kings.* New York: Walter de Gruyter, 1988.

Rad, G. von. "The Levitical Sermon in I and II Chronicles." Translated by E. Dicken. In *The Problem of the Hexateuch and Other Essays,* 267–80. New York: McGraw-Hill, 1966.

———. *Deuteronomium Studien.* Göttingen: Vandenhoeck & Ruprecht, 1947.

———. *Old Testament Theology.* New York: Harper & Row, 1962.

Randellini, L. "Il Librow delle Cronache nel decennio." *Rivista Biblica* 10 (1962): 136–56.

Redditt, Paul L. "Zerubbabel, Joshua, and the night visions of Zechariah." *Catholic Biblical Quarterly* 54 (1992): 249–59.

Rehm, M. *Textkritsiche Untersuchungen zu den Parallelstellen der Samuel-Königsbücher und der Chronik.* Münster: Aschendorff, 1937.

Reventlow, H. G. *Liturgie und Prophetisches Ich bei Jeremiah.* Gutersloh: Moher, 1963.

Richardson, H. N. "The Historical Reliability of Chronicles." *Journal for Biblical Review* 26 (1958): 9–12.

Robinson, J. *The Second Book of Kings.* Cambridge Bible Commentary. Cambridge: University Press, 1976.

Rofé, Alexander. "The Arrangement of the Book of Jeremiah." *Zeitschrift für die alttestamentliche Wissenschaft* 101 (1991): 390–98.

Rogerson, J. W. *The Supernatural in the Old Testament.* London: Lutterworth, 1976.

Romerowski, S. "Les règnes de David et Salomon dans les Chroniques." *Hohkma* 31 (1986): 1–23.

Rothstein, J. W., and Hänel, J. *Das erste Buch der Chronik.* Kommentar zum Alten Testament. Leipzig: A. Deichert, 1927.

Rowley, H. H. *Men of God: Studies in Old Testament History and Prophecy.* London: Nelson, 1963.

———. *The Growth of the Old Testament.* New York: Harper Torchbooks, 1963.

Rudolf, W. "Problems of the Books of Chronicles." *Vetus Testamentum* 4 (1954): 401–09.

Bibliography

———. "Zum Text des Königsbuches." *Zeitschrift für die alttestamentliche Wissenschaft* 63 (1951): 201-15.

———. *Jeremia*. Handbuch zum Alten Testament 10. Tübingen: Mohr, 1955.

———. *Chronikbücher*. Handbuch zum Alten Testament 21. Tübingen: Mohr, 1955.

Saebø, M. "Messianism in Chronicles? Some Remarks to the Old Testament Background of the New Testament Christology." *Horizons in Biblical Theology* 2 (1980): 85-109.

Saggs, H. W. F. "Assyrian Prisoners of War and the Right to Live." In *Vorträge gehalten auf der 28. Rencontre Assyriologique in Wien 6.-10. Juli 1981*, edited by H. Hirsch and H. Hunger, 85-93. AFO Beiheft 19: Horn, 1982.

———. *The Greatness that Was Babylon*. New York: Hawthorn, 1962.

Sanda, A. *Die Bücher der Könige*. Exegetisches Handbuch zum Alten Testament. Munster: Aschendorff, 1911-1912.

Schalit, Abraham. *Namenwörterbuch zu Flavius Josephus*. Leiden: Brill, 1968.

Schedl, C. "Nachmals das Jahr der Zerstörung Jerusalems." *Zeitschrift für die alttestamentliche Wissenschaft* 74 (1962): 209-13.

Schultz, S. J. "Jehoiachin." In *International Standard Bible Encyclopedia*, edited by Geoffrey W. Bromiley, 2:975-76. Grand Rapids: Eerdmans, 1982.

Schumacher, J. H. "The Chronicler's Theology of History." *The Theologian* 13 (1957): 11-21.

Scott, R. B.Y. "The Hebrew Cubit." *Journal of Biblical Literature* 77 (1958): 201-15.

Seeligman, I. L. "Die Auffassung von der Prophetie in der deuteronomistischen und chronistischen Geschischtsschreibung (mit einem Exkurs Über das Buch Jeremiah)." Congress Volume, Vetus Testamentum Supplement 29, 254-84. Leiden: Brill, 1978.

———. "The Beginnings of Midrash in the Book of Chronicles." *Tarbiz* 49 (1979-1980): 14-32.

Seitz, Christopher R. *Theology in Conflict: Reactions to the Exile in the Book of Jeremiah*. Berlin: Walter de Gruyter, 1989.

———. "The Prophet Moses and the Canonical Shape of Jeremiah." *Zeitschrift für die alttestamentliche Wissenschaft* 101 (1989): 3-27.

Skinner, John. *Prophecy and Religion: Studies in the Life of Jeremiah*. Cambridge: University Press, 1922.

———. *The Books of Kings*. Century Bible. Edinburgh: T.C. & E.C. Jack, 1904.

Slotki, I. W. *Chronicles*. London: Soncino, 1952.

Smend, R. *Elemente alttestamentlichen Geschichtsdenkens*. Textus Testamentum 95. Zurich: EVZ, 1968.

Snaith, N. H. *The First and Second Books of Kings*. Interpreter's Bible. Nashville: Abingdon, 1954.

Soggin, J. A. *A History of Ancient Israel*. Philadelphia: Westminster, 1985.

———. *Introduction to the Old Testament from Its Origins to the Closing of the Alexandrian Canon*. Translated by J. Bowden. London: SCM, 1976.

Solomon, A. M. V "Fable." In *Saga, Legend, Tale, Novella, Fable*, edited by G. W. Coats, 114-125. Sheffield: JSOT, 1985.

Souroyer, B. "Le litige entre Josias et Nechao." *Revue Biblique* 55 (1948): 388-96.

Southwell, P. J. M. "Theology of Manasseh." In *New International Dictionary of Old Testament Theology and Exegesis*, edited by W. A. VanGemeren, 4:930-32. Grand Rapids: Zondervan, 1997.

Bibliography

Spalinger, A. "Egypt and Babylonia: A survey c. 620–550 BC." *Studien zur altägyptischen Kultur* 5 (1977): 232.

Spieckermann, H. *Juda unter Assur in der Sargonidenzeit*. Göttingen: Vandenhoeck und Ruprecht, 1982.

Spronk, K. "Aanhangsel of uitvloeisel? Over het slot van het deuteronomistische geschiedswerk (2 Köningen 25:27–30) (Appendix or Development? Concerning the Conclusion of the Deuteronomistic History [2Ki 25:27–30])." *Gereformeerd theologisch Tijdschrift* 88 (1988): 162–70.

Stern, E. "Israel at the Close of the Period of the Monarchy: An Archaeological Survey." *Biblical Archaeologist* 38 (1975): 26–54.

Stinespring, W. F. "Eschatology in Chronicles." *Journal of Biblical Literature* 80 (1961): 209–19.

Stipp, Hermann-Josef. "Zedekiah in the Book of Jeremiah: On the Formation of a Biblical Character." *Catholic Biblical Quarterly* 58 (1996): 627–48.

Stuart, Douglas. *Old Testament Exegesis*, 2nd ed. Philadelphia: Westminster, 1984.

Stuhlmueller, C. *Haggai and Zechariah: Rebuilding with Hope*. International Theological Commentary. Grand Rapids: Eerdmans, 1988.

Swart, J. de. *Theologie von Kronieken*. Groningen: Gebroeders Hoitsema, 1911.

Sweeney, M. A. *King Josiah of Judah: The Lost Messiah of Israel*. New York: Oxford University Press, 2001.

Tadmor, H. "Chronology of the Last Kings of Judah." *Journal of Near Eastern Studies* 15 (1956): 226–30.

Tadmor, H., and Mordechi Cogan. *2 Kings*. Anchor Bible 11. New York: Doubleday, 1988.

Talmon, S. "The History of the 'am-ha'aretz in the Kingdom of Judah." *Beit Mikra* 12 (1966–1967): 27–55.

―――. "Case of Faulty Harmonization." *Vetus Testamentum* 5 (1955): 206–08.

―――. "Divergences in Calendar Reckoning in Ephraim and Judah." *Vetus Testamentum* 8 (1958): 48–74.

Thackeray, H. St. J. "The Greek Translators of the Four Books of Kings." *Journal of Theological Studies* 8 (1907): 262–78.

―――. *The Septuagint and Jewish Worship*. London: British Academy, 1923.

Thenius, W. *Die Bücher der Könige*. Kurzgefasstes Exegetisches Handbuch zum Alten Testament 9, 2nd ed. Leipzig: Hirzel, 1873.

Thiele, E. R. *The Mysterious Numbers of the Hebrew Kings*. Grand Rapids: Zondervan, 1983.

Thomas, D. W. "The Age of Jeremiah in the Light of Recent Archaeological Discoveries." *Palestine Exploration Quarterly* 82 (1907): 1–15.

Thompson, John A. *The Book of Jeremiah*. New International Commentary on the Old Testament. Grand Rapids: Eerdmans, 1980.

Throntveit, M. *When Kings Speak: Royal Speech and Royal Prayer in Chronicles*. Alanta: Scholars, 1987.

Toombs, Lawrence E. "When Religions Collide: The Yahewh/Baal Confrontation." In *The Yahweh/Baal Confrontation and Other Studies in Biblical Literature and Archaeology*, edited by F. L. Horton and J. M. O'Brien, 13–46. Lewiston, NY: Edwin Mellen, 1995.

Torrey, C. C. "The Chronicler as Editor and Independent Narrator." *American Journal of Semitic Languages and Literatures* 25 (1908–1909): 157–75, 188–217.

Bibliography

———. *The Chronicler's History of Israel*. New Haven: Yale University Press, 1954.

Tov, E. "Some Aspects of the Textual and Literary History of the Book of Jeremiah." In *Le Livre de Jérémie*, edited by P. M. Bogaert, 145-67. Leuven: Leuven University Press, 1981.

———. "Exegetical Notes on the Hebrew Vorlage of the LXX of Jeremiah 27 (34)." *Zeitschrift für die alttestamentliche Wissenschaft* 91 (1979): 73-93.

Tsevat, M. "The Neo-Assyrian and New-Babylonian Vassal Oaths and the Prophet Ezekiel." *Journal of Biblical Literature* 78 (1959): 199-204.

Unger, E. "The deposed rulers in Babylon, dating from about 570." *Theologisch Literaturzeitung* 50 (1925): 481.

Unterman, Jeremiah. "Jehoiachin." In *Harper's Bible Dictionary*, edited by Paul Achtemeier, 451. San Francisco: Harper & Row, 1985.

Urman, D. "A Signet Ring of Bar-Kokhba." *Bulletin of the Anglo-Israel Archaeological Society* 15 (1996): 51-54.

Ussishkin, D. "Royal Judean Storage Jars and Private Seal Impressions." *Bulletin of the American Schools of Oriental Research* 223 (1976): 1-13.

VanGemeren, W., editor. *New International Dictionary of Old Testament Theology and Exegesis*. Grand Rapids: Zondervan,1988.

Vannutelli, P. *Libri Synoptici Veteris Testamenti*. Rome: Pontifical Biblical Institute, 1931.

Vaux, R. de. "The Decrees of Cyrus and Darius on the Rebuilding of the Temple." In *The Bible and the Ancient Near East*, edited by R. de Vaux, translated by D. McHugh, 63-96. London: Darton, Longman, and Todd, 1972.

———. "Le sens de l'expression 'peuple du pays' dan l'Ancien Testament et le rôle politique du peuple en Israël." *Revue d'assyriologie et d'archéologie orientale* 58 (1964): 167-72.

Verhoef, P. A. *The Books of Haggai and Malachi*. New International Commentary on the Old Testament. Grand Rapids: Eerdmans, 1987.

Vermes, Geza. *Scripture and Tradition in Judaism: Haggadic Studies*. Leiden: Brill, 1961.

Vogelstein, M. "Nebuchadnezzar's Reconquest of Phoenicia and Palestine and the Oracles of Ezekiel." *Hebrew Union College Annual* 23 (1950-1951): 197-220.

Walton, John H. "Vision Narrative Wordplay and Jeremiah xxiv." *Vetus Testamentum* 39 (1989): 508-09.

Watson, W. G. E. "Archaic Elements in the Language of Chronicles." *Biblica* 53 (1972): 191-207.

Watts, J. D. W. "The Deuteronomic Theology." *Review and Expositor* 74 (1977): 371-87.

———. *Isaiah 34-66*. Word Biblical Commentary 25. Waco: Word, 1987.

Weidner, E. F. "Jojachin König von Juda in babylonischen Keilschrifttexten." In *Mélanges Syriens offerts à M. René Dussaud*, vol 2, 923-35. Paris: Geuthner, 1939.

Weinberg, J. P. "Die Natur im Weltbild des Chronisten." *Vetus Testamentum* 31 (1981): 325-45.

Weinfeld, M. "The Origin of the Apodictic Law: An Overlooked Source." *Vetus Testamentum* 23 (1973): 63-75.

Weippert, H. "Die deuteronomistisches Beurteilung der Könige von Israel und Juda und das problem der Redaktion der Königsbücher." *Biblica* 53 (1973): 301-39.

Welch, A. C. *The Work of the Chronicler: Its Purpose and Date*. London: British Academy, 1939.

Bibliography

Wellhausen, J. *Prolegomena to the History of Ancient Israel*. Translated by Menzies and Black. New York: Meridian, 1957.

Wells, Roy D., Jr. "Indications of Late Reinterpretation of the Jeremianic Tradition from the LXX of Jer 21:1–23:8." *Zeitschrift für die alttestamentliche Wissenschaft* 96 (1984): 405–20.

Welten, P. "Kulthöhe und Jahwetempel." *Zeitschrift des deutschen Palästina-Vereins* 88 (1972): 19–37.

———. *Geschichte und Geschichtsdarstellung in den Chronikbüchern*. Wissenschaftliche Monographien zum Alten und Neuen Testament 42. Neukirchen: Neukircherner, 1973.

Wenham, J. G. "Large Numbers in the Old Testament." *Tyndale Bulletin* 18 (1967): 19–53.

Wessels, W. J. "A Proposed Ideological Reading." *Zeitschrift für die alttestamentliche Wissenschaft* 101 (1989): 232–49.

Westermann, C. T. C. *Basic Forms of Prophetic Speech*. Philadelphia: Westminster, 1967.

Wevers, J. W. "Double Readings in the Books of Kings." *Journal of Biblical Literature* 65 (1946): 307–10.

———. "Principles of Interpretation Guiding the Fourth Translator of the Books of the Kingdoms." *Catholic Biblical Quarterly* 14 (1950): 40–56.

———. *Ezekiel*. New Century Bible, edited by H.H. Rowley and M. Black. London: Thomas Nelson & Sons, 1969.

White, N. J. D. "Jehoiakim." In *Anchor Bible Dictionary*, edited by James Hastings, 3:557–58. Edinburgh: T&T Clark, 1902.

Whitelam, K. W. "Israel's Traditions of Origin: Reclaiming the Land." *Journal for Biblical Literature* 44 (1989): 19–42.

Wifall, W. "David, Prototype of Israel's Future." *Biblical Theology Bulletin* 4 (1974): 94–107.

Wilcock, M. "1 & 2 Chronicles." In *New Bible Commentary, 21st Century Edition*, edited by G. J. Wenham, J. A. Motyer, D. A. Carson, and R. T. France, 388–419. Downers Grove, IL: InterVarsity, 1994.

Wilda, G. *Das Königsbild des chronistischen Geschichtswerkes*. Bonn: Rheinische Friedrich-Wilhelms-Universitat, 1959.

Wilkinson, J. "The Road from Jerusalem to Jericho." *Biblical Archaeologist* 38 (1975): 10–24.

Willi, T. *Die Chronik als Auslegung*. Forschungen zur Religion und Literatur des Alten und Neuen Testaments. Göttingen: Vandenhoeck und Ruprecht, 1972.

Williamson, H. G. M. "Ezra and Nehemiah." In *New Bible Commentary, 21st Century Edition*, edited by G. J. Wenham, J. A. Motyer, D. A. Carson, and R. T. France, 420–41. Downers Grove: InterVarsity, 1994.

———. "The Problem with 1 Esdras." In *After the Exile, Essays in Honour of Rex Mason*, edited by J. Barton and D. J. Reimer, 201–16. Macon, GA: Mercer University Press, 1996.

———. *1 and 2 Chronicles*. New Century Bible Commentary. Grand Rapids: Eerdmans, 1982.

———. "Eschatology in Chronicles." *Tyndale Bulletin* 28 (1977): 115–54.

———. *Israel in the Books of Chronicles*. London: Cambridge University Press, 1977.

———. "Sources and Redaction in the Chronicler's Genealogy of Judah." *Journal of Biblical Literature* 98 (1979): 351–59.

Bibliography

Wilson, R. R. *Prophecy and Society in Ancient Israel*. Philadelphia: Fortress, 1980.
Wiseman, D. J. *Notes on Some Problems in the Book of Daniel*. London: Tyndale, 1965.
———. *Peoples of Old Testament Times*. Oxford: Clarendon, 1973.
———. *Chronicles of the Chaldean Kings*. London: British Museum, 1956.
———. "Jehoiachin." In *Illustrated Bible Dictionary*, edited by J. D. Douglas, 2:737–38. London: InterVarsity, 1980.
Wolff, H. W. *Haggai: A Commentary*. Translated by M. Kohl. Minneapolis: Augsburg, 1988.
———. "The Kerygma of the Deuteronomistic Historical Work." In *The Vitality of Old Testament Traditions*, edited by W. Brueggemann and H. W. Wolff, 83–100. Atlanta: John Knox, 1975.
Zenger, E. "Die deuteronomistische Interpretation der Rehabilitierung Joiachins." *Biblische Zeitung* 12 (1968): 16–30.

General Index

Additions to Esther, 133–34, 147
Allen, L.C., 79, 102, 104
Amel-marduk, xi, 21–22
Antiquities of the Jews (Josephus), 127–30, 132, 133
Auld, A.G., 20n41
Avigad, N., 86

Babylon, South Citadel of, xvi
Babylonian Chronicle, xv–xvi, 1, 8, 9, 18, 31
Barnes, W.E., xix, 116–17
Baruch
   as author, 69
   book of, 140–43, 147
   reading Jeremiah's scroll, 35–36
Becking, B., 22
Begg, C.T., 23n55, 105n9, 106, 107
Benzinger, I., 13n30
Bertheau, E., 13n30
Bible, rewritten, 127, 133
Bright, John, 22, 27, 48, 64, 68

captives, denuding of, 51
Carroll, Robert P., 26, 48, 71
Cassel, P., 95, 96
cedar, allegory of, in Ezekiel, 101–5, 120
circularity, 114
clemency, 28–29
Clements, R.E., 21n47, 28
Clines, D.J., 115
Cogan, M., 30
Coniah. *See* Jehoaichin

covenants, sanctity of, 119, 122, 143, 152
Craigie, P.C., 49, 50
Curtis, E.L., 12–13
Cyrus, 31

Dahood, Mitchell J., 39
Dancy, J.C., 134
dating, historical, 9
Davidic covenant, x
Davidic line, x, xi, *xiv*, 104, 105
   blessings upon, parameters for, 47
   last five kings to rule on throne of Judah and Jerusalem, 5
   lineage of, 82, 83–87
   naming of, xiii
   primogeniture succession of, xviii
   rabbis' interest in, 139
   study of, xi
   threat to succession of, 37
Davidson, Robert, 23
Davis, J.D., xiii
Dempster, Stephen G., 153
deuteronomistic history, x, 86
Dillard, R.B., 12–13
Dubberstein, Waldo H., 79–80
Duguid, I.M., 105
Duhm, Bernhard, 42, 114

eagles, in Ezekiel's cedar allegory, 102–5, 120
Edict of Cyrus, 18
editor, function of, 76
Ehrlich, 4 [QY: need first name or initial, or delete entry? Arnold?]

General Index

Eliakim seal impressions, xvi
Esther
    book of, 94, 96, 97, 133
    role of, 95, 96–97
exile
    catalog of, in Jeremiah, 65
    dating of, 73
    interpretation of, x
Ezekiel
    book of, dating of, 76–77, 78–81, 98
    cedar allegory in, 101–5, 120
    lioness motif in, 105–9
    prophecy relating to Jehoiachin, 78
    referring to Jehoiachin as "king," 98
    vine imagery in, 108, 120

fable, 102
Feldman, Louis H., 131–32, 140
figs
    Jeremiah's vision of, 52–56
    metaphor of, 65, 67, 74, 75–76, 97, 99
First Esdras, book of, 121, 122–27, 146–47
Freedy, K.S., 79

Genesis Apocryphon, 127
Gibeon, 63
Goulder, Michael, xix, 113–16, 118–19, 120, 151–52
Gray, J., 3, 8n15

haggadah, 134, 147
Haggai, book of, 89, 99
Hagner, D.A., 143, 146
Halakhah, 134, 147
Hamilton, V.P., 51n32
Hananiah, 56–57, 62, 63–65
Hillers, D.R., 111
Hobbs, T.R., 3, 4
Holladay, W., 28, 36–37, 45, 48, 53
Hughes, J., 20n42, 28
humiliation, prophecy of, 41

idolatry, 11

inscriptions informing Jehoiachin study, xv–xvi
Isbell, Charles D., 36
Ishtar Gate, xvi
Israel, exile of, xx

Janzen, J.G., 45
Japhet, S., 13, 84, 85, 86
Jeconiah. *See* Jehoaichin
Jehoahaz, 11, 15
Jehoiachin (also Coniah; Jeconiah)
    accolades for, 128, 131–32
    in Additions to Esther, 133–34
    age of, when beginning reign, 12–13
    in Baruch, 142–43
    becoming king, xv
    biblical significance of, 67
    captivity of, 81, 98
    Chronicler's report of, 17, 86
    compared to other kings, 108–9
    contrasted with Zedekiah, 71–73
    contributor to Judean monarchy's plunge into exile, 44, 52
    death of, xi, 25, 29, 31
    evil of, 11
    as example of repentance, 138
    exile of, xiii, xv, 26, 27, 71, 146
    Ezekiel's prophecies relating to, 78
    family of, 22
    in 1 Esdras, 122–24
    freed from prison, 2, 19, 24, 29, 30
    giving forth a fragrance, 136
    information about, sources for, x
    installed as king, 1
    Jeremiah's prophecies about, 38–76
    Josephus's characterization of, 128–30, 131
    life of, setting for, xiv–xv
    linked with characters in book of Esther, 93
    linked with Lamentations, 110, 112
    linked with psalms, 116–19
    linked with Suffering Servant of Isaiah, 113–16, 119
    longevity of, 81
    in Matthew, 143–46

General Index

mentions of and allusions to, xi–xii
name of, xiii, 43, 70, 81, 123
optimistic portrait of, 32
perception of, positive, 23
in rabbinical literature, 135–40
referred to as "king of the Jews," 77
rehabilitation of, 31, 121, 132–33, 136–37, 140, 145–46, 147
reign of, xiii, 7, 9, 13, 80, 146
rejected as king, xiii
reminiscences of the life of, 121
returning the temple keys, 135, 139–40
singled out for favorable attention, xi
studies about, ix–x
taken prisoner by Nebuchadrezzar, 64
and his wife, in captivity, 135–36
Jehoiakim, 16–17
associated with lion cub in Ezekiel, 107
changing allegiance to Nebuchadrezzar, 35
contrasted with Zedekiah, 70–71
death of, 128
evil of, 7, 11
in 1 Esdras, 124–25
Jeremiah's prophecy about, 33, 35–38
lifestyle of, 47
struggles of, 10–11
Jeremiah, 78
catalog of exiles, 65
prophecies about Jehoaichin, 38–76
prophecy about Jehoiakim, 33, 35–38
temple sermon of, 35
Jeremiah, book of
condemnatory tone of, 33, 73
dating of, 79
Jerusalem
condemned to destruction, 9, 10
destruction of, 71, 72
fall of, 27
Jesus, set in world context, 143

Jewish communities, conflict between, 55
Jones, D., 23, 69
Jones, G., 3, 22n46
Josephus, xx, 127–33, 147
Judah, last kings of, x, 14–15, 18

Kalimi, I., 14n33
Kebar Canal, 79
Keown, Gerald L., 26, 36, 70–71
Kimchi, 42, 102
King David (McKenzie), xi
King Josiah (Sweeney), xi
Kutsch, E., 9n16

Lachish Ostracon III, xvi, 69–70, 74
Lamentations, book of, 109–11
lioness motif, in Ezekiel, 105–9
Long, Burke, 6n9, 23
Lord, ignoring, punishment for, 34
Lowery, K.E., 123
Luke, genealogy in, 144
Lundbom, J.R., 39, 41
Lysimachus, 133

Malamat, Abraham, 27, 60, 69
Marduk, 95
Margaliyot, Eliezer, 140
Mason, S., 133
Matthew, book of, 143, 153
genealogy in, 121–22, 143–46, 147
May, H.G., 10
McConville, J.G., 70
McKane, W.A., 45, 48, 51
McKenzie, S., xi
menstrual purity, 134–35
messianic titles, 92
Metzger, B.M., 133
Midrash, 134
monarchy, impermanence of, 51
Montgomery, J.A., 3
Moore, C.A., 95
Mordecai, portrayal of, 93, 95–96, 97
Murray, D.F., 20n41
Myers, J.M., 10, 13

Nebuchadrezzar (Nebuchadnezzar), 16, 104

175

General Index

capitulation to, 65
Josephus's account of, 127–29
scourging Zedekiah, 71
treatment of Zedekiah, 129
Noth, M., 23n55, 30

Omanson, R.L., 96
Origen, 78

Parker, Richard, 79–80
paronomasia, 47
Person, Richard, 20n41
poetry, analysis of, methods for, 100–101
Porteous, Norman W., xix, 109, 110–11, 112–13, 120
Provan, I.W., 23, 111–12
psalms, Jehoiachin linked to, 116–19
Purvis, J.D., 14n33

rabbinic Judaism, xx
Rashi, 42
reclothing, 29
Redford, D.B., 79
riddle, 102
Robinson, J., 3
Rowleym H.H., 76
Rudolph, Wilhelm, xix, 109, 110–11

salvation history, 143–44, 146
Samaria, siege of, 5
seals, xvi, 27, 32
Second Kings, book of, dating system of, 79
Second Temple, rebuilding of, 87–90, 91–92
Seitz, Christopher R., 3, 21, 23, 32, 70
Selah, as literary convention, 119
Sellin, E., 113
Servant Songs, 114
signet, metaphor of, 44, 48, 49, 73–74, 88, 91, 92
Southwell, P.J.M., 5
Spalinger, A., 69
succession protocol, 6n9
Suffering Servant, 113–16, 119, 151–52
Sweeney, M.A., xi

Tadmor, H., 22, 30
Talmon, S., 20n41
Tate, Marvin E., 116–17
telescoping, literary effect of, 95–96
temple, impermanence of, 51
Thomas, D. Winton, 53
Thompson, John A., 48
Tov, E., 45, 57–58, , 59–60n41, 60

Unger Prism, xvi, 22, 25, 32
Uzza, garden of, 7

vassal covenant, 103–4
Verhoef, P.A., 91
Vermes, Geza, 127
vessels, care of, 4, 9, 14, 60–61, 64
vine, imagery of, in Ezekiel, 108, 120
Von Rad, Gerhard, 23n55, 30, 90

Wars of the Jews (Josephus), 127, 131, 133, 146
Weidner tablets, xv, xvi, 22, 24–25, 27–28, 32
Wells, Roy D., Jr., 45
Wilcock, M., 86–87
Williamson, H.G.M., 13, 85, 86–87, 127
Wolff, H.W., 90, 91

Yahweh
    oaths of, 48–49, 105
    response to, 42, 49
yoke sign-prophecy, 60, 61, 74

Zedekiah, 17, 18
    contrasted with Jehoiachin, 71–73
    contrasted with Jehoiakim, 70–71
    in Davidic succession, 86
    different spellings for, significance of, 84
    evil of, 11
    in 1 Esdras, 126
    rebellion of, 105
    reign of, 64–65, 72
    status of, 80
    treatment of, 26
Zerubbabel
    father of, 86, 87
    role of, 88, 92, 99

176

Ancient Documents Index

OLD TESTAMENT

Genesis

12	152
12:1–3	147
12:10–20	134
15:2	46
15:4–6	147
15:18–21	147
17:1–21	147
29:17	96
40:13	24
41:14	25, 29
46:27	96
49:9–11	105, 107–8

Exodus

5:13	24
5:19	24
6:24	85
16:4	24

Leviticus

19:28	16n34
20:20–21	46

Numbers

14:21	48
14:28	48

Deuteronomy

18:20	63, 65
26:10	55
28:36	44, 49, 51, 52
28:36–37	42
33:40	48

Judges

7:22	90
9:8–15	102
9:15	103

Ruth

4:18–22	143

1 Samuel

6:19	xiii n14
9:1–2	95
18:11	50
20:33	50

2 Samuel

7	x, x n7, xiii, 118, 119, 139, 147
7:5–8	91
16:5	95
17	152

1 Kings

2:19–25	29
5:13	103
11:32–34	91
16:34	7
21:29	7
25	8

2 Kings

4:1b	91
8:20	7
14:9	102, 103
17:4	25
18:9	5
18:13–16	9
18:17	5
19:35	9
20:16–18	5, 11
20:16–19	x, 7n11, 52
21	5
21–24	5, 10, 32
21:1–18	10
21:10	6
21:11–15	x, 7n11
21:13–14	6, 7, 10
21:18	6
21:23	6
21:24	6
21:26	6
22–23	36, 150
22:11–23:24	6
23	84, 122
23–24	14
23–25	14
23:26–27	5, 6, 7, 10
23:27	9
23:29	7
23:30	6
23:30–33	47
23:30b	124
23:30b–34	15
23:34	6, 6n9, 124
23:34–24:4	7
23:34–24:6	125
23:34–24:6a	16
23:35	7
23:36	42
23:37	7
24	12, 18, 19, 79, 82, 84, 103, 122, 145, 150, 152
24–25	69, 87
24:1	1, 7, 8, 9, 10, 16, 16n34, 24, 125
24:1–6	16
24:2	7n11, 40, 42, 107
24:3	9n15
24:3–4	5, 10
24:5	17
24:6	xiii, 7, 125
24:6–7	8
24:6–9	38
24:6–17	xvii, 1, 2–12, 10–12, 65
24:6a	2
24:6b–17	17
24:7	8, 17
24:8	xiii, xvii, 12, 13, 14, 40, 68
24:8–9	8
24:8–16	17
24:8–17	119
24:9	1, 11, 31, 74, 128, 146
24:10	9
24:10–11	9, 17, 32
24:10a	2
24:11	2, 125
24:11–15	107
24:12	xiii, 8, 11, 21, 40, 42–43, 65–66, 68, 71
24:12–15	67
24:12–16	9–10, 54–55, 74
24:13	xvii, 9n17, 9n19
24:13–16	31–32
24:14	9n17, 58
24:14a	2
24:14b	2
24:15	xiii, xv, 40, 68

24:15a	3
24:16	9n17
24:17	xiii, xvii, 6, 10, 13, 69, 84, 124n6, 126
24:17–25:7	17
24:18	71
24:18–20	69
25	xi, xx, 2, 8, 19, 21, 25, 26–27, 28, 30, 31, 38, 76, 79, 81, 82, 87, 150
25:1	24
25:1–7	21
25:1–26	23
25:3	70
25:3–6	112
25:4–7	43
25:5–7	104
25:8	24
25:19	70
25:22	19, 70
25:22–25	xvi
25:23	xvi
25:26	19
25:27	xiii, xvii, 20n43, 24, 25, 28, 30, 68, 98
25:27–30	x, xvii, 2, 8, 14, 15, 19–25, 23, 25, 26, 26n64, 29, 30, 43n14, 72, 114, 116, 140
25:27a	20
25:27b	20
25:27c	20
25:28	24, 25
25:28a–a	20
25:29	xiii, 24, 30, 68
25:29a	20
25:29b–b	20
25:30	24, 25
25:30a	20
25:30b	20
25:30c	20
25:30d–d	20
30	30
33:11	16
34:6–17	31

1 Chronicles

1–9	83
1:1–23	83
1:34	143
2:1–13	143
3	xi, xix, 82, 83, 145, 151
3:1	83
3:1–19	143
3:9	82
3:10	83, 85
3:15	6n9, 15, 70, 82, 83, 84, 124, 146
3:15–16	58
3:15–19	xviii, 82–87
3:15a	82
3:16	xiii, 8n14, 18, 68, 70, 71, 82, 84, 87
3:16–17	xv, 22, 125
3:16–19	76, 81
3:16a	82
3:17	68, 82, 84, 85, 98–99, 136, 137, 138, 145
3:18	84, 85, 87
3:19	51n32, 83, 85
3:19a	83
3:19b	83
3:20	84
3:20–21	83n13
3:21	84
3:21b	85
3:22	85
3:22b	85
3:23	84
3:24	83, 85
6:7	85
6:8	85
6:22	85
6:23	85
6:37	85
9:1–3	83
15:27	123
17	xiii

2 Chronicles

3:19b–24	153
31:12–13	123
35	122
35:9	123
35:22	123

2 Chronicles (*continued*)

36	8, 15, 18, 19, 31, 32, 38, 103, 122, 150, 152
36:1	124
36:1–4	15, 47
36:1–21	xvii, 18
36:3	15
36:4	49, 124
36:4–8	125
36:5–8	7, 16
36:6	16, 17
36:6–7	xv, 107, 125
36:7	14, 15, 62
36:8	xiii, 2, 7, 16n34, 17, 68, 125
36:8–9	18
36:8–10	xvii, 1–2, 8n13, 12–19
36:9	xiii, xvii, 8n13, 68, 128, 146
36:9–10	17
36:9a–a	12, 14
36:9b–b	13, 14
36:10	xvii, 14, 15, 18, 32, 49, 84, 105, 107, 125
36:10a–a	13
36:11–14	17
36:13	10, 17, 104
36:17–20	104
36:18	14, 15

Ezra

1–4	89
1–6	14n33
1:7	82n11
1:11ff.	82n11
2:2	xv, 95
3:2	xv, 85
3:8	85, 89
4:3	xv
4:24	89
5:2	xv, 85
6:15	89
8:26–30	9n18

Nehemiah

7:2	95

12:1	85

Esther

1:11	97
2	151
2:3	97
2:4	93n37
2:5	94
2:5–6	xix, 81, 92
2:5–7	xviii, 76, 93–98
2:5a	93
2:6	xiii, 39n10, 58, 68, 96, 125
2:6a–a	93
2:7	96
2:7a	93
2:7b	94
2:8	93n37, 96
2:17	94
9:29	94

Job

10:15	24
12:14	42
41:4b	91

Psalms

2	xiii
61	xii, xix, 101, 116–17, 120, 151
61:2–4	116–17
61:5	116
61:6	116
61:7	116
78:70	91
89	xii, xix, 100, 117–19, 120, 151, 152
89:1–2	118
89:2	119
89:3	91
89:3–4	92, 118
89:4	119
89:5	119
89:5–18	118

89:12	118	39:5–8	7n11
89:19–37	118	40–55	88, 91
89:19–51	118	45:1	42
89:20	91	49:18	48
89:21	119	52	xix
89:37	119	52–53	xix
89:38	119	52:13–15	114
89:38–51	119	52:13–53:12	xii, 101, 113–16, 119, 120, 152
89:39	117		
89:40	117	53	xix, 114, 115, 151
89:41	117	53:1–3	114, 115
89:42	117	53:2	115
89:43	117	53:3	115
89:44	117	53:4	116
89:45	117	53:4–6	114, 115
89:46	118, 119	53:5	116
89:48	118	53:6	116
89:49	119	53:7–9	114
89:50	118	53:9	116
89:51	118	53:10	116
89:52	118	53:10–12	114
110:7	24	53:11b–12	114
132:10	91	53:12	116
137:1–2	79		
140:9	24		

Ecclesiastes

Jeremiah

12:5	137	1:3	84
		2:16	24
		3:2	41–42

Song of Songs

		4:3	34
		4:4	34
5:15	103	4:5	39n8
7:20	136	7:1–15	35
		7:3	51
		7:4	46
		7:14–15	7n11
		11:2	34

Isaiah

		11:9	34
6:3	46	13	150, 151
10:33	103	13:9	38
11:1	viii	13:15–16	38
22:15–19	50	13:18	41, 71
22:17	50	13:18–19	xviii, 24, 33, 38–43, 40, 42, 43, 73, 74
22:18	50		
22:22	42	13:18–20	41
28:4	55	13:18a	39
39:5–7	5, 11	13:18b	39
		13:18c	39

Jeremiah (*continued*)

13:19	39, 41, 42
13:19a	39
13:19b–b	40
13:20	41, 42
13:20–27	38
15:2	138
16:10	50
16:13	50
17:25	34
18:11	34, 39n8
20:10	72
21:1–10	70
21:3–7	x, 7n11
21:10–12	72n64
22	103, 145, 150
22:1–30	52
22:3	47
22:3–4	10, 49, 52
22:4	47
22:5	47
22:6	58
22:10–11	115
22:10–12	x, 7n11, 47, 84, 106
22:10–23:8	105n9, 107
22:11	15, 124
22:11–12	49
22:13–19	x, 7n11, 10, 47
22:13–23	42
22:17	17, 107
22:18–19	128
22:19	10n22
22:20–23	47
22:24	viii, xiii, 48, 69, 70, 81, 91, 125, 137
22:24–27	49, 50, 92
22:24–30	x, xix, xviii, 7n11, 33, 37n7, 43–53, 54, 73, 75, 76, 91, 98, 99, 107, 115, 136, 138, 148, 153
22:24a	45
22:25	49
22:25a	45
22:26	29, 31, 40, 49, 50
22:26a–a	45
22:27	44, 49, 61
22:27a	45
22:28	viii, xiii, 45, 50, 69, 70, 72, 88
22:28–30	44, 45, 50, 52
22:28a	45
22:28b	46
22:29	51
22:29a	46
22:30	38, 51–52, 52n32, 80, 88, 92
22:30a	46
22:30b	46
22:30c	46
23:1–2	47
23:2	58
23:5	47
23:5–6	105, 120
23:15	58
23:22	72n64
23:40	53
24	30, 54, 67, 71, 151
24:1	xi, xiii, 52, 54–55, 56, 67, 68, 74, 139
24:1f.	136
24:1ff.	136
24:1–3	xviii, 33, 43n14, 44, 49, 52–56, 67, 78
24:1–4	65
24:1a	53
24:1b	53, 65
24:1c–c	53
24:1d	53
24:2–3	x, 55, 65
24:4–10	54
24:5	29, 31, 54, 55
24:5–7	55, 61
24:6–10	74
24:8–10	x, 7n11, 55
25:13	66
25:14	59
26:1	35, 59
26:3	59
26:12	59
26:16–22	59
26:20–23	35, 42
26:24	67
27	56, 61, 63
27–29	31
27:1	59, 61
27:3	60, 67
27:3–11	56
27:7	59

Ancient Documents Index

27:9	56	29:1	66, 67
27:10	56	29:1–3	xviii, 33, 43n14, 44, 49, 55, 65–67, 78, 141
27:12	60		
27:12–15	23n55, 56	29:1a	66
27:13	60	29:1b	66
27:14	60	29:1c	66
27:16–22	23n55, 56, 60	29:2	xiii, 40, 58, 65–66, 67, 68
27:18	57, 59, 60	29:2a–a	66
27:18–19	58	29:3	67
27:19	60	29:4	65
27:19–20	60	29:5–9	x
27:19–22	xviii, 33, 44, 56–61, 74, 78	29:8	29, 31
27:19a	57	29:8–9	61
27:19b–b	57	29:9	29, 31
27:19c	58	29:10	60n
27:19d–d	58	29:15–17	65
27:20	xiii, 60–61, 62, 68	29:16	73
27:20a	58	29:16–19	67
27:20c–c	58	29:25	66
27:20d–d	58	29:29	66
27:21	57, 58, 60, 61	31:7	39n8
27:21a	58	31:10	39n8
27:22	60, 61, 150	31:23	34
27:22a	58	32:29	72n64
27:22b–b	58, 59	32:32	34
27:22c–c	58, 59	33:14–26	25
28	59, 63	34:2	72n64
28:1	62n43, 64	34:2–3	7n11
28:1–4	xviii, 33, 43n14, 44, 52, 56–57, 61–65, 66, 74, 78	34:19	70
		35:13	34
28:1a	62	36	35, 36, 69, 70, 141, 150, 151
28:1b–b	62	36:1–8	35
28:1c	62	36:5	35, 41, 42, 73
28:2	64	36:9	35
28:2a	62	36:9–26	35
28:3	62, 64	36:10	67, 141, 147
28:3a	62	36:11–12	36
28:3b	62	36:20–26	33
28:4	x, xiii, 50, 58, 64, 68	36:25	67
28:4a	62	36:26	8n14
28:4b	62	36:27	35
28:4c	62	36:27–32	35, 37
28:6	29, 31	36:28	35, 58
28:12–17	63	36:29	33
28:16	29, 31, 63	36:29ff.	17
28:16–17	61		
28:17	63, 64		
29	40, 80, 151		

183

Jeremiah (continued)

36:29–31	x, 7n11
36:30	29, 31, 37, 41, 43, 44
36:30–31	xvii, 33–38, 40, 42, 47n20, 73
36:31	29, 31, 37, 52
36:31a	34
36:31b	34
36:32	35, 36
37	69, 151
37–39	69, 70
37–43	69
37:1	xiii, 34, 69, 70, 71, 73, 84, 104
37:1–2	xviii, 33, 43n14, 44, 67–73, 69, 70, 73, 74, 77, 78
37:1a	68
37:1b–b	25, 68, 70, 77
37:1c–c	68
37:1d–d	68
37:2	17, 70
37:2a	68
37:4	25
37:5	69, 104
37:6–10	104
37:7	59
37:8	72n64
37:10	72n64
37:11	104
37:13–17	70
37:15	70
37:20	70
38:3	70
38:14	70
38:17–18	70
38:18	72n64
38:23	70
39:1–5	112
39:4	70, 71
39:5–6	71
39:6	58
39:6–7	71
39:8	71
40	23n55
43:6–7	140, 147
44:21	70
46:14	39n8
46:18	48
48:17	39n8
48:19	39n8
50:2	39n8
52	xi, xx, 27, 29, 30, 31, 61, 76, 81, 87, 150
52:6–9	112
52:7–11	104
52:9	71
52:9–10	71
52:9–11	71
52:11	21, 72
52:12–13	71
52:13	58
52:27–30	9n17
52:31	xiii, xvii, 20, 24, 28, 30, 32, 68, 81, 98
52:31–33	140
52:31–34	xvii, 2, 8, 14, 20n41, 23, 24n60, 25–29, 26n64, 30–31, 43n14, 72
52:31a	25
52:31b	25
52:31c	25
52:31d	25
52:31e	25
52:32–33	28
52:32a	25
52:33	xiii, 20, 30, 32, 68
52:33a	25
52:34	xi, 28, 29, 30
52:34a–a	25
52:34b–b	25
52:34c–c	26

Lamentations

1	111
1–2	110, 113
1:1	109
1:11	111
1:19	111
3	xii, xix, 101, 109–13, 151
3:1	110, 111, 112
3:1ff.	113
3:2	110
3:4	110
3:6	110
3:7	110

3:8	110	17:1–2	102
3:9	110	17:1–10	102–3
3:11	110	17:1–21	102
3:14	110	17:3	104, 108
3:18	110	17:3–4	102–3
3:19	110	17:3–10	101–5
3:22	112	17:4	104, 108
3:31–33	112	17:5	103, 105
3:32	112	17:5–6	101, 103, 108
3:34	110	17:5–8	101
3:53	110	17:6	103, 105
4	xii, xix, 101, 109–13	17:7	103
4:20	110, 112, 113, 120	17:7–8	103
		17:7–10	104
		17:8	103, 106, 108
		17:9–10	103
		17:11–12	102

Ezekiel

1	79, 151	17:11–15	103
1–4	91	17:11–21	103–4
1–24	81	17:12	102, 105, 125
1:1	68, 76, 78–79	17:12–13	105
1:1–3	xviii, 76–81	17:13	105
1:2	xiii, 72, 76, 79, 81, 98	17:13–14	119
1:2–3	76–77, 78	17:13–15	101, 126
1:2a	77	17:13–21	80, 102
1:3	76, 80	17:13b	104
1:3a–a	77	17:14	103–4
1:3b	77	17:15	101, 104
1:4ff.	76, 79	17:16	48n26, 73, 101, 105
3:15	79	17:18	101
3:23	79	17:19	101, 105
5:11	48n26	17:19–20	102
8:1	77n3, 79n8	17:20	101, 108
12:10–13	72, 80	17:22	102
14:16	48n26	17:22–23	102
14:18	48n26	17:22–24	73n66, 104, 105, 120
14:20	48n26	17:23	105
16	101, 109, 119	18:3	48n26
16:7	101	19	xii, xix, 78, 98, 101, 105–9, 120, 139, 151
16:8	101, 119		
16:12	43	19:1–9	105
16:15	101	19:2–4	106
16:15–34	101	19:3	105
16:25	101	19:4	105, 106
16:29	102	19:5	106
16:48	48n26	19:5–9	80, 106–7
16:59	101, 119	19:6a	106
17	xii, xix, 47n20, 78, 98, 101, 108, 109, 119, 120, 151	19:6b	106

Ezekiel (continued)

19:7a	106
19:7b	106
19:8	107
19:8–9	107
19:9	106, 107, 109, 120
19:10	106, 107, 108
19:10–14	105, 107–8
19:11	106
19:11–12	108, 120
19:11a	108
19:11b	108
19:12	108
19:13	108
19:14	106, 108
20:1	77n3, 79n8
20:3	48n26
20:31	48n26
20:33	48n26
21:21	53
24:1	77n3, 79n8
24:23	138
25–32	81
26:1	77n3, 79n8
29:1	77n3, 79n8
29:17	77n3, 79n8, 98
30:20	77n3, 79n8
31:1	77n3, 79n8
32:1	77n3
32:17	77n3, 79n8
33–48	81
33:11	48n26
33:21	xix, xv, 77n3, 79n8
33:27	48n26
34:8	48n26
34:23ff.	91
34:24	104
35:6	48n26
35:11	48n26
37:24	91
37:24–25	104
38:21	90
40:1	77n3, 79n8, 81
43:3	79

Daniel

1:1–2	xv, 80
1:1–3	147, 153
1:5	24

Hosea

9:10	55

Amos

1:6	40
1:9	40
7:17	79

Micah

7:1	55

Zephaniah

2:9	48

Haggai

1:1	88, 90, 94
1:8b	91
1:12	85, 88, 90
1:12–14	89
1:14	85, 90
2	151
2:2	85, 88, 90
2:6	88, 90
2:6–7	89
2:9b	91
2:10	87, 90
2:18	87, 90
2:19b	91
2:20	90
2:20–23	xviii, 76, 87–92, 99, 136
2:21	viii, 90
2:21–22	89
2:21a	88
2:21b	88

2:22	90
2:22a	88
2:23	81, 85, 86, 88, 90, 91, 99, 137, 148, 153

Zechariah

1:1	94
4:9	xv
6:11–12	92
9:11	136
9:16	43
14:13	90

Malachi

1:6–7	55

APOCRYPHA AND SEPTUAGINT

Baruch

1	152
1:1	140
1:1–14	141–42
1:2	140
1:3	xiii, 68, 140
1:3–9	xix, 140–41
1:5–14	140
1:9	xiii, 68
1:10	140
1:12	140

1 Esdras

1	121–27, 139, 146–47, 150, 152
1:1–33	122–23
1:9	xiii, 68, 123
1:9ff.	xix
1:22	122
1:28	123
1:33	123
1:34	xiii, 68, 124

1:34–35	124
1:34–36	122, 124
1:37–42	122, 124–25
1:38	122, 122n3, 124
1:39	125
1:40–41	125
1:42	13, 125
1:43	xiii, 12, 18, 68, 125
1:43–45	122, 125–26
1:45	125
1:46–48	122, 126
1:48	126
1:52–53	126
1:56	126
3:1–5:6	147

Additions to Esther

11	147
11:2–4	xix, 93n38, 133–34
11:4	xiii

Sirach

49	153
49:11–12	92

NEW TESTAMENT

Matthew

1	xi, 72n65, 147, 152, 153
1:1	143
1:1–16	92
1:1–17	xx, 143–46
1:2	145, 146
1:2–6	144
1:2–6a	143
1:6	145
1:6b–11	144
1:11	xiii, 144–46
1:11–12	145
1:11–16	145–46
1:11a	144–45
1:11b	145
1:12	xiii

Ancient Documents Index

Matthew (continued)

1:12a	145
1:12b	145
1:16a	145
1:17	143, 145

Luke

3	153
3:23–38	92
3:27	144
3:32–34	144

Acts

8:34	116
16:13	79

DEAD SEA SCROLLS

1QIsa[b]	153
4Q174	153
4QJer	153
4QPs[e]	153
5QLam[a–b]	153

JOSEPHUS

Antiquities of the Jews

6:194	128
9:166	128
9:260	128
10:96–98	128
10:96–102	127
10.98	150
10:99–102	128–29, 139
10:100	146
10:101	132
10:138–39	129
10:139	127
10:229–30	127, 129–30
11:183	128

Wars of the Jews

6:93–102	130–31
6:103	127, 146
6:103–6	131

MISHNAH, TALMUD, AND RELATED LITERATURE

Ma'asroth Middoth

2	139

Ma'asroth Sanhedrin

183	153
37b–38a	138, 153

Ma'asroth Sheqalim

2.18	140n21
6	139

Megilla

13a	96

Soncino Zohar, Shemoth

Section 2, Page 106a	138